D0887295

Technological
Entrepreneurship

A Volume in
Research in Entrepreneurship and Management

Series Editor: John Butler, Hong Kong Polytechnic University

Technological Entrepreneurship

Edited by
Philip H. Phan
Lally School of Management and Technology
Rensselaer Polytechnic Institute

INFORMATION AGE
PUBLISHING

80 Mason Street • Greenwich, Connecticut 06830 • www.infoagepub.com

Library of Congress Cataloging-in-Publication Data

Technological entrepreneurship / edited by Philip Phan.
    p. cm. -- (Research in entrepreneurship and management ; v. 2)
Includes bibliographical references.
 ISBN 1-930608-80-2 (Paperback) -- ISBN 1-930608-81-0 (Hardcover)
 1. High technology industries–Management. 2. Entrepreneurship. I.
Phan, Philip. II. Series.
 HD62.37 .T428 2002
 658.4'21--dc21

                                    2002007465

ISBN: 1-930608-80-2 (paper); 1-930608-81-0 (cloth)

Printed in the United States of America

CONTENTS

Part III
Case Studies in Technological Entrepreneurship:
Managing in Turbulent Environments

LIST OF CONTRIBUTORS

Pier A. Abetti

Lally School of Management and Technology,
Rensselaer Polytechnic Institute
abettp@rpi.edu

Michael Armstrong

School of Business
Carleton University
armstrong@carlton.ca

Chee-Leong Chong

Department of Management and Organization
NUS Business School, National University of Singapore
biz@nus.edu.sg

Maw Der Foo

Department of Management and Organization
Faculty of Business Administration
National University of Singapore
mawder@nus.edu.sg

David H. Gobeli

Department of Management
Oregon State University
gobeli@bus.orst.edu

Lisa K. Gundry

Department of Management
DePaul University
lgundry@depaul.edu

Rueylin Hsiao

Department of Decision Sciences
NUS Business School, National University of Singapore
rueylin@nus.edu.sg

Jill Kickul	Department of Management DePaul University jkickul@condor.depaul.edu
Bruce Kirchhoff	School Of Management New Jersey Institute of Technology kirchhoff@njit.edu
Harold F. Koenig	Department of Marketing Oregon State University koenig@bus.orst.edu
Moren Lévesque	Weatherhead School of Management Case Western Reserve University moren.levesque@weatherhead.cwru.edu
Andy Lockett	Department of Management Nottingham University Business School andy.lockett@nottingham.ac.uk
Qing Lu	Department of Business Policy National University of Singapore bizql@nus.edu.sg
Chandra S. Mishra	Department of Finance Oregon State University mishra@bus.orst.edu
Sarika Pruthi	Center for Management Buy-out Research Nottingham University Business School sarika.pruthi @nottingham.ac.uk
Dean A. Shepherd	Leeds School of Business University of Colorado at Boulder dean.shepherd@colorado.edu
Hwee Hoon Tan	Department of Management and Organization Faculty of Business Administration National University of Singapore biztanhh@nus.edu.sg
Gregory Theyel	Institute Global Perspective Program Worcester Polytechnic Institute theyel@wpi.edu

Steve Walsh   Department of Management
                         University of New Mexico
                         walsh@mgt.unm.edu

Clement K. Wang   Department of Business Policy
                         National University of Singapore
                         cwang@nus.edu.sg

Poh Kam Wong   Department of Business Policy
                         National University of Singapore
                         bizwpk@nus.edu.sg

Mike Wright   Center for Management Buy-out Research
                         Nottingham University Business School
                         mike.wright@nottingham.ac.uk

Toru Yoshikawa   College of Commerce
                         Nihon University
                         toruyoshik@aol.com

Part I

THE CONTEXT OF
TECHNOLOGICAL ENTREPRENEURSHIP:
VALUE CREATION AND OPPORTUNITY IN
TURBULENT ENVIRONMENTS

CHAPTER 1

STRATEGIC VALUE CREATION

**David H. Gobeli, Harold F. Koenig, and
Chandra S. Mishra**

ABSTRACT

We develop a fundamental, value-added model, which revolves around the entrepreneur and accounts for traditional business models, pure e-commerce models, and combined or integrated models. The three levels of value for this model are firm value, value drivers and value levers. The value drivers are at the heart of the model and they account for the core value creation activities: product innovation, operations efficiency, and delivery effectiveness. The value levers enhance or multiply the value created by the drivers. Typical value levers are leadership qualities, executive incentives, information technology, and strategic investments such as foreign investment. For illustration, we will discuss information technology in its role as a strategic value lever. Entrepreneurial implications from the model are provided.

INTRODUCTION

An issue addressed by economists in the first half of the 1900s was what comprised economic development. Schumpeter (1934) discusses *production* as the combination of materials and forces within our reach, and *development* as the creation of a "new combination" of materials and forces. These new combinations can include the introduction of a new good, the use of a new method of production, opening a new market, finding a new source of supply, or creating a new market structure within an industry.

3

When new combinations begin to replace older combinations, the transition is typically not smooth; the introduction of new combinations produces disequilibrium in the system. This disequilibrium requires firms to adapt; new firms may move to the front of the industry, some firms fade into the background, and others that cannot adapt may close their doors forever (Schumpeter, 1939). Schumpeter (1942) described this as "creative destruction"—where capital is continuously destroying the current economic structure and simultaneously creating the new economic structure.

The person who generates these new combinations is the entrepreneur. Hayek (1945, p. 524) referred to this person as the "man on the spot" who has knowledge of and recognizes the "particular circumstances of time and place." The nexus of these two—the entrepreneur and opportunities—is at the heart of Shane and Venkataraman's (2000) conceptual framework of entrepreneurship. Schumpeter (1949) states that it is not particularly important whether we refer to this person as the entrepreneur or business leader or innovator. What is important is that this person creates increased value in the system through the "incessantly different use" of the existing factors of production (Schumpeter, 1949, p. 257). As discussed above, entrepreneurial activity upsets the market equilibrium, forcing a revision of values of all elements in the system; but this "disharmonious or one-sided increase" will offset any losses and the new equilibrium is characterized by an increase in the aggregate output (Schumpeter, 1939).

So, strategic value is based upon innovation, but Schumpeter's "materials and forces" used to create the new combinations can produce a stronger competitive advantage when they are broadly defined and also involve the firm's operational efficiency and delivery. If sufficient amounts of these intangible assets exist, *then* information technology, for example, which could be used to launch an e-commerce initiative, can serve as a lever to effectively multiply critical resources, or to help create them in the first place.

To understand the unfolding drama of strategic value creation in the brave new electronic world, this article first presents a general framework, the Value-Added Model, for mapping and understanding the underlying value creation of businesses. Finally, conclusions and implications for entrepreneurs are drawn, based on the theories and study results presented here.

FRAMEWORK

Our Model includes three levels of value creation: the value of the firm, value drivers, and value levers. Table 1 presents a summary of value-adding elements and measures for each level among the variables. Each level will be described further below.

Table 1.   Value-Added Model Elements and Measures

Value Level	Value Element	Value Measure
Firm	Accounting-based (historical)	ROI, ROA, ROE
	Value-based (forward-looking)	Stock price, Q Value
	Consumer-based perceptions	Brand Equity (consumer's knowledge of firm and perception of image)
Value Drivers	Innovation (value shop)	R&D expenses
	Operations Efficiency (value chain)	Operating Margin (OM)
	Delivery Effectiveness and Customer Contact (value network)	M&S expenses, market share, shelf space
Value Levers	Leadership	Management Incentives
	IT	Technology investment
	DFI, M&A	Investment level
	TQM, REE, FCT, TNS	Cost savings, Cycle time

Firm Value as the Final Purpose

Firm value can be assessed as an historical, accounting-based perspective by examining profitability in the form of ROI or ROA. This is a traditional measure of performance that can be used within and between industries. But, as start-up businesses take off, measuring performance in the traditional way, however comforting, become problematic, given the lack of profitability in the early stages of many such businesses. So, forward-looking, value-based measures are either more appropriate, or at least desirable as complementary measures. One useful variable for assessing the future level of sustainable competitive advantage is stock price, in that it represents investors' perceptions of what the firm is likely to do. This is also not perfect, as many investors found out with technology stocks in the late 1990s—group think or a herd mentality can push values away from reasonable levels.

A related measure is Q value, popularized in several forms by scholars, but measured most simply as the ratio of the market value of the stock to the book value of equity. As such, it reflects the value investors assign to the organization above and beyond its adjusted book value. Researchers have shown the utility of this measure in determining the impact of R&D

expenditures and advertising expenditures (Hirschey & Weygandt, 1985), and in assessing the level of the firm's sustainable competitive advantage (Grant, 1991).

Another measure of the firm's value is one provided by consumers—brand equity. Two issues are important to assess brand equity; (1) how many consumers are aware of the brand, and (2) what is the brand's reputation or image among consumers (Keller, 1993). The brand is more valuable when many consumers know of the brand and consumer's image of the brand is very positive.

Value Drivers

Three common, fundamental value drivers create firm value: product development, operations, and effective delivery. These match the three types of technology described by Thompson (1967), which Stabell and Fjeldstad (1998) used in their descriptions of value shops, value chains and value networks. The *intensive technology* of the value shop creates value by solving unique problems, which is the goal of *product/service development*. The *long-linked technology* of the value chain creates value by changing inputs into products, which is the purpose of *operations*. Finally, the *mediating technology* of the value network creates value by enabling direct and indirect exchanges, which is the goal of *effective delivery* (see Figure 1).

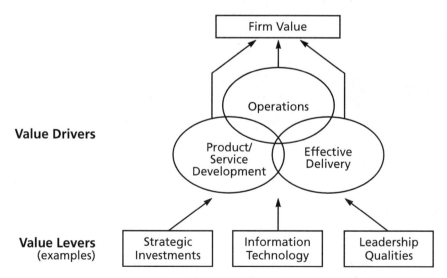

Figure 1.   Creation of Firm Value.

The firm's product or service may rely on only one of these technologies, and in that case, the firm would focus on the corresponding driver. But the firm may use more than one technology, in which case, emphasis may be on more than one driver and the overlap of the value drivers must be recognized. The major caveat is recognition that an emphasis on the value chain alone, or this paper's closest match to the value chain, operations efficiency, is not adequate to sustain a competitive advantage (Porter, 2001). Rather, product or service development striving for real innovation, significant advances in delivery effectiveness, or a combination are required to carve out a unique position in the marketplace. This is a lesson many dot.coms have not yet learned. However, as we shall see, operations efficiency efforts such as Total Quality Management, Reengineering, or Fast Cycle Time may serve as effective *levers* to enhance true value drivers.

Operation Efficiency as a Value Driver

The operational efficiency of an organization (also termed operational effectiveness by some authors), is a construct that includes efficiency and quality of operations. This driver is key to running a viable business or, more simply, providing the products and services in a profitable way. Hence, operations are at the center of the value chain, which is primed by product/service development and enhanced by effective delivery.

E-commerce activities can improve this efficiency and quality through simplification and automation, often resulting in reduced cycle times for such routine activities as order processing and billing. These activities are not fundamentally different from those emphasized in "Reengineering" by Hammer and Champy (1993), who recommended the creative use of information technology to improve such processes as order fulfillment. This "Productivity Revolution" is likely to spread (Reingold et al., 2000) as more industries seek the benefits of information technology-based reengineering.

However, we agree with Porter (1998) when he separates operational effectiveness from strategy, arguing that operational effectiveness is a necessary rather than a sufficient condition for competitive advantage. The entrepreneur's efforts can be fruitful here, but gains are typically "at the margin," and not breakthrough opportunities. At best only a temporary advantage can be gained through a focus on efficiency and quality, since competitors can imitate these improvements. The increased use of information technology has made the quest to remain competitive in operations even more frantic, but only provides limited strategic advantage from such efforts.

Product/Service Development as a Value Driver

To build firm value, products and services that match customers' needs and expectations are essential. The new products and services are Schumpeter's (1934) "new combinations," that keep "the capitalist engine in motion" (Schumpeter, 1942, p. 82). Whether it is Henry Ford's automobiles replacing the horse and wagon, or Microsoft Excel replacing Lotus 1–2–3 which replaced VisiCalc, this is the heart of creative destruction (Schumpeter, 1942).

The investments required to develop new products and services for the marketplace are typically classified as research and development (R&D). Adapting ideas from Cohen and Levinthal (1989), R&D goes beyond operational effectiveness improvements, and provides two primary benefits: generation of new knowledge, and/or the ability to assimilate and exploit others' knowledge. This includes, but is not limited to, using IT to create entirely new business models as E*TRADE and ebay.com have done.

The first benefit is to enhance the ability to create truly competitive product innovations within the firm itself. These could be new products or new processes, possibly creating new intellectual property that can be protected by patents or trade secrets. Using information technology as a lever, AOL has demonstrated its ability to add value though its proprietary bundled services, and Amazon.com has even sought patent protection on how it processes payments with its partners ("one-click").

The second benefit is often called the "spillover" phenomenon—more simply technological competence—which is the general ability of the firm to develop obvious product improvements or extensions, possibly adopting ideas from industry. As an example, Amazon.com would likely have little trouble modifying its services to respond to competitive initiatives.

Effective Delivery as a Value Driver

Effective delivery comprises two components: delivering information to customers, this includes channel partners as well as the ultimate consumers, and the delivery of the product or service. This can be assessed through a variety of measures. An aggregate measure is the firm's marketing and sales expenditures. Admittedly crude, this measure provides a starting point in assessing efforts to communicate and deliver value to consumers. Measures of market share assess the percentage of consumers that seek out and purchase a brand. Related to market share is the number of shelf facings (linear feet of shelf space) or square feet of the producer's merchandise on display at the retail level. This encompasses two related ideas, first, the level of demand for the merchandise by consumers, and second, the willingness of the retailers to stock more merchandise from one producer and less of another.

The second point illustrates the formal network or channel of distribution the entrepreneur must establish. Typically, wholesalers and retailers must be contacted and agree to carry the product—Schumpeter's reference to opening a new market. Or the entrepreneur could decide to market directly to the consumer, in which case they must create the network of warehouses and employees to perform the fulfillment function.

Informal networks may begin to form by connecting customers in an effort to build brand loyalty. The development of "brand communities" is facilitated by interaction among customers as well as company employee to customer interaction. Events such as Jeep Jamborees, Harley-Davidson H.O.G. rallies or events sponsored by DeWalt power tools for building contractors, are examples of ways to facilitate this interaction (McAlexander et al., 2002).

THE ENTREPRENEUR'S ROLE

For the entrepreneur to be successful, their place in the value-added model is the intersection of operations, product/service development, and delivery. Paraphrasing Hayek and Schumpeter, the entrepreneur is the person that recognizes how existing resources can be combined in a different way that creates additional value. This is most likely to happen when the entrepreneur is at the center of the model.

Value Levers

There is growing support that the market value of the stock (and hence Q value) will increase only if the firm has significant intangible assets, such as historical investments in R&D and advertising. Internalization Theory posits that if a firm engages in such activities as international expansion, then the Q value will be greater, but only if significant R&D or advertising equity already exists (Buckley & Casson, 1976; Dunning, 1980; Mishra & Gobeli, 1998; Morck & Yeung, 1991; Rugman, 1980).

We are extending this theory to include other value levers such as the organization of resources (e.g., mergers and acquisitions, TQM programs, reengineering efforts), leadership qualities, and so forth. But the lever we will focus on for this article is Information Technology. Information Technology is another way to leverage intangible assets and increase competitive advantage. This leads directly to the management implication that entrepreneurs engaging in e-commerce must either already have, or must concurrently develop, substantive operational effectiveness, research and development efforts, and channels for delivery to be successful.

These intangible resources can be better understood through the Resource-Based Theory of the firm (Barney, 1991; Dierickx & Cool, 1989; Grant, 1991; Hall, 1992). This variation on the strategic management model explains how effective management of resources can lead to a sustainable competitive advantage, providing the foundation for the internalization of equity (e.g., prior advertising or R&D expenditures) through e-commerce. To summarize the essence of this theory, a firm can sustain a competitive advantage if resources are heterogeneously distributed among firms in an industry, and these differences are stable over time (immobile). Common empirical attributes of resources that assess how they contribute to sustainable competitive advantage include value, non-tradability, inimitability, and non-substitutability.

Therefore, the entrepreneur's ability to create a sustainable competitive advantage is enhanced when resources are valuable, non-tradable, difficult to imitate, and lack viable substitutes. These are the exact attributes that programs to build operational efficiency, innovation, and effective delivery should focus on, in order to build a solid foundation of firm value and competitive advantage. Our proposition is that leveraging these intangible assets through IT serves to further enhance them, providing a "multiple equity effect" on firm value.

Information Technology as a Lever

Information technology (IT) is a lever for multiplying the effect of these three strategic intangibles, and thereby allows for the chance to enhance competitive advantage. Yet, information technology itself has tangible as well as intangible elements. The tangible elements include investments in equipment and services (fixed assets supporting operations) that make e-business possible. The intangible elements include the knowledge of the technology in the entrepreneur's team: how to design and implement information technology systems. These intangible assets can, of course, directly support entrepreneurial product and service research and development.

Bharadwaj et al. (1999), point out that these IT investments could result in cost reductions and reengineering efforts. But, IT investments could also lead to improved customer service and provide higher quality products and services, hence supporting all three strategic variables. Measuring IT as expenditures on staff, hardware, software and data communications, they found that such investments associate positively with Q value.

Based on the model discussed above, a two-stage process of value creation is possible, as shown in Figure 1. First, an entrepreneurial firm must create or have the fundamental value drivers in place; at least one or a combination of product/service development, operations efficiency and delivery effectiveness must be used to provide competitive advantage. Second, one or more value levers can be used to enhance these value drivers, and this relationship can be mapped to see how value levers enhance which value drivers, and how in turn the value drivers contribute to firm value.

Fortunately, the value of such activities has had promising results. Investments in business-to-business (B2B) e-commerce are generally well grounded (Field, 1999; Sager et al., 1999). Intel has quickly increased its business to a billion dollars a month, representing a majority of its total business (Venkatraman, 2000). However, operational efficiency improvements have had mixed results. Davenport (1998) provides evidence that enterprise resource planning (ERP) systems can pay off handsomely, but only if properly implemented to support the competitive advantage of the firm. Nonetheless, as discussed by Hartman et al. (2000), these "new fundamentals" must be addressed before an entrepreneurial company can move onto more sophisticated e-business activities.

Meanwhile, businesses that depend on neither the traditional bricks and mortar model, nor a pure e-commerce model, but rather blend the traditional model with the e-commerce model, are looking better and better. IBM, which has won praise because "They get it," is showing what an integrated business model can do (Sager et al., 1999). Alliances such as Wal-Mart with AOL, and outright mergers such as AOL and Time-Warner, further demonstrate the growing perceived strategic value of an integrated business model. This has been termed the "right mix of bricks and clicks" by Gulati and Garino (2000), who allow for a spectrum of integration.

With regard to effective delivery, IT provides a potential competitive advantage, since it provides a new way for the consumer to navigate the competitors and their distribution systems in a more extensive model of what the economists call "free competition." This new model is described in detail by Evans and Wurster (1999) in their discussion of the three dimensions of navigational advantage: reach, affiliation and richness. Reach (access and connection, or number of customers and products served) has been the primary competitive differentiation for e-businesses so far. Richness (depth and detail of information available on customers and products) is a developing opportunity for customer relationship management. Affiliation (whose interests the business represents) often gravitates toward the customer in e-business. AOL has done well on all these dimensions, and has demonstrated real operational profits from the effort. AOL serves to illustrate both a pure e-commerce model and an integrated bricks and clicks model in its merger with Time-Warner.

IT's influence on company-customer contact is not limited only to the customer's search for a product. In the early part of the twentieth century, before the rise of "big retail," retailers knew their clientele by name, their preferences, and the quantity of each item purchased on a weekly or monthly basis. As multi-unit retailers proliferated, they were less likely to know each customer, and they worked on predicting what to stock based on demographic and economic trends because they had inadequate knowledge to simply sum up individual customers' needs. Customer relationship management (CRM) uses IT to track customer purchases so a better understanding of purchase patterns and trends is gained. One example of how the database of customer purchases can be used is targeting promotions to customers that are most likely to respond; customers that respond to direct mail are contacted with that method, while those that redeem coupons receive more coupons.

AOL as the Pure E-commerce Model

AOL is especially relevant since it began operation under the pure e-commerce business model, but transitioned to an integrated clicks and mortar business. The traditional business model (bricks and mortar) is based on the development of brand equity through advertising and related activities, development of product and service innovations through R&D, and development of operational effectiveness through process improvement or reengineering. To move into an integrated business model, the firm would then have to leverage IT much as described by Griffith and Palmer (1999).

But, it is important to note that the underlying processes must also support both customer delivery and product development activities. Increasingly, these processes have been enhanced by business-to-business e-commerce, various types of enterprise resource planning systems (ERP), and other electronic support activities, even in the alleged traditional business model. It is becoming increasingly difficult to find a pure bricks and mortar organization. IBM is one firm that has made this journey of integration quickly and effectively (Sager et al., 1999).

AOL as the Integrated Model

Returning to Figure 1, the pure e-commerce business model is based on a nearly simultaneous development of products and services through research and development, contact with customers and e-commerce capabilities, supposedly without the benefit of significant fixed assets (other than IT) in operations. In reality, even a supposedly pure e-business firm cannot open its website for business unless it has some baseline of all three of these strategic variables; a product or service must be ready, the ability for customer delivery must exist, and some bricks and mortar (e.g., warehouses and shipping facilities) is inevitable.

And, if these value drivers are well developed with an eye toward competitors and the market, which might be labeled a "strategic approach to entrepreneurship," the chance of developing a real competitive advantage exists. Nonetheless, the implicit promise made to many investors is that these strategic variables will be developed as the firm converts investment capital into market share, and will eventually convert market share into profits. This premise breaks down, at least in the long run, if the only focus is imitating a traditional business and simply upgrading operational effectiveness or marketing activities through information technology. A long term competitive advantage requires a solid combination of effective delivery and innovative product and service technology, which then lead to profitability, as AOL has demonstrated.

SUMMARY AND ENTREPRENEURIAL IMPLICATIONS

Internalization theory, complemented with resource-based firm theory, has been presented as a value creation framework for three different e-business models. This framework allows us to explain how to increase the sustainable competitive advantage of an entrepreneurial firm using information technology as a lever to enhance the value of the delivery system, research and development and operational effectiveness. Entrepreneurial implications are provided below within the context of this framework.

Increasing Effective Delivery

More effective contact with consumers is associated with higher firm value, although the relationship may appear even stronger if only because of the more immediate and obvious payoffs from marketing activities. Whether for new products or product improvements that make use of existing technology, a new marketing program is likely to be required to enter existing or new markets.

Although a greater return on investment may accrue for delivery and contact efforts at one point in time, it is still not a substitute for sustaining the technological advantage of new product and service development; substitution of one form of equity for another will simply not work. This was shown in a more extensive analysis of the impact of foreign direct investment (Mishra & Gobeli, 1998). The R&D foundation must not only be maintained, but developed further, in order to fuel the ongoing development of firm value.

Increasing Research and Development

An increased value of research and development is associated with a higher firm value. An implication for the entrepreneur is that significant R&D expenditures over several years will enhance the market value of the firm. Increasing the average level of R&D expenditures will lead to improved benefits for both base technological competence and innovative potential for true breakthroughs. It is thus advantageous to have substantive historical R&D expenditures. Furthermore, the investments in R&D (for new products and services, not just IT) should be ongoing, in order to maintain a sustainable advantage.

Increasing Operational Effectiveness

This is the easiest and most basic e-commerce strategy. In fact, few businesses can escape the necessity of keeping in touch with the electronic frontier just to retain its competitiveness. But, by itself this is not really a viable strategy; it must be combined with efforts to develop new products and services, and to support more effective contact with consumers.

Using IT as a Strategic Lever

Our final conclusion is that increased e-commerce investment will be associated with higher firm values when the investment enhances delivery/ customer contact, research and development and operational effectiveness. The implications for entrepreneurs are significant for two reasons. One, having a solid foundation of these strategic variables will likely enhance the chances of success through e-commerce investment. Second, firm value increases not only with higher values of each equity, but the increases are even greater with higher e-commerce investment.

This "equity multiplication effect" on competitive advantage can occur through any or all of the three strategic variables. Contributions through customer contact can build brand equity and are not only essential, but are the most seductive and apparent, given sufficient investors' funds. Contributions through product and service research and development are perhaps the most fundamental to competitive advantage, but due to the longer term return on investment, may not appear to be so.

Finally, contributions through leveraging operational effectiveness, while essential, are limited, as other competitors also pursue the productivity boundaries described by Porter (1998). This is why many dot-coms are doomed if they simply apply the IT lever alone.

REFERENCES

Barney, J. (1991). Firm resources and sustained competitive advantage. *Journal of Management, 17*(1), 99–120.

Bharadwaj, A. S., Bharadwaj, S. G., & Konsynski, B. R. (1999). Information technology effects on firm performance as measured by Tobin's q. *Management Science, 45*, 1008–1024.

Buckley, P., & Casson, M. (1976). *The future of the multinational enterprise.* London: Macmillan.

Cohen, W., & Levinthal, D. (1989). Innovation and learning: The two faces of R&D—Implications for the analysis of R&D investment. *Economic Journal, 99*, 569–596.

Davenport, T.H. (1998). Putting the enterprise into the enterprise system. *Harvard Business Review*, 121–131.

Dierickx, I., & Cool, K. (1989). Asset stock accumulation and sustainability of competitive advantage. *Management Science, 35*, 1504–1511.

Dunning, J.H. (1980). Toward an eclectic theory of international production: Some empirical tests. *Journal of International Business Studies, 11*, 9–31.

Evans, P., & Wurster, T.S. (1999). Getting real about virtual commerce. *Harvard Business Review*, 85–94.

Grant, R.M. (1991). The resource-based theory of competitive advantage: Implications for strategy formulation. *California Management Review*, 114–135.

Griffith, D.A., & Palmer, J.W. (1999). Leveraging the web for corporate success. *Business Horizons*, 3–10.

Gulati, R., & Garino, J. (2000). Get the right mix of bricks & clicks. *Harvard Business Review, 78*, 107–114.

Hall, R. (1992). The strategic analysis of intangible resources. *Strategic Management Journal, 13*, 137–144.

Hammer, M., & Champy, J. (1993). *Reengineering the corporation.* New York: Harper Business.

Hartman, A., Sifonis, J., & Kador, J. (2000). *Net ready: Strategies for success in the E-conomy.* New York: McGraw-Hill.

Hayek, F.A. (1945). The use of knowledge in society. *The American Economic Review, 35*, 519–530.

Hirschey, M., & Weygandt, J. (1985). Amortization policy for advertising and research and development expenditures. *Journal of Accounting Research, 23*, 326–335.

Keller, K.L. (1993). Conceptualizing, measuring, and managing customer-based brand equity. *Journal of Marketing, 57*, 1–22.

McAlexander, J., Schouten, J., & Koenig, H. (2002, in press). Building brand community. *Journal of Marketing.*

Mishra, C., & Gobeli, D. (1998). Managerial incentives, internalization, and market valuation of multinational firms. *Journal of International Business Studies, 29*(3), 583–597.

Morck, R., & Yeung, B. (1991). Why investors value multinationality. *Journal of Business, 64*, 165–187.

Porter, M.E. (1998). What is strategy. *Harvard Business Review, 74*, 61–78.

Porter, M.E. (2001). Strategy and the internet. *Harvard Business Review, 79*, 63–78.

Reingold, J., Stepanek, M., & Brady, D. (2000). What the productivity revolution will spread. *Business Week*, February 14, pp. 112–118.

Rugman, A.M. (1980). Internationalization as a general theory of foreign direct investment: A reappraisal of the literature. *Weltwirtschaftliches Archiv, 116,* 365–379.

Sager, I., Burrows, P., Rocks, D., & Brady, D. (1999). Inside IBM: Internet business machine. *Business Week,* December 13, pp. EB20–EB40.

Schumpeter, J.A. (1934/1961). On the theory of economic development. Reprinted in B. Okun & R.W. Richardson (Eds.), *Studies in economic development* (pp. 89–95). New York: Holt, Rinehart and Winston.

Schumpeter, J.A. (1939/1961). The contours of economic evolution. Reprinted in B. Okun & R.W. Richardson (Eds.), *Studies in economic development* (pp. 95–100). New York: Holt, Rinehart and Winston.

Schumpeter, J.A. (1942/1975). *Capitalism, socialism and democracy.* New York: Harper.

Schumpeter, J.A. (1949/1951). Economic theory and entrepreneurial history. Reprinted in R.V. Clemence (Ed.), *Essays of J.A. Schumpeter* (pp. 248–266). Cambridge, MA: Addison-Wesley.

Shane, S., & Venkataraman, S. (2000). The promise of entrepreneurship as a field of research. *Academy of Management Review, 25,* 217–226.

Stabell, C.B., & Fjeldstad, O.D. (1998). Configuring value for competitive advantage: On chains, shops, and networks. *Strategic Management Journal, 19,* 413–437.

Thompson, J.D. (1967). *Organizations in action.* New York: McGraw-Hill.

Venkatraman, N. (2000). Five steps to a dot-com strategy: How to find your footing on the web. *Sloan Management Review, 41,* 15–28.

CHAPTER 2

ENTREPRENEURS' OPPORTUNITIES IN TECHNOLOGY-BASED MARKETS

Steve Walsh and Bruce Kirchhoff

ABSTRACT

This paper examines the statement made by Christensen (1997) that disruptive technologies are introduced into markets with innovations that cost more and perform more poorly than existing products. This is likely to be an industry specific observation observed in part because of an imprecise definition of "disruptive innovation." Empirical evidence suggests that start-up independent firms are more successful at the innovation process because they are unaffiliated with an existing product line, do not have an existing customer base, and so search for applications where their technology can provide immediate profitability. This "fresh start" advantage means that *The Innovator's Dilemma* provides major opportunities for independent entrepreneurial firms.

INTRODUCTION

Since Christensen's publication of *The Innovator's Dilemma* in 1997, there has been a renewal of interest in R&D procedures and a plethora of new ideas on how to create disruptive technologies in order to avoid the innovator's dilemma of relying on sustaining technologies. The definition of disruptive technologies builds upon the strategic categorization scheme originally suggested by Bower and Christensen (1995). They view technologies as either those that *sustain* the current manufacturing practices and technological capabilities required in an industrial setting or alternatively *disrupt* the current capability set required by a given market. Furthermore disruptive technologies are those that do not support current firm based manufacturing practice. In addition, Bower and Christensen (1995) state that a technology is considered disruptive when its utility generates service products and/or physical products with different performance attributes that may not be valued by existing customers. Moore (1991) adds clarity to this aspect of disruptive technologies by noting that they generate discontinuous innovations that require users/adopters to significantly change their behavior in order to use the innovation.

Christensen in the *Innovator's Dilemma* (1997) notes that many firms slip into an operating mode that avoids disruptive technologies in favor of sustaining technologies that have a greater time adjusted rate of return. Firms find that the disruptive technology-based innovations "disrupt" existing profitable products thereby reducing revenues in the short run. While disruptive technologies promise considerable opportunities for early and strong entry into existing and new markets, they also involve high risk of failure because of customer resistance. There are a growing number of corporate executives, especially in large, established firms who believe that the commercialization of disruptive technologies is an increasingly more costly endeavor with greater uncertainty of success in a more rapidly changing technological environment. This raises the question of whether commercial activities based on disruptive technologies can deliver appropriate payoffs to investors.

Christensen (1997) provides anecdotal evidence that shows large firms who commercialize innovations based upon disruptive technologies face enormous internal and market problems. It is not unusual for these firms to experience conflict among technologists about the value of the technology, difficulty with manufacturing processes, plus resistance and occasionally refusal by marketing managers to promote and sell such high risk product(s) to existing, satisfied customers. Internal problems are compounded by resistance from users regarding adoption, and, when adopted, resistance to make the major changes in user behavior necessary to implement the technology.

In other words, a firm that has established an existing technological competence that yields profits and expanding revenues finds it difficult to commercialize the next disruptive technology and destroy the market that it currently serves so well. In this way, the highly successful innovator is unprepared for and falls victim to the next emerging disruptive technology (Christensen, 1997).

Disruptive technology creation and commercialization has become the focus of financial concerns for both large and small firms. In large firms disruptive technologies have traditionally emerged from R&D organizations. But, Christensen (1997) notes that because of its unstructured nature and the uncertainty of the technological outcomes, commercialization of disruptive technologies is hard to quantify and therefore justify in financial terms. Commercial yield or "big payoffs" can take a long time to emerge, many years as compared to the commercialization of sustaining (sustaining) technologies which are more incremental in nature and may find widespread application within months.

Small business organizations, on the other hand, have lower fixed costs and involve all of the organization's employees in the commercialization process. The business exists for the purpose of successfully commercializing a particular technology.

This paper provides an alternative perspective of technological innovation's role in development of competitive markets based on Schumpeter's (1934, 1942) economic theory. This model argues contrary to much of the literature on technologically based market competition. For example, standard design has long been an accepted basis of competitive advantage as noted by Abernathy and Clark (1985). They develop the concept of the Transillance map to demonstrate how a dominant design is derived in an industrial setting and that firms compete along those design parameters. Elsewhere, Anderson and Tushman (1990) directly discuss technological discontinuities and dominant designs as the major factors defining market competition. Most of the conventional literature on innovation and competition suggests that industries with dominant standards appear to be bereft of opportunities for new start ups. We believe that reality frequently demonstrates that early in the development of new technology based innovations, entry opportunities exist that reshape competitive markets.

Christensen (1997, p.125) concludes that this contrast between established firms and small firms suggests that new, small organizations are the preferred mechanism for introducing disruptive technologies. So, he recommends that large firms form small organization units to launch and manage the growth of a disruptive technology for its entire life. Match the size of the organization to the size of the market. With this statement, Christensen basically equates small size to entrepreneurial behavior.

ENTREPRENEURIAL FIRMS

In the new, independent, entrepreneurial firm, the linkage of technology to markets is the responsibility of everyone, especially the founders, of the firm. And, new entrepreneurial firms, have low fixed costs, low overhead, a single technology focus, and willingly risk current income for potential capital gains they will receive if successful. With a lower cash burn rate, new entrepreneurial firms have longer staying power and no customer base to attend to while pursuing commercial acceptance. And success can generate phenomenal increases in firm valuation simply because the potential revenues are not diluted by a wide variety of other product sales.

Historically new entrepreneurial firms have handled the commercialization process more successfully. Research on product innovations introduced in the early 1970s showed that small independent firms produced 2.5 time more innovations per employee than large firms (Gellman, 1976). Later research of product innovations in the United States during 1982 yielded confirmation of these results (Futures Group, 1984).

If new, small, independent technology intensive firms outperform their larger more established and resource rich cousins in the commercialization of disruptive technologies, then the source of their advantage should be searched out and identified so that technological progress of such firms can be enhanced. Especially important are questions about the technologies selected and the commercialization methods that new firms apply. Formulated in strategic terms, we need to learn what core competencies and capabilities successful new, tech intensive small firms use. And, we need to know what market strategies they choose and why they choose these. It is possible that appropriate identification of the innovation process can provide a foundation for improved effectiveness in launching new disruptive technologies.

We do not yet have answers to all of the questions we raise in the above paragraph. But we begin our own research effort by developing a model of the innovation process that provides a foundation for future research. The model begins with technology creation and ends with user application. By examining this model, we gain insight into the advantages that entrepreneurial firms have in commercializing disruptive technologies and some understanding of why it may not be enough to follow Christensen's recommendation of simply "...matching the organization size to the market" (Christensen, 1997, p. 125).

DISRUPTIVE TECHNOLOGY MODEL

Figure 1 provides a diagram that describes the overall innovation process. From left to right, the diagram shows the process of technology becoming an invention that emerges as an innovation with market success. We focus our discussion with the upper half of the diagram that begins with disruptive technology. But first, we need to define disruptive and sustaining technologies.

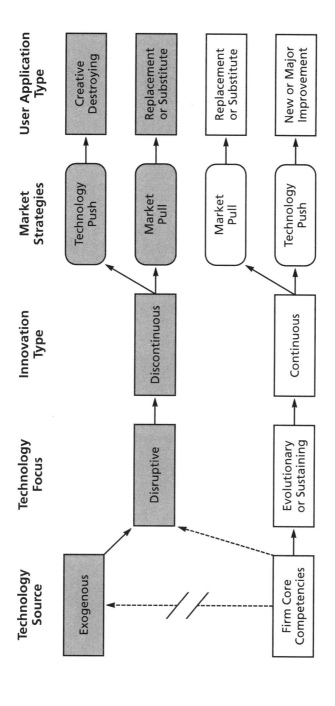

Figure 1. Disruptive Technology Innovation Model. *Source:* Walsh and Kirchhoff, 1998, "Strategies for HTSF's Embracing Autonomous Disruptive Technologies;" a paper presented at the 6th Annual International High-Technology Small Firms Conference, June 1998.

Disruptive Technology

Christensen (1997), Morone (1993), Bower and Christensen (1995), Bitindo and Frohman (1981), SEST-Euroconsult (1984) and many others identify two classes of technology: (1) disruptive, radical, emergent or step-function technologies; and (2) sustaining, evolutionary, incremental or "nuts and bolts" technologies. Although there is considerable ambiguity and overlap in these multiple terms, we will use the terms disruptive and sustaining as categories encompassing the major characteristics of these two technology types.

Bower and Christensen (1995) note that disruptive technologies may not be radically new from a technological point of view but have superior performance trajectories along critical dimensions that customers value. Disruptive technologies typically emerge from a combination of information drawn from a mix of technical disciplines. As such, disruptive technologies are exogenous, i.e., external to the mainstream (sustaining) technologies that dominate a particular industry or firm. For example, the transistor emerged as a mix of chemistry, physics and electrical technical knowledge. No vacuum tube manufacturer had this combination of knowledge and none of the vacuum tube manufacturers were able to enter the transistor manufacturing industry. Yet, transistors (and their eventual evolution into integrated circuits) are the main technology in electronics today with vacuum tubes a shadow memory of the past.

Disruptive Technology and Creative Destruction

Schumpeter (1942) argues that innovations with major impact upon economic activity originate from outside the industry that they affect. To the extent that Schumpeterian innovations are technology based, he argues that they are brought from outside the existing industry structure and introduced by entrepreneurs. On the other hand, it is apparent that when disruptive technologies are converted into discontinuous innovations, they have a tremendous impact upon markets. Schumpeter (1934) describes capitalism as an economic system that finds its competitive strength in innovation. This innovative activity he calls "creative destruction" is clearly driven by what we call disruptive technologies. And discontinuous innovations have the power to destroy market structure by shifting market shares from old technologies to new technologies. For example, the personal computer had an economic impact that continues to positively affect world economic growth. Applications of personal computers have expanded exponentially. At the same time the market for main frame and minicomputers has been destroyed and producers such as Digital

Equipment, Data General, and Univac have been driven out of the business. This is creative destruction.

Abernathy and Utterback (1988) confirm this as they describe disruptive technologies as those that underlie discontinuous innovations that create entirely new technology-product-market paradigms to the world markets that may be opaque to customers. Opaqueness, they note, constrains buyer enthusiasm for varying their established behavioral habits.

Opaqueness may, in fact, be too circumspect a word to use for buyer reaction. Buyers resist adopting discontinuous innovations because such innovations cause them grief in an important way. Moore (1991) states that all discontinuous innovations require buyers to change their behavior in some significant way. For example, during the 1980s, as businesses acquired personal computers, the information processing divisions of these organizations had to change from one central group running batch programs on large mainframe computers to a dispersed group assisting many employees to comprehend and use a bevy of independent machines spread throughout the firm. This changed both the organization structure and power relationships in all large firms that adopted microcomputing and networking.

Moore (1991) notes that the mechanism for overcoming buyer/user resistance to adopting discontinuous innovations is to demonstrate that such innovations provide significant cost reductions and/or offer performance improvements. In this way, customers are found who are willing to take the risks of newness (Mansfield, 1968). But, customers are not usually resident in a new, single-product/single-industry market. A truly disruptive technology finds its uses in many different markets among "lead user" groups (Von Hipple, 1986). Christensen (1997) argues that "disruptive innovations"[1] rarely enter a market with well developed, user enhancing advantages. Thus, their entry is slow to take root and entry rarely yields early profits for suppliers. However, as noted below, such blunt entry may not be the norm used by new, entrepreneurial firms and this may be their major advantage.

Furthermore, disruptive technologies have an unfortunate (for researchers) characteristic since they can only be identified after their effects are known. As yet, it is impossible to identify disruptive technologies early in their life. Christensen (1997) describes disruptive technologies from several industries and products in his book. But, this is with the benefit of hindsight. In Chapter 8, Christensen makes an effort to provide guidance for identifying disruptive technologies early in their life. However, much of this depends on a market analysis that implicitly contains the assumption that new disruptive technologies will enter the existing market(s). Lots of anecdotes exist to show that disruptive technologies actually create new industries that only with time replace the old markets—Schumpeterian creative destruction. The internal combustion engine was around for years before it found its home in automobiles—which displaced horse drawn carriages and wagons. Microprocessors were around for seven years before the Apple II became commercial. And then the microprocessor-based computers did not seriously impact on the market for mainframe and minicomputers for another 12 years after that (Freiberger & Swaine, 2000).

Technology is evolutionary, i.e., unpredictable. Christensen knows this and indicates that he chose an industry that was changing rapidly so that he could observe it over a short period of time and learn about disruptive technologies (1997, pp. 3–4). However, this causes him to develop a one industry perspective, a perspective that is too narrow to capture the vital role of replacement and substitute innovations as the critical step to developing disruptive technologies.

Sustaining Technologies

Sustaining technologies are those that foster improved product performance "…along the dimensions of performance that mainstream customers in major markets have historically valued" (Christensen, 1997, p. xv). Given this definition, it becomes apparent that disruptive technologies not only provide their originators with sustainable competitive advantage but they provide proprietary markets for subsequent sustaining technologies. The mechanism by which this occurs is that innovations derived from disruptive technologies lead buyers to change their behaviors to accommodate the advantages of the innovations (Moore, 1991). Once user behaviors are changed, the new technology becomes part of the customer's organization. Foster (1986) states that sustaining technologies improve incrementally from a body of existing knowledge. Sustaining technologies create innovations that are modifications of, improvements to, or replacements for existing products. These are called continuous innovations (Morone, 1993). Such technologies often change incrementally moving from the simple to the more complex. Sustaining technologies do not alter markets the way that disruptive technologies do and they often are driven by customer demand for improvements of existing products, improvements that make better products to fit current customer behaviors.

As users identify new needs, sustaining technologies emerge from research based upon core competencies developed from the disruptive technology to create continuous innovations that satisfy users' growing needs. In this way, a disruptive technology leads to a stream of sustaining technologies that produce continuous innovations that constantly update and improve the current customer-based products. Thus, a discontinuous innovation, when successful, creates its own market for follow-on continuous innovations that provide improvements and upgrades of customer-based products. Therefore, companies build on disruptive technologies to remain competitive.

INNOVATION AND MARKET STRATEGIES

Innovation, by Schumpeter's definition, means the commercialization of invention (Schumpeter, 1934). Commercialization is widely perceived as the process of bringing an invention into a working product that has commercial acceptance and derives adequate revenues and profits to at least maintain the operations of a profit making business. This is heavily dependent upon the process we call marketing. Here two steps in our model, market strategies and product are so closely linked that we discuss them together.

Our model suggests a two-tier approach to the commercialization of technologies: (1) products that creatively destroy markets; and (2) products for replacements, substitutes or improvements. Discontinuous innovations can emerge as either replacement products or new major creative destroyers. New creative destroying products require a long time to penetrate the market and realize their full profit potential. But, replacement products can be made to meet identifiable buyer needs and enter the market rather quickly with little buyer resistance.

Replacement Products

The stream of sustaining technologies that flow from the core competencies that are built during the creation of the disruptive technology will tie the customer to continuous innovations from the manufacturer for many years. However, the incidence of intellectual property protection among sustaining technologies is less common than among disruptive technologies so there is less opportunity for achieving sustainable competitive advantage based upon intellectual property protection. This opens the market for innovative replacement and/or substitute products that offer better performance and/or lower cost.

The corollary to this logic is that entrepreneurial firms may find their greatest market advantage through offering proprietary disruptive technologies in the form of innovative products that replace or augment the continuous innovations offered to customers of large established firms. Thus, the entrepreneur's best strategy is to seek an entirely new (to the entrepreneurial firm) set of customers to adopt the firm's proprietary technology as a replacement or enhancement to the existing products of the established, dominant supplying firms. And these replacements should be both cost and performance improvements over the offerings of the established firms. This allows the entrepreneur to construct a customer base rather quickly. And revenues begin to flow into the firm, revenues that are necessary to launch a full creative destroying innovation based upon the disruptive technology.

Replacement products can also emerge from sustaining technologies (i.e., continuous innovations). Thus, in total, our model suggests four classifications of innovations and market strategies: (1) discontinuous/market-pull innovations (i.e., replacement products); (2) discontinuous/technology-push innovations (i.e., creative destroying new products); (3) continuous/market-pull innovations (i.e., replacement products); and (4) continuous/technology-push innovations (i.e., new products). Here we only discuss the discontinuous/market-pull innovations that represent the greatest opportunity for entrepreneurial entry strategy since these provide a viable entry mechanism that entrepreneurial firms can use and larger firms have difficulty implementing.

DISCONTINUOUS/MARKET-PULL

This combination of disruptive technology and market strategy of replacement products may be the lifeblood of true creative destruction. Although not in itself the basis for creative destruction, it nonetheless provides a bridge for entrepreneurs between the old and new technologies. Disruptive technologies need to evolve over time so that the disruptive technology can be refined and improved, innovations can gradually acquire appropriate characteristics, and production infrastructure can be established, i.e., raw material suppliers, process methods, and production procedures can be identified and matched with the technology's capabilities. A major way to accomplish this is by using a disruptive technology to create innovations that are replacements and/or substitutes for existing user applications where user needs are not being met by the mainstream technologies. As mentioned above, replacement or substitute products are usually much easier to sell because, if properly designed, such innovations require minimal changes to customer behavior and offer cost and performance advantages.

For example, silicon based, large scale integrated circuit, microprocessors were first manufactured by Intel Corporation. Intel was a new firm that began as a "me too" manufacturer of RAM chips for mainframe and minicomputers. At that time, there was no buyer need for unique, small, independent computing power. But, at the request of an existing customer, Intel developed a microprocessor for a calculator in 1970. Although not requested, Intel made the processor programmable and more powerful than necessary based upon its own creative interest. Eventually, in 1971,

Intel's 8008 processor, applicable to calculators, but more powerful because of its programmability, became commercially available (Freiberger & Swaine, 2000). Hobbyists bought it and made the first microcomputers. Intel also found a market for its microprocessors in mainframes and mini-computers. In these applications, manufacturers used them to manage peripheral operations (printers, card readers, etc.) so as to improve the capabilities of their computers by making more of the expensive RAM memory available for calculation. These replacement applications (and several others) allowed Intel to generate revenues and gradually improve its technology until it created the chip that became the microprocessor for the IBM-PC in 1981. During this gradual improvement process, Intel never targeted a mass market for independent (personal) computing machines. Yet, the IBM-PC became the standard for a host of commercially successful, mass marketed personal computers leading to the phenomenal expansion of personal computers that changed the entire computer world—an excellent example of creative destruction (Frieberger & Swaine, 2000).

Christensen's (1997) observations of the hard disk drive manufacturing industry caused him to conclude that new "disruptive" innovations often begin life as cost inefficient, poorly performing products. But, innovations in hard disks were marketed with technology-push strategies, i.e., pushing the new technology in direct competition with the existing technologies. There was only one major market for small, high capacity, hard disk drives—personal computers. Not surprisingly, buyers who were connected to the dominant product suppliers had no defined need for the new product. The entrepreneurial firms with the new technology had a very difficult sales job since the new technology required the user to completely redesign the users' product (microcomputers). Customer resistance resulted in long start-up times and unprofitable operations that threatened survival of the firms introducing the new technology. Also, in terms of Schumpeter's definition, none of these technologies were creative destroyers. Hard disk manufacturers are a good example of sustaining technology myopia, but not of disruptive technologies. Hard disk drives did not creatively destroy the microcomputer industry nor creatively destroy any existing industry. Christensen's definition of disruptive technology is ambiguous, an ambiguity that prevents this example to become definitive.

However, examples such as Intel abound to refute Christensen's assumption that the hard disk industry is necessarily typical of entrepreneurial entry or of disruptive technology.

CONCLUSIONS

New entrepreneurial firms with disruptive technologies can find survival and even profitability in replacement or substitute products directed at filling an existing need among customers of established, market dominant firms. Entrepreneurs find that their technology can provide innovations that offer improvements over existing products provided by large firms operating in the mainstream of a sustaining technology. The wise technological entrepreneur chooses a buyer-pull strategy balanced with technology-push by finding a replacement or substitute product that fulfills buyer needs. This strategy provides revenues and profits while the disruptive technology matures into a Schumpeterian creative destroyer innovation. It is the creative destroyer innovation that also produces long term core technological competencies and competitive advantages. These in turn provide long-term growth and success for the enterprise.

Christensen's perception that early innovations of new disruptive technologies have higher costs and poorer performance characteristics are not correct for all such technologies. But, this difference may be why he misses the important advantages held by new, small entrepreneurial firms. Small units of established firms undoubtedly will experience pressures to meet the needs of the existing customer base and technological mainstream of the parent firms. In this way, they will be inclined to look for new products or replacement products to fit existing markets. This focus will inhibit their efforts to develop the creative destroying innovations that could make a major impact.

But, new, independent, entrepreneurial firms have no existing markets, no existing customers. They look for any market where their technology offers cost and performance advantages over existing products, i.e., replacements for existing products. And, the existence of replacement/ substitute product opportunities assures new technology entrepreneurs that they can succeed in creating market destroying innovations that will benefit the economy as well as their own pockets.

There are subtle and not so subtle research implications of this logic. As researchers, we have the difficulty of identifying nascent disruptive technologies or disruptive technologies prior to their full effect being realized. To date this has been impossible. We have concluded that if researchers are going to understand disruptive technologies, they need to carry out ongoing research on new technologies for long periods of time in hope of documenting the early life of those people and ideas that eventually become a creative destroying innovation.

The authors' research efforts are following such a path. We are following a new industry based on Microand Nano systems technology that is currently blossoming in its twentieth year of innovative activity. We have been and are observing through biennial surveys the status of the firms in the industry and waiting for the "disruptive" technologies to emerge. So far, there are many replacement innovations in the industry and more entering many different markets annually. No "creative destroyer" has yet been observed. But, we are watching.

NOTE

1.   Christensen does not differentiate between disruptive "technologies" and "innovations" thereby allowing ambiguity to enter into his arguments.

REFERENCES

Abernathy, W.J., & Utterback, J.M. (1988). Patterns of industrial innovation. In M.L. Tushman & W. Moore (Eds.), *Readings in the management of innovation* (2nd ed., pp. 25–36).Cambridge, MA: Ballinger.

Anderson, P., & Tushman, M. (1990). Technological discontinuities and dominant designs: A cyclical model of technological change. *Administrative Science Quarterly, 35*, 604–633.

Bitindo, D., & Frohman, A. (1981, November). Linking technological and business planning. *Research Management,* 19–23.

Bower, J.L., & Christensen, C.M. (1995, January-February). Disruptive technologies: Catching the wave. *Harvard Business Review,* 43–53.

Christensen, C.M. (1997). *The innovator's dilemma.* Boston: Harvard Business School Press.

Foster, R.N. (1986). Timing technological transitions. In M.L. Tushman & W. Moore (Eds.), *Readings in the management of innovation* (2nd ed., pp. 215–228).Cambridge, MA: Ballinger.

Freiberger, P., & Swaine, M. (2000). *Fire in the valley.* New York: McGraw Hill.

Futures Group. (1984). *Characterization of innovations introduced on the U.S. market in 1982.* Washington, DC: U.S. Small Business Administration, Office of Advocacy.

Gellman Research Associates. (1976). *Indicators of international trends in technological innovation.* Washington, DC: U.S. Small Business Administration, Office of Advocacy.

Mansfield, E. (1968). *The economics of technological change.* New York: W.W. Norton.

Moore, G. (1991). *Crossing the chasm.* New York: Harpers Business.

Morone, J. (1993). *Winning in high tech markets.* Boston: Harvard Business School.

Schumpeter, J. (1934). *The theory of economic development.* Boston: Harvard University Press.

Schumpeter, J. (1942). *Capitalism, socialism, and democracy.* London: Allen & Unwin.

SEST-Euroconsult. (July, 1984) *Le Bonzai de l'industrie japonais, Elements de reflexion sur l'integretion de technologie dans la function strategique des enteprises japonaises.* French Ministry of Research and Technology.

Utterback, J.M. (1994). *Mastering the dynamics of innovation*. Boston: Harvard Business School Press.

Von Hippel, E. (1986). Lead users: A source of novel product concepts. In M.L. Tushman & W. Moore (Eds.), *Readings in the management of innovation* (2nd ed., pp. 352–366). Cambridge, MA: Ballinger.

Walsh, S., & Kirchhoff, B. (1998, June). *Strategies for HTSF's embracing autonomous disruptive technologies*. Paper presented at the 6th Annual International High-Technology Small Firms Conference.

CHAPTER 3

BEYOND THE BOUNDARYLESS ORGANIZATION

The Value of E-Commerce Technologies in Entrepreneurship Behavior

Lisa K. Gundry and Jill Kickul

ABSTRACT

The rise of electronic commerce has created one of the most challenging environments for entrepreneurship in recent history, where market needs and the technology required to meet these needs can change even while the product or service is still under development. This demands that founders of organizations strive for "relentless innovation," leading their firms through the continual infusion of new ideas, emphasizing constant innovation, experimentation, and rapid change. The overall purpose of our paper is to examine how the changes associated with e-commerce technology influence the way entrepreneurs identify and exploit market opportunities and add value through the introduction and design of new innovations and practices for their businesses. A new set of core business values appears to distinguish Internet entrepreneurial teams from others. These values are constant innovation, experimentation, and rapid change. Future research questions that emerge center on whether such "hyper-innovative" behaviors are truly required in these organizations that go beyond what would be considered in traditional firms to be novel, different, and change embracing.

INTRODUCTION

Entrepreneurship has always been a vibrant force in the economy, and at the forefront of adaptation and growth of new markets. As the twentieth century draws to its closure, it has been described as the "century of the entrepreneur" (Bangs & Pinson, 1999). The entrepreneurial landscape continues to transform and as the twenty-first century unfolds, a new form of entrepreneurship is taking shape. With the rapid acceleration and availability of technology, electronic commerce is changing the nature of business.

Electronic commerce has experienced dynamic and rapid growth in the late 1990s. By the end of 2000, it was estimated that there were 407.1 million web users worldwide. In the United States and Canada alone consumers spent more than $45 billion shopping online in the year 2000 while net-commerce (both B2B and B2C) accounted for more than $657 billion worldwide ($488.7 billion in the United States). Total Worldwide Net commerce—both B2B and B2C—is expected to hit $6.8 trillion in 2004 (Forrester Research, 2001). By some estimates, annual online sales will reach $200 billion by 2004 and will exceed $1 trillion a year within ten years (Birnbaum, 2000). It is projected that by 2003, forty million U.S. households will shop on the web, and revenues from this will approach $108 billion (Forrester Research, 1999). These statistics reflect the increasing number of ventures that will be launched on the Internet.

This rise of electronic commerce has created one of the most challenging environments for entrepreneurship in recent history, where market needs and the technology required to meet these needs can change even while the product or service is still under development (Iansiti & MacCormak, 1997). This framework demands that founders of organizations strive for "relentless innovation," leading their firms through the continual infusion of new ideas, emphasizing constant innovation, experimentation, and rapid change (Cohen & Jordan, 1999).

The overall purpose of our paper is to examine how the changes associated with e-commerce technology influence the way entrepreneurs identify and exploit market opportunities and add value through the introduction and design of new innovations and practices for their businesses. Many of our answers will inform the development of the growing research base in this area, and will facilitate the subsequent comparison of key variables and relationships found in firms engaging in e-commerce with those of traditional brick and mortar firms.

We will present the emergent practices and processes of e-commerce entrepreneurship, and will explore the key challenges facing these new ventures. We will also present a research agenda to guide future work in this area. The paper draws on recent research findings, and focuses on founders and organizations whose activities *encompass* the Internet, conducting multiple transactions on the web, rather than on organizations that use the web only as an additive to their business for customer advertising and information gathering purposes. It is the premise of this paper that the first major step in developing a model of e-commerce entrepreneurship is to examine the processes and behaviors found within these ventures. This is conducted along several dimensions and contributes to our understanding of the nature, opportunities, challenges, and future directions of these entrepreneurial firms.

DISCONTINUOUS CHANGE AND E-COMMERCE TECHNOLOGIES

Schumpeter's (1943) notion of "creative destruction" appropriately characterizes how Internet technology has revolutionized the way organizations function and operate to bring value to their multiple customers and business partners. As mentioned by McKnight (2001), "Internet businesses are founded on and rely on nothing more remarkable than the technological and economic forces of creative destruction—as usual" (p. 51). The overall reach, speed, and influence of both destructive and economic pressures are accelerated by the global interconnectivity of businesses and consumers through the Internet. In many ways, the Internet can be seen as destructive change that undermines previously established business models and practices. However, at the same time, new opportunities and possibilities are being created and established (Schwartz, 1999). New forms of arranging work are observable, such as collapsing boundaries between firms, suppliers, customers, and competitors. New and expanding markets are creating increased competition, and greater consumer choice (Morino, 1999). The rapid acceleration and availability of Internet technology is also shaping an evolution in how emerging and existing organizations establish their value position in their markets/industries as well as how they structure and design new processes and management practices within their own businesses.

This new environment forces organizations to rapidly try new approaches, quickly share successes and failures, and monitor what is new and useful (Oliva, 1998). E-commerce and its enabling technology will allow managers to become quicker in how they gather, synthesize, utilize, and disseminate information, and those that are willing to experiment with new product and service offerings will be positioned to compete most effectively (Hodgetts, Luthans, & Slocum, 1999).

The extents to which these entrepreneurs capitalize on the conditions presented by e-commerce and engage in experimentation and innovation is of major interest in contemporary research. Because of the demand for innovative organizational behavior present in e-commerce, this is an important domain in which to study entrepreneurship. E-commerce can be seen as an integrated, flexible approach to deliver differentiated business value that enables new and existing organizations to run core business operations, systems, and processes (Amor, 2000).

The Entrepreneurial Landscape: Emergent Trends in E-Commerce Entrepreneurship

Prospective entrepreneurs who wish to capitalize on Internet technology will need to identify the factors necessary to successfully found and sustain this type of business. Effective "e-businesses" will seek out and act upon the demands of the market, differentiating themselves through customer management, relationship marketing, and community building (Shannon, 1999). In order to meet many of their financial and operating goals and objectives, many e-businesses are engaging in a variety of corporate initiatives that emphasize new market penetration, mergers and acquisitions, mass customization, and technology and process improvements (Drucker, 1997; Hitt, 1998; Morgan & Smith, 1996).

In order to achieve many of these initiatives and goals, many e-businesses have had to find innovative ways to increase levels of efficiency, lower costs, and improve technological processes throughout the entire organization. In addition, these companies and their management teams have had to formulate strategies that are flexible to allow for continual redesign and reconfiguration of the organization as it grows and matures. Internet technology can assist businesses in building new strategies that add value to the organization through the development of new markets, opportunities, and relationships. By utilizing the appropriate technology, entrepreneurs and existing businesses can pursue new opportunities by placing processes in place to gather information, organize it for the market, select what is valuable, synthesize it, and finally distribute the product/service (see Figure 1). These value-added steps when combined with Internet technology make up the virtual value chain that can be used to identify and exploit market needs, demands, and opportunities (Rayport & Sviokla, 1998).

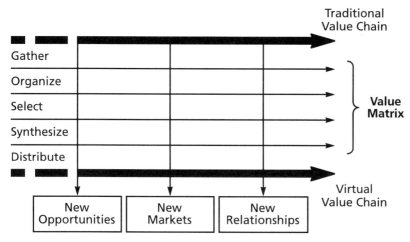

Figure 1.   The Virtual Value Chain.

In order to realize the value of the opportunities made possible by introducing Internet technology into a business, entrepreneurial and forward-thinking organizations will need to consider several dimensions paramount to effective performance (Morino, 1999). According to Morino, these are: speed (advances in computing and globalization have changed stakeholders' expectations about the pace of change); adaptability (the business must be much more flexible and able to identify and respond to changes in technology, competition, and buyer patterns); multidisciplinary and collaborative (integrating such diverse disciplines as technology, services, and graphics). The boundary where the enterprise starts and ends will become blurred, as extranets connect vendors and information networks of capabilities (Cohen & Jordan, 1999).

Evident from this analysis of recent trends in e-commerce is the expression of a new set of entrepreneurial values and behaviors that are increasingly coming to characterize an emerging model of Internet entrepreneurship. In the next section, we identify from recent research some of the primary variables that shape the entrepreneurial actions in these organizations.

The Key Values and Strategic Orientations of Internet Entrepreneurs

The rise of the World Wide Web and electronic commerce has created one of the most challenging environments for product and service development in recent history, where market needs and the technology required to meet these needs can change even while the product or service is still under development (Iansiti & MacCormak, 1997). This framework demands that entrepreneurs strive for "relentless innovation," leading their firms through the continual infusion of new ideas (Cohen & Jordan, 1999). A new set of core business values appears to distinguish Internet entrepreneurial teams from others. These values are constant innovation, experimentation, and rapid change. Such an orientation is similar to what Miller and Blais (1992) characterize as "maverick" behaviors in which firms adopt innovative modes based on their competencies, competitive situations, or managerial preferences. The environment of e-commerce enables firms to rapidly try new approaches, quickly share successes and failures, and monitor what is new and useful (Oliva, 1998). As founders of Internet ventures attempt to meet the opportunities and demands of this new economy, a set of entrepreneurial orientations and behaviors will emerge that can begin to characterize the nature and process of e-commerce ventures.

Strategic Posture of Internet Entrepreneurs

The ability of entrepreneurs to be proactive in their orientation has been described as a critical dimension of entrepreneurship. It includes the propensity to act on perceived market opportunities and entering into new or existing markets (Lumpkin & Dess, 1996). Miller and Friesen (1983) first characterized the entrepreneurially-oriented firm as one that innovated and fully exploited environmental opportunities while repressing environmental threats. Researchers have since identified two key dimensions that underlie an entrepreneurial strategic posture (Covin & Slevin, 1990; Covin & Covin, 1990) or an entrepreneurial strategy-making mode (Dess, Lumpkin, & Covin, 1997). These are the competitive aggressiveness entrepreneurs display as they pursue new opportunities, innovation, and experimentation; and their proactivity that leads to being the first mover among their competitors. An entrepreneurial strategic posture emphasizes a value for innovation. Page (1997) characterized the entrepreneurial strategic posture as the identification or recognition of opportunity and its proactive pursuit.

Interestingly, while new ventures are often the result of entrepreneurs who recognized strategic opportunities within turbulent environments and capitalized upon them (Cooper, Folta, & Woo, 1995; Palich & Bagby, 1995), research has suggested that entrepreneurs are less successful in identifying and pursuing new opportunities beyond the start-up phase (Meyer & Dean, 1990). A significant challenge for young technology ventures is their ability to recognize a highly competitive environment and proactively change their strategic orientation to survive and grow (Page, 1997).

Research findings in this area have been mixed: Miles, Arnold, and Thompson (1993) found that the degree of perceived environmental hostility was negatively correlated with the CEO's entrepreneurial orientation. Other studies point to the positive relationships between hostility and entrepreneurial posture. For example, Smart and Vertinsky (1984) described an entrepreneurial posture as a function of the entrepreneurial personality and that it is deliberately adopted as a strategic response to an uncertain environment. Covin and Slevin (1989) introduced the possibility of positive financial benefits tied to the adoption of an entrepreneurial posture in hostile environments.

The role of strategy in the Internet start-up is evolving as the contrast between traditional planning in organizations and the demand for flexible, responsive experimentation in electronic commerce is increasingly evident. Kanter (2001) describes strategy in Internet firms as "improvisational theater," in which the performances of many "troupes" accumulate to take the organization in a new direction. Entrepreneurs perceive it as emerging and revealed through action, where the action itself reveals the goal. Thus, the primary mode of strategic operation in these ventures is sense-and-respond, as opposed to the traditional make-and-sell (Bradley & Nolan, 1998). This orientation enables entrepreneurs in these organizations to move at Internet speed, and consequently the traditional strategic plan is one on which these entrepreneurs can no longer rely.

The strategic orientation of Internet entrepreneurs includes behaviors such as experimentation, going to the customer and building the customer into the venture as an "actor" (Oliver, 2000). This is similar to Kanter's metaphor of strategy as improvisational theater, in which the "audience" or customers, interact with the venture and influence its outcomes. Further, strategy tends to flow through the organization in all directions, rather than from the top down as it has conventionally moved.

Opportunity Recognition Behaviors of Internet Entrepreneurs

A recent study (Kickul & Gundry, 2000a) measured the relationship between the entrepreneurial posture of Internet business owners who operate within a highly uncertain environment (i.e., their rapid response to change, value for innovation, and development of inter-firm alliances), and their opportunity recognition behaviors. Further, the researchers investigated whether this relationship influences the technological innovations implemented by Internet entrepreneurs (see Figure 2).

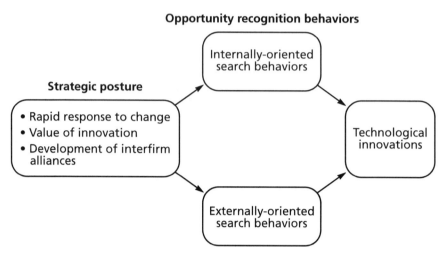

Figure 2.

This study found that the strategic orientations of rapidly responding to change as well as placing value on innovation were linked to externally-oriented opportunity search behaviors. According to Koshiur (1997), Internet entrepreneurs must be continually prepared to make changes within the infrastructure of their businesses to meet and prepare for future opportunities and technological advancements. In addition, flexibility further allows the business to be a successful player in the virtual value chain—"converting the raw information into new services and products in the information world" (Koshiur, 1997, p. 103).

The current electronic marketplace will necessitate new innovative models that deal with firm organization, production, and overall market institutions (Choi, Stahl, & Whinston, 1997; Lange, 1999). Indeed, as others have suggested (Cohen & Jordan, 1999; Oliva, 1998), Internet firms that emphasize innovation and rapid response to change are best positioned for success in this new form of entrepreneurship.

Developing relationships with other firms was also shown to be a determining factor associated with externally-oriented opportunity search behaviors. A promising application for entrepreneurs and their firms in electronic commerce is to use web technology for business-to-business interactions (Choi et al., 1997, Shannon, 1999). Contracting with other organizations allows the entrepreneur to have a more decentralized, nonhierarchical organization that may foster the recognition and implementation of opportunities associated with new product/service ideas and solutions (Morino, 1999). Moreover, having inter-firm relationships that are fluid may also be necessary in uncovering opportunities related to the marketing and distribution of information about the value of the firm's products and services.

Finally, this study also found that Internet firms who engaged in opportunity search behaviors that are externally-focused had implemented technological innovations dealing with new information technology, new computer technology, as well as new methods of advertising. Our results suggest that Internet entrepreneurs tend to rely on network activity (Hills, Lumpkin, & Singh, 1997) in order to enable them to capitalize on opportunities and to reach technological innovations for their businesses and for the marketplace. The significance of these findings is that the net now uniquely enables entrepreneurs to recognize opportunity, thus influencing the subsequent innovations in which they are able to engage.

Given the rapid pace of technology and business, Davis and Meyer (1998) have asserted that there is a greater need to be connected with their suppliers, customers, and business partners. This need for connectivity forces Internet-based organizations to re-evaluate the intangible benefits of the company's technology infrastructure and its product/service offerings. It is expected that as more Internet entrepreneurships are established and identified, research attention will grow and focus on additional strategies and behaviors of this pioneering group.

E-Commerce Technology's Influence on Entrepreneurial Behavior

Drucker (1998) described four areas of innovative opportunities that exist within a company or industry, including unexpected occurrences, incongruities, process needs, and industry and market changes. While these innovative opportunities may be present to Internet entrepreneurial teams, there may be additional areas such firms may identify for potential innovative actions.

This emphasis on innovation and change will be oriented not only to the outcomes of these organizations (e.g., products, services, new markets, etc.) but also to the structure and work arrangements of the ventures themselves. Oliva (1998) has noted that a successful Internet study needs to be designed to assess the following research questions:

- To what extent have these entrepreneurs been engaged in innovations?
- Additionally, what is the direction (type) of these business innovations?

Kickul and Gundry (2000b) examined the type and direction of innovative actions incorporated by Internet entrepreneurs in their businesses. Six distinct innovative behaviors displayed by entrepreneurs were uncovered, ranging from continuous product/service improvements to managing human resources. These innovations varied to the extent that they were considered and implemented into the operations and business of the Internet firm. Improving products/services, seeking alternative markets and opportunities, and incorporating additional marketing strategies were the critical factors associated with initiating innovation and change. According to Koshiur (1997), entrepreneurs must be continually prepared to make innovations and changes within the infrastructure of their business to meet and prepare for future opportunities and market/industry advancements.

Moreover, creative behavior and flexibility further allow the business to be a successful player in the virtual value chain—"converting the raw information into new services and products in the information world" (Koshiur, 1997, p. 103). The current electronic marketplace will necessitate new innovative models that deal with firm organization, production, and overall market institutions (Choi, Stahl, & Whinston, 1997; Lange, 1999). Indeed, as others have suggested (Cohen & Jordan, 1999; Oliva, 1998), Internet firms that emphasize innovation and rapid response to change are best positioned for success in this new form of entrepreneurship.

While this study examined the various types of innovations engaged in by Internet entrepreneurs, future research should investigate how these innovations are related to the firm's strategic focus and orientation. More work should test the strategic requirements for successful Internet enterprise developments that have been proposed in the literature, including: How do the strategic orientations of first-to-market, first-follower, competitive aggressiveness, and rapid response to change predict innovative behavior? Does the enactment of innovative marketing behaviors, for example, give competitive advantage to these firms? What types (direction) of innovative actions seem to matter most to the firm's ability to respond rapidly to change?

Many of the entrepreneurs in this sample reported innovative behaviors that can be characterized as growth-extending, as they adapt to market conditions and negotiate a position for their ventures in the rapidly expanding e-commerce environment. Of further research interest is to determine the degree to which these entrepreneurs eventually increase their growth-enabling behaviors as a means to sustain performance. What role, for example, does recruiting or training actions play in the development of technological innovations (a growth-extending behavior)? More research is needed to ascertain the behavioral supports found in such firms.

Additionally, more research should investigate how Internet entrepreneurs form and develop strategic relationships and alliances with other organizations. That is, how are partnerships formed and dissolved to meet clearly defined business goals and imperatives? As discussed by Hartman, Sifonis, and Kador (2000), Internet firms that are able to define their core competencies and work side-by-side with complementary partners will be able to exploit many of the opportunities existing in the marketplace. Moreover, those firms who are able to continuously improve their businesses and competencies as well as their alliance structure will also be at an advantage in meeting the next new opportunity (Choi et al., 1997; Griffith & Palmer, 1999; Shannon, 1999).

Contracting with other organizations allows the entrepreneur to have a more decentralized, nonhierarchical organization that may foster the implementation of new product/service ideas and solutions (Morino, 1999). Kelley and Rice (1999) found that the rate of alliance and interfirm formation was directly related to the rate of new product introductions in new firms. Moreover, having interfirm relationships that are fluid may also be necessary in the marketing and distribution of information about the value of the firm's products and services. Alternative methods of marketing found in electronic marketplaces that depend on business-to-business cooperation and communication include: soliciting and exchanging web links, soliciting listings from search services, and endorsing and reviewing products/services on newsgroups by firms.

More work should also examine the *strength* of the association between the Internet firms and their suppliers, value-added resellers (VARs), and customers in determining organizational effectiveness and performance. Value-chain migration (Hartman et al., 2000) is one strategy that integrates both the supply-chain and customer-facing system into a single, integrated process. Innovations and improvements are made in the ordering, configuration, and manufacturing processes to bring real-time data, knowledge, and information to multiple partners along the value chain. This increased connectivity may allow Internet entrepreneurs to become responsive and flexible to meeting each of their customers' particular needs and demands (Neese, 2000).

While our study was able to uncover multiple dimensions of innovative actions in Internet firms, future research should examine the effects of these ideas and solutions on several non-quantitative factors related to organizational effectiveness and performance. McGrath, Venkataraman, and MacMillan (1992) emphasize three such factors: enhancing the value of the firm, creating worth for customers, and insulating the firm from its competition. By incorporating this set of criteria to evaluate innovations, researchers would be able to capture a more complete assessment of an Internet entrepreneur's innovations and solutions from an immediate and/or long-term perspective. For example, while the financial benefits of implementing new methods of advertising or promoting a product or service on the Internet may not be readily visible, such innovations may give the business a sustainable competitive advantage in building brand loyalty and customer satisfaction. Over a period of time, however, these innovations may lead to positive financial rewards and benefits for all involved stakeholders in the Internet firm.

As more entrepreneurs enter the arena of electronic commerce, future research is also needed to examine how these entrepreneurs effectively design and integrate new business processes and practices. Although researchers have made important first steps in identifying dimensions of innovative behavior associated with and found inside Internet firms, more work should concentrate further on how these innovations relate to changes in organizational training and development, channel management, and client and customer relationships. These are all particularly relevant given that the expanded description of electronic commerce includes on-line information technology and communication that are used to enhance customer service and support (Choi et al., 1997; Koshiur, 1997). Keeney (1999) has outlined several areas of customers' concerns and values that can be used by an entrepreneur to design and grow their Internet ventures.

In order to build and grow an entrepreneurial organization around e-commerce strategies and initiatives, several factors need to be considered. As shown in Figure 3, entrepreneurial firms should use the opportunities and possibilities of the Internet, Intranets and extranets to *transform* their core e-business processes. As noted earlier, they fundamentally change the

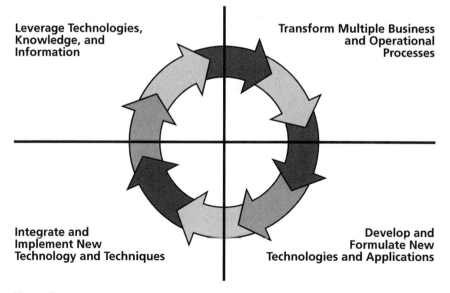

Figure 3.

way they do business. These companies should be not only be very open to changing core processes but also have a vision of how such a transformation will improve their business. Building upon existing systems and applications, e-businesses should also build new and improved applications and systems quickly and easily, in response to the ever-changing market and customer demands. Moreover, e-commerce organizations should establish a hardware infrastructure that can grow easily with the business. They also need to understand how to manage a network computing environment and how to keep it secure. Finally, e-commerce firms need to take a strategic approach in order to leverage their knowledge and information over time. Ultimately, they should be able to capitalize on the information and experience they already have and quickly apply new intelligence and knowledge (Jones, 2000).

Moving Toward New Entrepreneurial Roles

The explosive commercial growth of the Internet presents both new opportunities and challenges to entrepreneurs in how they formulate, develop, and implement new innovations into their businesses. As Drucker (1998) has asserted, innovation is the specific function of entrepreneurship. Moreover, distinctive innovative behaviors appear to characterize the emerging group of Internet entrepreneurs in comparison to ventures not fully dedicated to electronic commerce. "What sets netpreneurs apart is not that they are different from other entrepreneurs, but that they are operating in a universe of transforming change. As pioneers of the new networked society, they are both defining and learning new ways of doing business" (Morino, 1999, p. 1). Because of the rapid acceleration of technology, it is becoming more critical that Internet entrepreneurs have the ability to respond quickly to changes by bringing revolutionary new ideas into their businesses and the electronic marketplace.

In this way, they are creating new patterns of entrepreneurial behavior and performance. The results uncovered in this research represent one of the first empirical investigations into the processes associated with e-business founders. This study attempts to increase our understanding of the phenomena surrounding the formation and growth of these businesses, and has focused on the distinctive innovative actions of a group of these entrepreneurs. Exploring the direction of such behavior should facilitate the development of new entrepreneurial models for predicting the successful identification and exploitation of e-commerce opportunities.

Whether the managerial emphasis on innovation and change results not only in the creation of new products, services, or markets, but also on the nurturing and establishment of innovative internal and external relationships is the focus of a recent study (Kickul & Gundry, 2001) on the impact of top management team functional diversity and creative processes on the assessment of new e-commerce opportunities for the organization. Further, it investigates the relationship between opportunity assessment and innovative organizational practices. These innovative practices are operationalized as external relationships (network membership with vendors, customers, and competitors), internal relationships (recruitment, retention, and rewarding of top talent in the organization) and generating new products and services (see Figure 4).

The results uncovered in this research represent one of the first empirical investigations into the managerial roles and processes associated with e-commerce firms. As a first and foundational step to increasing our understanding of managerial practices in e-commerce organizations, this study examined CEOs' perceptions surrounding key firm behaviors that foster innovation. The emphasis of recent work by Iansiti and MacCormak (1997), Hodgetts et al. (1999), and Shannon (1999) has been on the significant roles of adaptation, innovation, experimentation, and change in the environments of e-commerce organizations. The necessity of realigning managerial roles and practices so that these organizations can take advantage of emerging opportunities has been proposed. Accordingly, our study attempted to empirically measure some of the managerial processes that stimulate innovation. If, as scholars have suggested, e-commerce firms

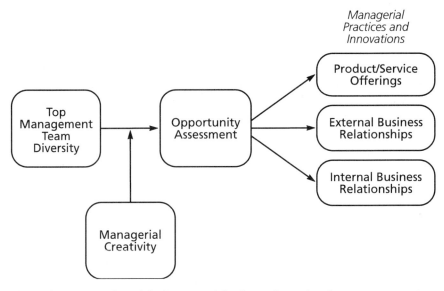

Figure 4.   Proposed model of managerial roles and practices in e-commerce organizations.

must innovate to survive, we have begun to explore the prerequisites and primary influences on this critical set of actions. The results of our study yield information that will be useful in guiding future research addressing key factors present among these top management teams, including comparative studies between e-commerce and traditional, brick-and-mortar organizations. Exploring the new managerial roles and practices, such as the development of innovative relationships with suppliers, customers, competitors, and employees of these businesses, will facilitate the construction of new models to predict success factors for managing e-commerce organizations.

Managing Relationships in E-Commerce Firms: Emergent Practices and Needs

A recent study by Inmomentum, Inc., an organization that researches the best practices of Internet economy businesses, reported that companies that helped their employees feel connected to their vision and values were growing at a rate of 141%, compared to a 10% growth rate for companies that did not do this well. This emphasis on the development of internal relationships in the e-commerce firm is an interesting one to watch as entrepreneurs continually search to recruit and retain top talent for their ventures. Confounding this requirement, however, is the reality that in the early part of 2001, there were more than two hundred CEO searches underway in Silicon Valley. Further, three hundred CEOs had been in their positions for less than one year. This renders the ability to develop and deliver a clear vision and connect it to company values a very great challenge.

The Internet entrepreneur's ability to harness the richness in breadth of perspective made available to them by functionally diverse team members is a key component of innovative actions. But a further step is needed to make the creative exploration useful in the form of actionable ideas and opportunities. Our research has shown that effective opportunity assessment has a mediating effect on the interaction of diversity and managerial creativity, facilitating the formation of external and internal organizational relationships as well as the introduction of new products and services. Thus, it enables managers to form strategic alliances necessary to achieve market growth and to develop methods to attract and retain the top talent so in demand by Internet organizations. Exploring the direction of such behavior contributes to our understanding of the changing roles, challenges and opportunities confronting managers in e-commerce firms.

The development of innovative internal management relationships was operationalized in the Kickul and Gundry (2001) study as finding unusual and creative ways to recruit, retain, and reward employees. These are emerging as one of the most significant entrepreneurial challenges of the information age. The predominance of knowledge workers has shifted the balance of traditional organizational resources of equipment, capital and people; while historically production workers have been replaced with technology leading to strong productivity gains, the same scale of substitution is not possible in knowledge-based organizations (Pottruck & Pearce, 2000). These authors concluded that the most critical parts of the human resource in an organization cannot be synthesized, and these are the creative brain, imagination, and spirit that fuel the information economy. Some of the new managerial practices of the CEOs in our sampled firms included unusual methods of retaining top talent in their organizations, as show in these responses:

> We are more than an employee's paycheck. The firm is committed to the belief that it shares a large part of the responsibility for the overall well-being of a given employee and this spiritual belief alone is what helps us keep our best employees. They see us putting their welfare at a higher priority than the numbers on the quarterly profit reports, and they wind up sticking around when the going gets rough for a while.

> A guarantee that their voice will always be heard in decision-making.

> Our arrangements permit a literal network of top level, talented and proven services and professionals to "morph" to suit the problematic demands of new clients. The organization is truly a team, with me as "leader" but without any hierarchical or concomitant structure. Only via affiliate resourcing can this be accomplished in the information sector where "trust is paramount" and "content is everything" in terms of both branding and perceived reliability.

One CEO represented the feelings of many in the following expression of frustration in response to the challenge of attracting and retaining employees:

> Whatever we do, it is not enough, as the competitive arena in this location makes success for us extremely difficult.

This scenario undoubtedly contributes to the necessity of taking innovative steps to meet the organization's internal strategic goals. Ester Dyson, one of the foremost thinkers on the implications of the Internet for business and for society as a whole (Pottruck & Pearce, 2000) has said:

> The limitation on the application of technology will never be ideas or capital. It will be finding enough people who are trained and excited about taking the ideas of the technologist and making them real in the world. (Dyson, 1997, p. 69)

Kickul and Gundry also found that CEOs engaged in forming innovative external relationships with their key constituents including suppliers, customers, and competitors. This increased connectivity may allow e-commerce organizations to become responsive and flexible in meeting each of their customers' particular needs and demands (Neese, 2000). Contracting with other organizations also allows the e-commerce firm to have a more decentralized, nonhierarchical organization that may foster the implementation of new product/service ideas and solutions (Morino, 1999). Kelley and Rice (1999) found that the rate of alliance and inter-firm formation was directly related to the rate of new product introductions in new firms. Having inter-firm relationships that are fluid may also be necessary in the marketing and distribution of information about the value of the firm's products and services. The nature of these relationships is described by the following responses of CEOs in our study:

> We use what others would call competitors a lot. We have no competition, just resources we have not used yet!

> We rely upon strategic partners around the globe. They are the keys to our success.

Entrepreneurial Skill Requirements for Internet Firms

Some of the most important competencies that entrepreneurs must have to survive and thrive in the new Internet economy are discussed in this section. Above and beyond the skill repertoire needed by all entrepreneurs, for Internet entrepreneurs the ability to think creatively and to "relentlessly innovate," as we have seen in previous sections, is paramount. The field is moving from an acceptance of "good" ideas to a need for truly "unique" ideas or business concepts. Leadership ability is essential, and this includes visioning and setting clear direction. Acting quickly involves creating economies of structure, such as the use of intranets to get information out to employees rapidly so they can make decisions. This is one example of how these entrepreneurs are using technology to stimulate communication and action in their organizations.

An Agenda for Future Research in E-Commerce Entrepreneurship

The primary purpose of our research was to examine how changes associated with e-commerce technology influence entrepreneurial behaviors such as identifying and exploiting market opportunities. We also sought to understand how e-commerce technology adds value to a business through the introduction and design of new innovations and managerial practices. Although we believe that we have made an important first step in identifying dimensions of innovative behavior associated with and found inside e-commerce firms, several issues emerge from this research that can be addressed in subsequent investigations.

For example, what other types of entrepreneurial behaviors such as risk-taking are associated with successful innovation in Internet firms, and which behaviors tend to be most important? More research is needed to determine whether, in fact, "hyper-innovative" practices are required in these organizations that go beyond what would be considered in traditional firms to be novel, different, and change embracing. Further, does the presence of e-commerce technologies influence the degree of entrepreneurial proactivity demanded in organizations?

Many of the CEOs in the study affirmed the need to stay ahead of the customer, as evidenced by the following response: "We must get in front of our clients in both technology and the way in which we leverage that technology. You need to know your customer and his needs better than he knows them himself!" Work has been conducted on the role of entrepreneurial proactivity and its relationship to new venture creation and other outcomes (Bateman & Crant, 1993; Becherer & Maurer, 1999). This may prove an interesting variable to investigate in Internet organizations where it has not been previously studied.

Additionally, what degree of strength characterizes the association between the Internet firms and their suppliers, value-added resellers (VARs), and customers in recognizing new opportunities? Value-chain migration (Hartman et al., 2000) is one strategy that integrates both the supply-chain and customer-facing system into a single, integrated process. Innovations and improvements are made in the ordering, configuration, and manufacturing processes to bring real-time data, knowledge, and information to multiple partners along the value chain. This increased connectivity may allow Internet entrepreneurs to become responsive and flexible to meeting each of their customers' particular needs and demands (Neese, 2000).

While our study was able to uncover various innovations by Internet firms, future research should examine the effects of these ideas and solutions on several non-quantitative factors related to organizational effectiveness and performance. McGrath, Venkataraman, and MacMillan (1992) emphasize three such factors: enhancing the value of the firm, creating worth for customers, and insulating the firm from its competition. By incorporating this set of criteria to evaluate innovations, researchers would be able to capture a more complete assessment of an Internet entrepreneur's innovations and solutions from an immediate and/or long-term perspective. For example, while the financial benefits of implementing new methods of advertising or promoting a product or service on the Internet may not be readily observable, such innovations may give the business a sustainable competitive advantage in building brand loyalty and customer satisfaction. Over a period of time, however, these innovations may lead to positive financial rewards and benefits for all involved stakeholders in the firm.

It will also be useful to focus on one outgrowth of this research. Specifically, how can the entrepreneurial behavior of focusing on external relationships be sustained?

Our study disclosed the importance of networks, partners, and other key stakeholders in the development of the Internet firm's innovative capabilities. How do these relationships evolve and how are they sustained over time or the life cycle of the organization? Here is the view of one CEO, who echoed the words of others in the sample:

> We are strong believers in the Japanese concept of "Keiretsu." We have a cadre of long-term suppliers that we value. When we are in a hurry, they give us priority. When there is a problem, they always make it right. We understand their abilities, limitations, and quirks, and do things to make their jobs much simpler and easier. Most of all we LISTEN to them and they listen to us.

We have attempted to set out the foundation of a research agenda for e-commerce entrepreneurship. Much empirical research on these and other important questions is needed to build our knowledge base in this rapidly growing sector of the economy in general and entrepreneurship in particular.

KEY CHALLENGES FOR E-COMMERCE ENTREPRENEURS

In the attempt to utilize e-commerce technology to more effectively recognize market opportunities and then bring about subsequent innovation in business practice, several challenges confront entrepreneurs and intrapreneurs. Perhaps the economic downturn of recent months has created an even greater set of difficulties to overcome in this arena. One of these challenges is the slowed spending and decrease in the availability of outside capital to fund and grow the firm. There will be rigorous examination of future business models, and it is likely that entrepreneurs may turn to models that emphasize unique business processes and concepts. There are numerous legislative challenges that affect these entrepreneurs, including taxation of goods and services sold over the Internet, fraud and identity theft, introduction of new domain names (e.g., .biz and .auto), international management of the Internet, and others.

A significant challenge for young technology ventures is their ability to recognize a highly competitive environment and proactively change their strategic orientation to survive and grow (Page, 1997). It is estimated that nearly three out of every four e-business ventures will fail due to the lack of technological understanding and poor business planning (Steensma, Marino, & Weaver, 2000). Research findings in this area have been mixed: Miles, Arnold, and Thompson (1993) found that the degree of perceived environmental hostility was negatively correlated with the CEO's entrepreneurial orientation. Other studies point to the positive relationships between hostility and entrepreneurial posture. For example, Smart and Vertinsky (1984) described an entrepreneurial posture as a function of the entrepreneurial personality and that it is deliberately adopted as a strategic response to an uncertain environment.

The explosive commercial growth of the Internet presents both new opportunities and challenges to entrepreneurs in how they formulate, develop, and implement new innovations into their business. The issues, challenges, and future directions presented in this paper represent one of the first comprehensive discussions of the entrepreneurial strategies, values, and behaviors that describe the internal and external processes of emerging e-commerce firms. Although much work remains, it is our hope that future research will continue to examine how entrepreneurs build, realign, and grow their organizations within a marketplace that demands speed, agility, and constant innovation. Exploring these new entrepreneurial roles and practices, such as the development of innovative relationships with suppliers, customers, competitors, and employees of these businesses, will facilitate the construction of new models to predict the value of e-commerce technology on entrepreneurial organizational behavior.

REFERENCES

Amabile, T.M. (1998, September-October). How to kill creativity. *Harvard Business Review*, 77–87.

Amor, D. (2000). *The e-business revolution: Living and working in an interconnected world.* Upper Saddle River, NJ: Prentice Hall.

Bangs, D.H., & Pinson, L. (1999). *The real world entrepreneur.* Chicago: Upstart Publishing Company.

Bateman, T.S., & Crant, J.M. (1993). The proactive component of organizational behavior: A measure and correlates. *Journal of Organizational Behavior, 14,* 103–118.

Birnbaum, J. (2000, August). The taxman cometh. EcompanyNow. Cited at www.Ecompany.com

Becherer, R.C., & Maurer, J.G. (1999, January). The proactive personality disposition and entrepreneurial behavior among small company presidents. *Journal of Small Business Management,* 28–36.

Bigelow, J.D. (1998). Teaching managerial skills. *Journal of Management Education, 19*(3), 305–325.

Bradley, S., & Nolan, R. (1998). *Sense and respond: Capturing value in the network era.* Boston: Harvard Business School Press.

Choi, S., Stahl, D., & Whinston, A. (1997). *The economics of electronic commerce.* Indianapolis, IN: Macmillan Technical Publishing.

Cohen, A., & Jordan, J.M. (1999). *Electronic commerce: The next generation.* Chicago: Ernst & Young Center for Business Innovation.

Cooper, A.C., Folta, T.B., & Woo, C. (1995). Entrepreneurial information search. *Journal of Business Venturing, 10*(2), 107–120.

Covin, J.G., & Covin, T.J. (1990). Competitive aggressiveness, environmental context and small firm performance. *Entrepreneurship: Theory and Practice, 14*(4), 35–50.

Covin, J.G., & Slevin, D.P. (1990). New venture strategic posture, structure and performance: An industry life cycle analysis. *Journal of Business Venturing, 5*(2), 123–135.

Covin, J.G., & Slevin, D.P. (1989). Strategic management of small firms in hostile and benign environments. *Strategic Management Journal, 10*(1), 75–87.

Davis, S., & Meyer, C. (1998). *Blur: The speed of change in the connected economy.* New York: Warner Books.

Dess, G.G., Lumpkin, G.T., & Covin, J.G. (1997). Entrepreneurial strategy making and firm performance: Tests of contingency and configurational models. *Strategic Management Journal, 18*(9), 677–695.

Drucker, P.F. (1998). The discipline of innovation. *Harvard Business Review, 76*(6), 149–157.

Drucker, P.F. (1997). *The organization of the future.* New York: Jossey-Bass Publishers.

Dyson, E. (1997). *Release 2.0: A design for living in the digital age.* New York: Broadway Books.

Forrester Research. (1999). *E-commerce by the numbers.* Cited at: http://www.net-profit-center.net/bynumber.htm.

Forrester Research. (2001) *E-commerce by the numbers.* Cited at: http://www.net-profit-center.net/bynumber.htm.

Griffith, D.A., & Palmer, J.W. (1999). Leveraging the web for corporate success. *Business Horizons, 42*(1), 3–10.

Hartman, A., Sifonis, J., & Kador, J. (2000). *Net ready: Strategies for success in the economy.* New York: McGraw-Hill.

Hitt, M.A. (1998). Twenty-first century organizations: Business firms, business schools, and the academy. *Academy of Management Review, 23,* 218–224.

Hodgetts, R.M., Luthans, F., & Slocum, J.W. Jr. (1999). Strategy and HRM initiatives for the '00s environment: Redefining roles and boundaries, linking competencies and resources. *Organizational Dynamics, 28*(2), 7–21.

Iansiti, M., & MacCormack, A. (1997). Developing product on internet time. *Harvard Business Review, 75*(5), 108–117.

Kanter, R.M. (2001). *Evolve! Succeeding in the digital cultural of tomorrow.* Boston:Harvard Business School Press.

Keeney, R. (1999, April). The value of Internet commerce to the customer. *Management Science,* 533–542.

Kelley, D., & Rice, M. (1999). Sustaining innovation in the new firm: The role of technology portfolios and alliance formation. In P. Reynolds et al. (Eds.), *Frontiers of entrepreneurship research*. Wellesley, MA: Babson College.

Kickul, J., & Gundry, L.K. (2001). Breaking through boundaries for organizational innovation: New managerial roles and practices in e-commerce firms. *Journal of Management, 27*, 347–361.

Kickul, J., & Gundry, L.K. (2000a). Pursuing technological innovation: The role of Entrepreneurial posture in Internet firms. *Frontiers of Entrepreneurship Research*. Wellesley, MA: Babson College.

Kickul, J., & Gundry, L.K. (2000b). Transforming the entrepreneurial landscape: Strategic innovation in Internet firms. *New England Journal of Entrepreneurship, 3*(1), 23–32.

Koshiur, D. (1997). *Understanding electronic commerce*. Redmond, WA: Microsoft Press.

Lange, J.E. (1999). Entrepreneurs and the Internet: The great equalizer. In J. Timmons (Ed.), *New venture creation* (pp. 175–211). Boston: Irwin-McGraw Hill.

Lumpkin, G.T., & Dess, G.G. (1996). Clarifying the entrepreneurial orientation construct and linking it to performance. *Academy of Management Review, 21*(1), 135–172.

McGrath, R.G., Venkataraman, S., & MacMillan, I.C. (1992, August). Measuring outcomes of corporate venturing: An alternative perspective. *Academy of Management Best Paper Proceedings* (pp. 85–89). Las Vegas, NV.

McKnight, L.W. (2001). Internet business models: Creative destruction as usual. In L.W. McKnight et al. (Eds.), *Creative destruction: Business survival strategies in the global internet economy*. Cambridge, MA: MIT Press.

Meyer, G., & Dean, T. (1990). An upper echelons perspective on transformational leadership problems in high technology firms. *Journal of High Technology Management, 1*, 223–242.

Miles, M.P., Arnold, D.P., & Thompson, D.L. (1993). The interrelationship between environmental hostility and entrepreneurial orientation. *Journal of Applied Business Research, 9*(4), 12–23.

Miller, R., & Blais, R.A. (1992). Configurations of innovation: Predictable and maverick modes. *Technology Analysis & Strategic Management, 4*(4), 363–386.

Miller, D., & Friesen, P.H. (1983). Successful and unsuccessful phases of the corporate life cycle. *Organizational Studies, 4*(4), 339–356.

Morino, M. (1999, May). Netpreneurs: A new breed of entrepreneur. *E-Commerce*. Cited at: www.netpreneur.org.

Morgan, R.B., & Smith, J.E. (1996). *Staffing the new workplace: Selecting and promoting for quality improvement*. Milwaukee, WI: ASQC Quality Press.

Neese, T. (2000, January 24). Report gives new trends on e-commerce evolution, communication changes. *The Journal Record*, http://www.journalrecord.com

Oliva, R.A. (1998). Match your web page to your mission. *Marketing Management, 7*(4), 38–41.

Oliver, R.W. (2000, September-October). The seven laws of e-commerce strategy. *The Journal of Business Strategy, 21*(5), 8–10.

Page, G. (1997). Temporal dimensions of opportunistic change in technology-based ventures. *Entrepreneurship: Theory & Practice 22*(2), 31–52.

Palich, L.E., & Bagby, D.R. (1995). Using cognitive theory to explain entrepreneurial risk-taking: Challenging conventional wisdom. *Journal of Business Venturing 10*, 425–438.

Pottruck, D.S., & Pearce, T. (2000). *Clicks and mortar: Passion driven growth in an Internet driven world.* San Francisco: Jossey-Bass.

Rayport, J.F., & Sviokla, J.J. (1998). Exploiting the virtual value chain. In *Harvard Business Review on Strategies for Growth.* Boston: Harvard Business Review Press.

Schumpeter, J.A. (1943). *Capitalism, socialism, and democracy.* London: Allen & Unwin.

Schwartz, E. (1999). *Digital Darwinism: 7 breakthrough strategies for surviving in the cutthroat web economy.* New York: Broadway Books.

Shannon, J. (1999). Net brands lead by innovation. *Marketing Week, 22,* 28.

Singh, R., Hills, G.E., Hybels, R.C., & Lumpkin, G.T. (1999). Opportunity recognition through social network characteristics of entrepreneurs. In *Frontiers of Entrepreneurship Research.* Wellesley, MA: Babson College.

Smart, C., & Vertinsky, I. (1994). Strategy and the environment: A study of corporate responses to crises. *Strategic Management Journal 5*(3), 199–213.

Steensma, K.H., Marino, L., & Weaver, K.M., (2000). Attitudes toward cooperative strategies: A cross-cultural analysis of entrepreneurs. *Journal of International Business Studies, 31*(4), 591–609.

Weintraut, J.N., & Davis, J. (1999). Building the bulletproof net start-up: The five critical ingredients of online success. *Business 2.0* (http://business2.com/).

CHAPTER 4

TERTIARY EDUCATION AND ENTREPRENEURIAL INTENTIONS

Clement K. Wang, Poh Kam Wong, and Qing Lu

ABSTRACT

In this paper, we propose a comprehensive three-stage entrepreneurship model that incorporates the key demographic, educational, motivational attitude, perceived interest and feasibility factors that are postulated in the literature to influence entrepreneurial intentions. This model is developed to analyze, in particular, the residual influence of educational variables, after controlling for other variables.

Empirically, we test the model using a large-sample, nationwide survey of students from business and technical fields in six institutions of higher learning in Singapore. The empirical results are found to provide support for the efficacy of our three-stage model. Our findings also suggest a more complex pattern of influence than the originally proposed model. In particular, we find that attitude variables are better predictors for perceived desirability and feasibility compared to background demographic and educational variables, as they absorb a large proportion of the variance of these background variables. Similarly, self-perception variables measuring the perceived desirability and feasibility of entrepreneurship are better predictors of entrepreneurial intentions, and absorb the variance largely. However, we found that, contrary to the literature, attitudinal variables have a significant influence on perceived feasibility as well, rather than on interest alone. Moreover, self-efficacy is also found to influence interest in addition to perceived feasibility.

In interpreting our findings, we suggest that alternative career prospect may have a strong moderating effect on the influence of entrepreneurial interest on entrepreneurial intentions. Since the characteristics of alternative career prospects are a key variable of the national environment, their effect on entrepreneurial intentions is likely to be sensitive to the national context. In the case of Singapore, years of sustained rapid economic growth have created an environment characterized by high availability of lucrative jobs in the corporate and public sector, and as such, high interest in entrepreneurship need not translate into high intention. In contrast, in other countries characterized by persistent, high unemployment, high entrepreneurial interest may indeed lead to high intentions. In view of this, we believe that adding variables measuring the alternative career prospects to our model would improve its predictability on entrepreneurial intentions.

Our findings also provide a number of practical implications for educational planners and government policy makers who are interested in promoting high tech entrepreneurship among university and polytechnic students, particularly students in business and technical fields. Future research directions are also suggested to extend the entrepreneurship model to incorporate alternative career prospects, to conduct international comparative study of entrepreneurial intentions of university students in other countries, and to explore the effect of technological opportunities on entrepreneurial propensities in other settings.

INTRODUCTION

Since the 1990s, the growth of the knowledge-based economy has brought significant changes to entrepreneurial activities around the world. In particular, the phenomenal success of Silicon Valley has encouraged many countries to put greater emphasis on promoting high-growth, technology-based start-ups by highly educated technical professionals, rather than small business formation in general. In Asia, after the 1997–1998 financial crisis, many governments have similarly placed a higher priority in nurturing local, homegrown entrepreneurs, especially among the young, well-educated population.

Viewed as one crucial issue in developing the knowledge-based economy, entrepreneurial propensity among the more highly educated has attracted increasing research attention from both academia and practitioners worldwide. One important research question is why people choose to act as entrepreneurs (Stevenson & Jarillo, 1990). In particular, a good understanding of motivations behind the career choice for entrepreneurship among university students will help in the prediction and education of potential entrepreneurs for the knowledge-based economy.

Entrepreneurship can be viewed as an intentional, planned behavior (Krueger & Carsrud, 1993). Though a new venture needs a good opportunity to start, the entrepreneur must prepare for it with a strong desire for a substantial period of time. As the entrepreneurial act is rare (only less than 10% of graduates start their own business eventually), obscure (many early stage entrepreneurs keep a full-time or part-time job to survive), and involves unpredictable time lags, entrepreneurial intentions is one approach to study the motivation of the entrepreneurial act. Entrepreneurial intention is viewed as central to understanding the entrepreneurship process (Krueger, 1993). Empirical studies on intentions are easier and less biased compared to studies on actual entrepreneurial behavior, which inherit the survival bias. It can be studied in an early stage with a large sample covering various groups of undergraduates and postgraduate students.

Among entrepreneurship researchers, the role of entrepreneurship education has been recognized as one of the crucial factors that help youths to understand and foster an entrepreneurial attitude (Gorman et al., 1997; Kourilsky & Walstad, 1998). Due to the influence that education could have on the attitudes and aspirations of youths, there is a need to understand how to develop and nurture potential entrepreneurs even while they are still students in school. Research on entrepreneurial intention of students in tertiary educational institutions is more important in the knowledge-based economy since most of the formation of knowledge-intensive, high-tech ventures typically presupposes higher educational training. Nurturing the entrepreneurial desire of current tertiary students is important for future entrepreneurial activities and national economic growth. However, few empirical studies have examined the entrepreneurial intentions of tertiary students and the influence of their education on such intentions, particularly the issue of how the technical education nurtures the technopreneurship intentions. Their attitude and personality of entrepreneurship are likely to shape their inclination to start their own businesses in the future. This type of study will also help tertiary institutions understand the weakness of current education system and develop suitable educational programs to prepare students for future entrepreneurship. Finally, findings from such a study will have important policy implications for educational planners.

In this study, we synthesize findings from the literature on the factors that influence entrepreneurial intentions to develop a comprehensive three-stage model on entrepreneurial intentions with a focus on the influence of tertiary education. This model is then tested using a nationwide survey among tertiary students in technical and business fields of studies in Singapore. Besides providing the first such empirical study of entrepreneurial intentions of tertiary students in Asia, we believe that our research findings also contribute to the theory of entrepreneurial intention formation by providing a more comprehensive picture of the relative contributions of the various factors affecting entrepreneurial intention. In addition, our findings highlight a number of policy implications for university administrators and government agencies interested in promoting entrepreneurship and technopreneurship among university students.

The paper is organized as follows. We first review existing models of factors influencing entrepreneurship in the literature, and synthesize a new comprehensive model that incorporates these factors in a three-stage model. We then discuss the research design, variable measurement as well as the data sample description. The empirical results are then presented and their interpretation discussed. We conclude the paper by highlighting a number of implications for administrators and policy makers.

HYPOTHESES ON ENTREPRENEURIAL INTENTIONS

Many studies on entrepreneurship behavior have attempted to look for factors that lead to entrepreneurial decisions. Early studies concentrate on the personality traits and demographic characteristics of entrepreneurs (e.g., Brockhaus & Horwitz, 1986; Furnham, 1992; Hisrich, 1986), but these studies only meet with modest success. Their explanatory power is not strong, and they fail to explain why some individuals with the same demographic traits choose to be employees rather than entrepreneurs. Johnson (1990) highlighted the influence of achievement motivation, while Robinson et al. (1991) argue that business attitudes such as attitude to risk or independence are a better predictor of entrepreneurial intentions than demographic characteristics and suggest a more dynamic model of the entrepreneurship process. Krueger (1993) further argues that personality traits and demographics are exogenous issues that have an indirect impact on entrepreneurship via attitudes, while attitudes in turn have an indirect impact on entrepreneurship via intentions.

Responding to the call for more dynamic entrepreneurship models by Robinson et al. (1991), many models on entrepreneurship choice and intentions are proposed and tested. Dyer (1994) presents a model on career choice including individual factors, social factors, and economic factors. Understanding that entrepreneurial behavior is influenced by perceptions of the external conditions, rather than the external environment per se, later studies focus more on personal attitudes and self-perception of the environment. Krueger et al. (2000) test two two-stage models on entrepreneurship intentions. The first model is based on Ajzen's (1987) theory of planned behavior, and the second is on Shapero's (1982) model of the "entrepreneurial event." Input variables used in the two models include two first-stage variables, self-efficacy (the perceived ability to execute a target behavior) and expected values, and three second-stage variables, attitude toward entrepreneurial act, perceived feasibility, and perceived desirability. Empirical results show support for both models.

In a similar vein, Douglas and Shepherd (2000) present an economic model of the career decision with attitudes as input variables. The choice for an entrepreneur or an employee is measured by a utility function, and expected income, expected work effort, risk anticipated, independence anticipated are input variables. An individual with high tolerance of work effort, high tolerance for risk, and a strong preference for independence will prefer entrepreneurship. This model provides a greater number of variables to measure attitudes from several aspects crucial to entrepreneurial decision. Empirically, Kolvereid (1996) studies the reasons for career intentions choice between employees and entrepreneurs among MBA students in Norway and finds that risk, independence, and work efforts are the three most important factors that separate future employees from potential entrepreneurs.

To synthesize a model for explaining entrepreneurial intentions of university students, most of whom do not have prior work experience, we propose a number of adaptations to Krueger's two-stage model. Firstly, as many variables in Ajzen's and Shapero's model are very closely related, we believe that they can be combined and simplified into one two-stage model. Secondly, the attitude variables used in Douglas and Shepherd's model are used to represent the expected values used in Kruger's model, as they are easier to measure. Thirdly, attitude toward income and attitude toward work efforts are combined as one variable since it is not easy to differentiate for students without working experience. We further combine the three variables for attitude toward the entrepreneurial act, propensity to act and perceived desirability in Krueger's model into one since they are similar especially in the early stage of entrepreneurial intention formation. We present the adapted model in Figure 1. Although certain information is lost as a result of such a synthesis, we believe that the abstraction helps improve data validity by avoiding possible confusion by students in answering the questionnaire.

Figure 1 shows that entrepreneurial intentions are hypothesized to be determined by perceived desirability and feasibility. The entrepreneurial desirability is in turn influenced by attitude toward work effort, independence and risk, while perceived feasibility is influenced by self-efficacy.

However, this model is not enough to answer the main research question in this paper, i.e., the effect of tertiary education on entrepreneurial intentions. Therefore, we further extend the model scope to incorporate educational influences. One more stage is added to the model with educational factors as input variables. As previous studies such as Krueger (1993)

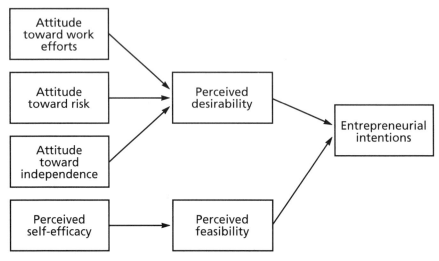

Figure 1.   Entrepreneurship intentions model summarized from literature.

have observed, demographic variables affect entrepreneurial intentions primarily through attitude variables. We therefore hypothesize that education affects entrepreneurial intentions through attitudes, and take demographic factors such as gender, family role model, socioeconomic status, and citizenship as control variables with education at the same stage. Although demographic variables per se are not strong predictors of the entrepreneurial intention, they may have some influences on attitudinal variables. Adding them into the model can also link our study with earlier research that examines the effect of demographic variables. In this way, our new, enlarged entrepreneurship model is able to incorporate demographics, education, and attitude factors. One variable, attitude toward work efforts is adjusted to attitude to work achievement in our model. As most respondents do not have working experience, their attitude to work efforts is less clear than their expectation on job achievement, measured by personal ambition and public recognition variables. These are hypothesized to be the relevant motivation behind a student's hard work. The expanded model is shown in Figure 2.

Demographic variables introduced in this model have been widely studied before. On the gender effect, it is expected and also observed that male students have stronger entrepreneurial intentions than females. Many studies have observed this phenomenon, such as De Wit and Van Winden (1989) in the Netherlands; Mesch and Czamanski (1997) on Russian immigrants in Israel; Matthews and Moser (1996) on business graduates in the United States; and Kourilsky and Walstad (1998) on U.S. high

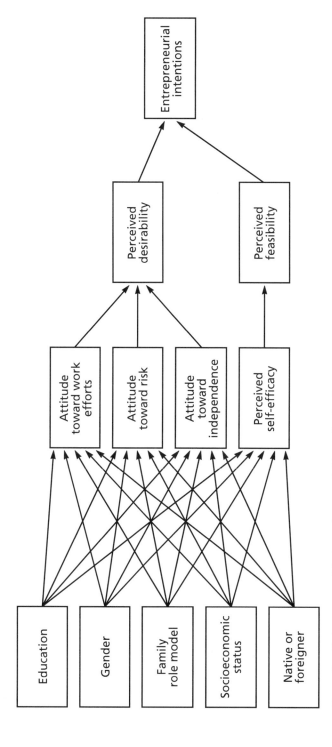

Figure 2. Entrepreneurship intentions model hypothesized.

school students. Matthews and Moser (1996) also discover through a longitudinal study that males' interests are consistent but females' interests decline with time.

There are many studies on the family role model as well. Scott and Twomey (1988) report that students whose parents own a small business demonstrate the highest preference for self-employment and the lowest for employment in a large business. Similar findings include Crant (1996) on U.S. undergraduates and MBAs, Schiller and Crewson (1997) on self-employment choice in the United States (only significant for females but insignificant for males), and Taylor (1996) on self-employment in the U.K. On the other hand, Brenner et al. (1991) find the influence of parental role on entrepreneurial intentions of U.S. business school undergraduates was insignificant. Ghazali et al. (1995) also report similar observation on the self-employment choice of graduates in Singapore.

On the comparison among natives and foreigners, Mesch and Czamanski (1997) find high entrepreneurial intentions among Russian immigrants in Israel due to the occupational closure in local employee market. As for the socioeconomic status of an individual, it may be expected that high family income may give support for one to start one's own business. Taylor (1996) reports positive correlation between housing equity and self-employment in the U.K. Evans and Leighton (1989) find men with higher assets were more likely to be self-employed in the United States. However, De Wit and Van Winden (1989) find that the effects of parents' social status are not significant in the Netherlands.

On the impact of education on entrepreneurial intentions, Stewart et al. (1999) study corporate managers, small business owners and entrepreneurs, and find that while on average, entrepreneurs are more educated than small business owners, it is the corporate managers who were the most highly educated. This suggests that while content knowledge is important for individuals to take the entrepreneurial plunge, a surfeit of knowledge can lead to risk aversion behaviors that reduce the propensity to engage in entrepreneurial activity. Van de Ven and Schroeder (1984) also suggest that entrepreneur's level of education and distinctiveness of the business idea are important contributions to new venture success. In Singapore, Ghazali et al. (1995) find that graduates with good honors or higher degrees are less likely to be self-employed. Since they can get good job prospects in the corporate sector, it would incur higher opportunity cost for them to start their own businesses. Thus, we observe two contrasting effects of education on entrepreneurial propensity. One is that good education could increase business knowledge and improve the self-efficacy of potential entrepreneurs. However, better career prospects for employees with good education may increase the risk of starting own business and thus hinder entrepreneurial behavior.

Besides educational level, the major field of study may also have an influence on entrepreneurial behavior. There has been little empirical evidence on this since most entrepreneurship education studies only focus on business students. A priori, students majoring in business are expected to be more equipped to start their own businesses due to their training, both in knowledge and attitudes molded in their field of study. However, with the growing importance of the knowledge-based economy, it can be argued that people trained in technical disciplines may be able to start business more easily than before. For example, students with specialized training in computer science or engineering may be able to start a new venture with their new technical inventions or specialized software skills. Their lack in management knowledge and business skills can often be complemented by their capital providers such as venture capitalists (Black & Gilson, 1998), and partners with good management skills and experience.

In summary, the existing literature suggests that the effect of education on entrepreneurship is mixed. In particular, most previous studies fail to demonstrate clearly how specific aspects of education, such as the disciplinary field, affect entrepreneurial intentions or behavior. By linking educational factors with attitude variables in our model, we hope to provide a better understanding of their effects on entrepreneurial intentions, leading to relevant policy implications for government policy makers and educators.

RESEARCH DESIGN AND DATA SAMPLE

To test the three-stage entrepreneurial intention model that we have synthesized, we utilize data from a nationwide survey in Singapore among full-time students in all the four polytechnics and two universities in existence in Singapore. Conducted by the first two authors in the first quarter of 2000, the survey was commissioned by the National Science and Technology Board (NSTB) of Singapore to examine the level of entrepreneurial interest among students of institutions of higher learning in Singapore who are majoring in business or technical fields of science, engineering and computing. The focus on students only in these fields reflects the Singapore government's interest in high tech entrepreneurship.

To test our three-stage intentions model, we carry out a three-stage hierarchy regression analysis. The first stage uses attitudes as dependent variables and demographic variables and education variables as independent variables. In the second stage we have attitudes as independent variables and self-perception variables as dependent ones. In the third and final stage, the ultimate output, entrepreneurial intentions is the dependent variable with self-perception variables as independent ones. The measurement of these variables is as follows.

Demographic Variables

Four demographic variables are included as control variables in our model: gender, family role model, citizenship, and socioeconomic status. The first three variables are binary variables. We define binary variable *Gender*, one for male and zero for female. We define binary variable *Family* to equal one if the respondent has at least one family member who is engaged in running his/her own business and zero if not. Similarly, we define binary variable *Citizen* as one if the respondent is a local Singaporean, and zero if a foreigner.

While socioeconomic status is usually measured by family income level, this is not done in the survey due to the sensitive nature of the question in the context of Singapore, and our concern with non-reliability of the responses, as the respondents, being students, are not the wage earners. As an alternative, the nature of the family housing of the respondent is used instead. Being a city-state without much land, the wealth of Singaporeans is largely reflected in the houses they live in. In general, families living in small public houses are poorer than ones living in larger public houses or private houses. Thus, we use the type of housing lived by the respondent's family as a proxy to measure his/her socioeconomic status. We divide type of housing into three groups, HDB (Housing Development Board) 3-room or 4-room (basic apartment for Singaporeans), HDB 5-room or executive (larger public apartments), and private houses. An ordinal variable *Income* is used to measure the socioeconomic status in five levels.

Educational Factors

As mentioned above, we study the educational factors from two aspects. First is the level of education. In the context of Singapore, the level of education can be classified into three levels: polytechnic students, university undergraduates, and university postgraduate students including Masters students and Ph.D. candidates. Education level is measured by two dummy variables, *University* and *Postgraduate*. *University* is one if the respondent studies in a university (including both undergraduates and postgraduates), and zero if he is in a polytechnic. *Postgraduate* is one if the respondent is a postgraduate student and zero otherwise.

The second aspect is the field of major of the respondent. Here we classify the major into three categories: sciences, engineering or computing/IT, and business/management-related. We hypothesize that the field of study may have an influence on the ease of starting a business. For example, students studying natural sciences may encounter more difficulties in applying their training to business venture directly, while engineering or computer science students may be able to do so more easily due to the applied nature of their training. Two dummy variables, *Business,* and *Engi-*

neering are used to measure the categorical variable on the major of education. *Business* is one if the respondent studies in business or management, and zero if otherwise. *Engineering* is one if the respondent studies in engineering or computer science/IT, and zero if otherwise.

Attitude Variables

There are four variables in our model to measure the four aspects of entrepreneurial attitudes. Attitude toward achievement is measured by three questions in the survey. In the motivation part, respondents are asked to value the importance on "accomplishing personal achievement," "achieving status and prestige," and "accumulating money and wealth" if they were to start their own business. The responses are measured by Likert scales from 1 (not at all important) to 5 (very important). We average the three scales to get the variable *Achievement*. The Cronbach alpha indicates that this construct is reliable.

Attitude toward risk is measured by the variable *Risk,* a Likert scale to measure whether students "enjoy personal challenges" as a motivation to start businesses, also ranging from 1 to 5. Similarly, attitude toward independence is measured by the variable *Independence*, the average of two Likert scales on response to "test my own ideas" and "becoming independent" as motivation to start business, ranging from 1 to 5. The Cronbach-alpha indicates that these constructs are reliable.

Perceived self-efficacy refers to the individual's self-confidence in doing business. For people still in school, it is not easy to test directly. In this survey we use the average of their evaluation on their business knowledge (more objective) and the sufficiency of their preparation for entrepreneurship (more subjective) as a proxy measurement. If they think they are well prepared for entrepreneurship with enough knowledge and confidence, their perceived self-efficacy will be higher. Here entrepreneurial knowledge is measured by the mean of two Likert scales measuring the knowledge in starting a business and knowledge in managing business. Entrepreneurship confidence is measured by evaluation to statement "education is enough to prepare me for entrepreneurship," ranging from 1 to 5. The average value is denoted by the variable *Efficacy*.

Self-Perception Variables

In the survey, perceived desirability is proxied by a variable that reflects the desire to start one's own business—entrepreneurial interest—as measured by the variable *Interest*. This variable consists of the maximum of two Likert scales from 1 to 5 measuring the interest in starting a new business in a respondent's area of study, and the interest in starting business not in the area of study. It is similar to the global perceived desirability variable in Krueger et al. (2000).

Perceived feasibility is measured by the variable *Feasibility*, a Likert scale response measure for the statement "becoming entrepreneur is a viable option for me," ranging from 1 (strongly disagree) to 5 (strongly agree). Again, it is similar to the measure used in Krueger et al. (2000).

Entrepreneurial Intentions

In Krueger et al. (2000), intention is measured by the probability of starting business in the next five years. Here we use a similar variable *Intentions*, but change the probability to the expected starting time categorized into six levels. First is "already started business," the second "immediately starting business after graduation," the third "starting within five years," the fourth "five to ten years," the fifth "more than ten years" and the sixth "don't know" (maybe never start business). *Intentions* is defined as 5 in the first case, 4 the second, till 0 for the last.

Survey Overview

The survey covers all six institutions of higher learning in Singapore with full-time students in Q1 of the year 2000, comprising of two universities and four polytechnics. Only students in technical fields of study or business management related programs are included in the study. The combined student population of these six institutions of higher learning in the defined fields is 71,000. Due to the large size of the universe, a stratified, random survey approach was adopted in the survey design, with the stratification variable being institutions, year of study, and field of majors. The final sample size realized is 8,036, or 11.3% of the whole population. Because of the large sample size, all strata are significantly represented. Analysis reveals no significant response biases by institutions and field of majors.

TESTING OF ENTREPRENEURSHIP MODEL

Descriptive Findings from the Survey

Before presenting our findings, it is useful to highlight a number of salient characteristics of the survey respondents. First, we find that the self-perceived level of business knowledge of the students is poor while their interest to start own business is high. While 65.4% of the students claim that their knowledge of doing business is below average (and only about 5.7% assert that their knowledge is good or very good), 47.0% of the students indicated they are quite interested or very interested to start their own business, with only 8.8% students expressing little or no interest. This finding is similar to other studies such as Kourilsky and Walstad (1998) on high school students in the United States.

Despite the relatively high level of interest in entrepreneurship, entrepreneurial intentions as measured by when they plan to start a business on their own are more moderate. Only around 30% of respondents plan to start own business within five years and 50% take neutral or unfavorable stand to the feasibility of becoming entrepreneurs.

The list of independent and intermediate variables, with their means and correlation are presented in Table 1. Due to the large sample size, only variables with strong correlation (p-value < 0.01) are denoted.

Table 1.   Variable List and Correlation

List of independent and intermediate variables

Gender	Taking value 1 if the respondent is a male, 0 if female
Family	Taking value 1 if family members starting own business, 0 if not
Citizen	Taking value 1 if the respondent is Singapore citizen, 0 if non-Singaporeans (including permanent resident)
Income	Ordinal variable taking value 1 if family resided in HDB 3-room or 4-room flat, 2 if HDB 5-room or executive/HUDC flat, 3 if private house (condominium, terrace, bungalow, etc.).
University	Taking value 1 if the respondent studies in a university, 0 if in a polytechnic
Postgraduate	Taking value 1 if the respondent is a postgraduate, 0 if undergraduate or polytechnic student
Business	Taking value 1 if studying in business or management school, 0 if otherwise
Engineering	Taking value 1 if studying in engineering or computer science/IT, 0 if otherwise
Achievement	Taking value 1 to 5 based on the valuation to the importance of three motivations, personal achievement, social status, and wealth
Risk	Taking value 1 to 5 based on the valuation to the importance of motivation—personal challenges
Independence	Taking value 1 to 5 based on the valuation to the importance of two motivations, independence and own idea testing
Efficacy	Taking value 0 to 5 based on the average of self-rated business knowledge and confidence for future entrepreneurship
Interest	Taking value 0 to 5 based on interest to start one's own business
Feasibility	Taking value 1 to 5 based on the valuation to the statement "becoming entrepreneur is a viable option for me"
Intentions	Taking value 0 to 5 based on the expected time of starting business. The higher the value, the earlier and stronger intentions

Table 1.   Variable List and Correlation[a] (Continued)

	Mean	s.d.[b]	1	2	3	4	5	6	7	8	9	10	11	12	13	14
1. gender	0.51	0.50														
2. family	0.48	0.50	-0.037*													
3. citizen	0.83	0.38	-0.094**	-0.089**												
4. income	1.60	0.75	0.009	0.163**	-0.127**											
5. university	0.48	0.50	0.040**	-0.020	-0.206**	0.157**										
6. postgraduate	0.03	0.16	0.068**	-0.001	-0.239**	0.059**	0.171**									
7. business	0.25	0.43	-0.229**	0.031*	0.094**	0.047**	0.066**	-0.014								
8. engineering	0.64	0.48	0.321**	-0.033*	-0.121**	-0.051**	-0.153**	0.042**	-0.781**							
9. achievement	3.77	0.71	0.052**	0.071**	-0.005	0.024	-0.023	-0.009	0.073**	-0.045**						
10. risk	3.92	0.93	0.012	0.056**	-0.018	0.024	0.044**	0.009	0.049**	-0.038*	0.449**					
11. independence	3.88	0.60	-0.012	0.076**	-0.010	0.017	-0.043**	-0.018	0.039**	-0.024	0.521**	0.562**				
12. efficacy	2.16	0.30	0.118**	0.127**	-0.036*	-0.001	-0.275**	-0.008	0.053**	0.039**	0.158**	0.128**	0.144**			
13. interest	3.30	1.32	0.119**	0.120**	-0.062**	0.035*	-0.012	0.050**	0.047*	0.009	0.287**	0.304**	0.327**	0.252**		
14. feasibility	3.54	0.89	0.127**	0.120**	-0.037*	0.054**	-0.013	0.033*	0.023	0.022	0.314**	0.297**	0.322**	0.271**	0.427**	
15. intentions	2.12	1.00	0.119**	0.091**	-0.095**	0.044**	0.004	0.051**	-0.012	0.056**	0.141**	0.140**	0.158**	0.205**	0.293**	0.279**

[a] N = 7844
[b] For multivariable constructs, Cronbach Alpha is presented in this column instead of the standard deviation.
*p < 0.01
**p < 0.001

Table 1 shows that the direct effects of demographic variables on entrepreneurial attitudes, interests and intentions are not strong in general. Gender and family role are more influential than socioeconomic status and citizenship. The direct effects of educational variables are also quite moderate. In contrast, attitudinal variables appear to be strongly correlated with self-perception variables as well as entrepreneurial intentions.

Effects of Background Factors

To test the effects of background factors and particularly educational variables on entrepreneurial attitudes, we apply hierarchical regression to each of the four attitude variables. The steps of the hierarchical regression are shown as follows.

Step 1: $Attitude = a + b_1 x_1 + \varepsilon$
Step 2: $Attitude = a + b_1 x_1 + b_2 x_2 + \varepsilon$
Step 3: $Attitude = a + b_1 x_1 + b_2 x_2 + b_3 x_1 x_2 + \varepsilon$

where
   Attitude is one of the four attitude variables, *Achievement, Risk, Independence,* or *Efficacy.*
   x_1 is demographic variables (*Gender, Family, Citizen, Income*)
   x_2 is educational variables (*University, Postgraduate, Business, Engineering*)
   ε is the random factor.

Regression analysis is conducted by step. Here we take *p*-value 0.01 instead of the normal 0.05 as the threshold of significance due to the large sample size. The results are presented in Table 2.

Table 2 shows that gender and family role model are the two main demographic factors affecting entrepreneurial attitudes while university and business major are the two main educational factors. The impact of demographic variables is similar to educational factors except self-efficacy, which is mainly influenced by education. Interaction factors are not significant in general. However, besides self-efficacy, the regression power of demographic and educational variables is not strong. Adjusted R^2 are less than 0.02 for attitudes toward achievement, risk and independence. We also find that gender is related to attitude toward achievement and self-efficacy but not attitude toward risk and independence, while family role model is the most influential demographic factor for all attitude variables. It is also noticed that citizenship and family income status have no influence on attitudes except the weak influence on self-efficacy from Table 2.

Table 2.   Result of Hierarchical Regression on Attitude Variables[a]

Independent Variable	Attitude toward achievement	Attitude toward risk	Attitude toward independence	Self-efficacy
Step 1: Demographic				
Gender	0.094**	0.031	−0.008	0.216**
Family	0.120**	0.104**	0.112**	0.249**
Citizen	0.001	−0.020	0.010	−0.092*
Income	0.013	0.017	0.004	−0.038*
ΔR^2	0.009**	0.004**	0.005**	0.033**
Step 2: educational				
University	−0.052*	0.081**	−0.074**	−0.541**
Postgraduate	−0.064	−0.017	−0.046	0.059
Business	0.161**	0.121*	0.081	0.316**
Engineering	−0.004	0.016	0.011	0.119*
ΔR^2	0.008**	0.004**	0.004**	0.094**
Step 3: interactions				
Gender * university	−0.056	0.059	0.032	0.131*
Gender * business	0.038	0.144*	0.103	0.108
Family * university Gender	−0.021	0.020	0.030	−0.070
Family * business	−0.040	−0.133*	−0.156**	−0.051
ΔR^2	0.001	0.002*	0.003*	0.002*
Overall Adjusted R^2	0.016**	0.009**	0.010**	0.128**
Overall Model F	11.1**	6.50**	7.02**	89.4**
s.e.	0.79	0.92	0.79	0.85

[a] N = 7219
* $p < 0.01$
** $p < 0.001$

Two education variables, *University* and *Business*, are significant for most attitude variables except the insignificance of *Business* to independence. It is interesting that the effect of the *University* variable is negative, i.e., students in university expressed less intense desire for achievement, independence and self-confidence as motivations for starting one's own venture than polytechnic students, although they do appear to be more risk tolerant than the latter. It is also interesting to note that postgraduate education has no additional influence on attitudes. Thus, the primary difference appears to be between university and polytechnics, not between undergraduate and graduate students.

The impact of student's major on attitudes is generally weak with the exception of the *Business* variable. Students majoring in business score significantly higher on three of the four attitudinal measures. Only the impact of business training on the desire for independence is insignificant. This may suggest that the current business training may put too much emphasis on cooperation, a quality more important for big corporations, but somehow does not promote enough desire for independence, an important element for entrepreneurship.

Among non-business students, the differences in major have no significant effect on attitudes, the exception being that students with technological backgrounds (engineering or computer major) exhibit higher self-efficacy.

Effects of Attitudes on Self-perception Variables

The second step of testing our entrepreneurship model is to test the relationship between attitudes and self-perception variables. We again use hierarchical regression to test the effects of the former on the latter variables. Here we take demographic and educational variables as independent variables first, and then add attitude variables to test whether attitudes improve the regression power. Interaction variables are not presented here since they are not significant. The steps of the hierarchical regression are similar. The results are presented in Table 3. To show the relative weights of variables, we also present adjusted β value in Step 2 regression.

Table 3 shows all four attitude variables are significantly related to the self-perception variables. Furthermore, it demonstrates that attitude variables are much better predictors compared to demographic and educational variables. R^2 is improved significantly from 0.04 to around 0.20. If we do the hierarchical regression the other way, step 1 starting with attitude variables and in step 2 adding demographic and educational variables, R^2 in step 2 will be 0.018 for perceived desirability and 0.016 for perceived feasibility. Thus our model is supported by the data as more than 50% of the variance from these background variables is absorbed into the four attitude variables. Table 3 also shows that self-efficacy significantly affects both perceived desirability and feasibility, while the attitudes toward achievement, risk and independence also affect feasibility. Thus the relationship between attitudes and self-perception variables is not isolated as originally postulated in Figure 2 but cross-related.

Focusing on the relative impacts of variables, we find that independence and self-efficacy are the two most important factors to enhance entrepreneurial interests and perceived feasibility. These findings suggest that the way to promote student interest in entrepreneurship is by increasing efficacy (by imparting more practical business knowledge and encouraging

Table 3.   Result of Hierarchical Regression on Self-perception Variables[a]

Independent Variable	Perceived desirability		Perceived feasibility	
	b	β (regression in step 2)	b	β (regression in step 2)
Step 1: Demographic and educational variables				
Gender	0.327**	0.089**	0.234**	0.090**
Family	0.306**	0.069**	0.204**	0.064**
Citizen	–0.167*	–0.026	–0.037	0.003
Income	0.013	0.003	0.040*	0.028
University	–0.078	0.027	–0.050	0.039*
Postgraduate	0.271	0.032*	0.090	0.016
Business	0.383**	0.078**	0.163**	0.025
Engineering	0.173*	0.052*	0.089	0.035
ΔR^2	0.044**		0.036**	
Step 2: Attitude variables				
Achievement	0.163**	0.099**	0.143**	0.129**
Risk	0.181**	0.128**	0.120**	0.126**
Independence	0.293**	0.176**	0.175**	0.156**
Efficacy	0.249**	0.174**	0.200**	0.207**
ΔR^2	0.155**		0.171**	
Overall Adjusted R^2	0.193**		0.206**	
Overall Model F	143.1**		155.1**	
s.e.	1.18		0.79	

[a] $N = 7129$
* $p < 0.01$
** $p < 0.001$

self-confidence of students in themselves) as well as by nurturing their desire for independence, aspects that are often missing in heavy tertiary course load by emphasizing narrow disciplinary specialization.

It is interesting to note that, after controlling for attitude variables in which polytechnic students are stronger, the effect of the *University* variable on perceived desirability and feasibility are both positive, and even significant for feasibility. It means that university students are found to have more interests in entrepreneurship (though not significant) as well as in its perceived feasibility than polytechnic students. The attitude advantage of polytechnic students somehow loses its impact when they come to evaluate the desirability and feasibility in starting one's own business.

Among the other educational factors, postgraduate, business, and students with technological background have more interests in starting own business, after controlling for attitudes. However, the same is not true for their perceived feasibility. It thus appears that while the field of majors may have an additional independent influence on the level of interests in entrepreneurship, they do not add to the perceived feasibility.

Effects of Self-perception to Entrepreneurial Intentions

The final step is to the test what affects entrepreneurial intentions, the most direct measure of entrepreneurial propensity. We use hierarchical regression to test the effects of the different types of variables as before. Same as above, we take demographic and educational variables as independent variables first, and then add perceived desirability and feasibility to test whether they improve the regression power. The steps of the hierarchical regression are similar to above ones. The results are presented in Table 4. To show the relative weights of variables, we also present adjusted β value in Step 2 regression.

Table 4. Result of Hierarchical Regression on Entrepreneurial Intentions[a]

Independent Variable	Entrepreneurial intentions	
	b	β (regression in step 2)
Step 1: Demographic & educational variables		
Gender	0.185^{**}	0.044^{**}
Family	0.166^{**}	0.038^{*}
Citizen	-0.168^{**}	-0.050^{**}
Income	0.021	0.008
University	0.001	0.004
Postgraduate	0.254^{*}	0.031
Business	0.149^{*}	0.034
Engineering	0.142^{**}	0.051^{*}
ΔR^2	0.027^{**}	
Step 2: Self-perceived variables		
Interest	0.150^{**}	0.197^{**}
Feasibility	0.200^{**}	0.178^{**}
ΔR^2	0.095^{**}	
Overall Adjusted R^2	0.121^{**}	
Overall Model F	90.6^{**}	
s.e.	0.93	

[a] N = 7144
* p < 0.01
** p < 0.001

Table 4 shows the two self-perception variables are indeed significantly related to entrepreneurial intentions, and they are better predictors compared with demographic and educational variables. If we do the hierarchical regression the other way, step 1 starting with self-perception variables and in step 2 adding demographic and educational variables, R^2 in step 2 will be 0.010. The model thus absorbs more than 60% variance from these background variables. Summarizing findings displayed in Table 2, Table 3 and Table 4, we present an entrepreneurial model in Figure 3 as empirical modification of the hypothesized model proposed in Figure 2.

Table 4 also shows the relative impacts of different variables. Perceived desirability and feasibility are two factors most significantly affecting entrepreneurial intentions. Among background controlling variables, gender and family role model have a significant influence on intentions. In addition, foreign students also exhibit higher entrepreneurial intentions, even though they do not exhibit significantly different attitudes

Looking at the influence of the educational factors to intentions, *University* has no influence, *Postgraduate* and *Business* are weakly significant, and *Engineering* is strongly significant. Business students are not very strong in intentions though they are found to score higher in motivational attitudes and interests. Their higher business knowledge and interests and stronger motivational attitudes do not generate stronger entrepreneurial intentions. A plausible reason for this may be that their good career prospects as employees in big corporations in Singapore may increase the perceived opportunity costs and hence lower entrepreneurial intentions. The prospect of being a manager in a large company may be more promising than being a hardworking entrepreneur in a small firm. This finding indicates the need for an additional item on alternative career prospective to improve the model predictability as suggested by Douglas and Shepherd (2000).

In contrast, students with technological background exhibit stronger entrepreneurial intentions, and the difference still exists after controlling for interests and perceived feasibility. However, for other educational factors, the difference disappears, i.e., the higher entrepreneurial intentions of students appear to be transmitted primarily through higher interest and perceived feasibility. Overall, educational differences are well absorbed into self-perception variables.

Besides the hierarchical regression, we also run the path analysis on variables in our model using SPSS Amos to test the validity of the analysis. The results are presented in Figure 4 and Table 5. For clarity, we remove the demographic variables. The path analysis results shown in Figure 4 and Table 5 confirm the results we derived from hierarchical regression.

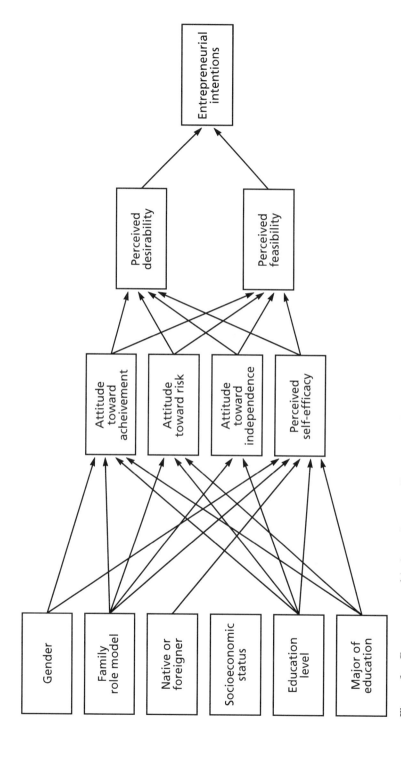

Figure 3.   Entrepreneurship intentions modle supported.

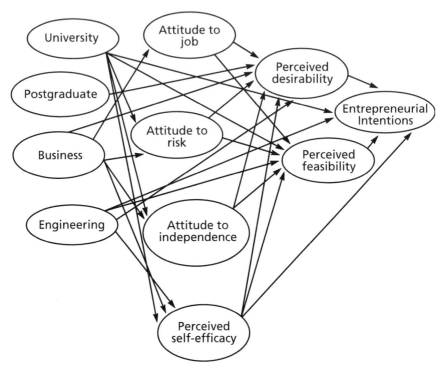

Figure 4.   Model results from path analysis (only paths with significant covariance are displayed).

Table 5.   Path Analysis Results[a]

Structural model	Covariance
University ‰ Risk	0.088
University ‰ Independence	−0.055
University ‰ Efficacy	−0.480
University ‰ Feasibility	0.081
University ‰ Intentions	0.070
Postgraduate ‰ Interest	0.304
Business ‰ Achievement	0.151
Business ‰ Risk	0.111
Business ‰ Independence	0.075
Business ‰ Efficacy	0.317
Business ‰ Interest	0.208
Engineering ‰ Efficacy	0.128

Table 5.   Path Analysis Results[a] (Cont.)

Structural model	Covariance
Engineering ‰ Interest	0.137
Engineering ‰ Feasibility	0.052
Engineering ‰ Intentions	0.093
Achievement ‰ Interest	0.159
Achievement ‰ Feasibility	0.155
Risk ‰ Interest	0.187
Risk ‰ Feasibility	0.108
Independence ‰ Interest	0.287
Independence ‰ Feasibility	0.157
Efficacy ‰ Interest	0.277
Efficacy ‰ Feasibility	0.203
Efficacy ‰ Intentions	0.122
Feasibility ‰ Intentions	0.164
Interest ‰ Intentions	0.136

[a] N = 7144, only significant covariance is presented.

CONCLUSIONS

In this paper, we propose a comprehensive three-stage entrepreneurship model that incorporates the key demographic, educational, motivational attitude and perceived interest and feasibility factors that are postulated in the literature to influence entrepreneurial intentions. The model is designed to test in particular the residual influence of educational variables, after controlling for other variables.

Empirically, we tested the model using a large-sample, nationwide survey of students business and technical fields in six institutions of higher learning in Singapore. We find the empirical results provide support for the efficacy of our three-stage model, but they also suggest a more complex pattern of influence than originally proposed model. In particular, we find that attitude variables are better predictors for perceived desirability and feasibility compared to background demographic and educational variables, as they absorb a large proportion of the variance of these background variables. Similarly, self-perception variables measuring the perceived desirability and feasibility of entrepreneurship are better predictors of entrepreneurial intentions, and absorb the variance largely. However, we found that, contrary to the findings of Krueger (2000), attitudinal variables are found to have a significant influence on perceived feasibility as well, rather than on interest alone. Moreover, self-efficacy is also found to influence interest in addition to perceived feasibility.

In interpreting our findings, we suggest that alternative career prospect may have a strong moderating effect on the influence of entrepreneurial interest on entrepreneurial intentions. Since the characteristics of alternative career prospects are a key variable of the national environment, their effect on entrepreneurial intentions is likely to be sensitive to the national context. In the case of Singapore, years of sustained rapid economic growth have created an environment characterized by high availability of lucrative jobs in the corporate and public sector; as such, high interest in entrepreneurship needs not translate into high intention. In contrast, in another country characterized by persistent, high unemployment, high entrepreneurial interest may indeed lead to high intentions. In view of this, we believe that adding variables measuring the alternative career prospects to our model would improve its predictability on entrepreneurial intentions.

Besides supporting the overall validity of the entrepreneurship model, our analysis also highlights the nature of the influence of educational factors on entrepreneurial intentions. While polytechnic students are found to have stronger motivational attitudes and self-efficacy toward entrepreneurship, this does not generate stronger intentions for entrepreneurship. Similarly, students in business majors also score higher in attitudes and have stronger interests in entrepreneurship, but these attributes likewise do not translate into higher entrepreneurial intentions after controlling for interest and perceived feasibility. On the other hand, postgraduate students and students majoring in engineering and computer science have stronger interest and intentions to start own business, despite having no significant difference in attitudes compared to other students. Thus, it appears that the technological education for these engineering or computer/IT students, and more advanced knowledge (gained through postgraduate studies), appear to exert an independent influence on entrepreneurial interest and entrepreneurial intentions, after controlling for attitudes. This finding suggests that technological educational background may be helpful in nurturing student interests and intentions for entrepreneurship even though it does not have a significant influence on their business attitudes. A possible reason for this may be that the possession of advanced technological knowledge in and of itself may expose students to the potential for creating value through new ventures. If true, this will lend support to the argument of Shane and Venkataraman (2000) that the likelihood of discovery of opportunity (technological opportunity in this case) could be an independent factor affecting entrepreneurial propensity, over and beyond the personal characteristics of the individuals concerned.

Our research findings above provide a number of insights on practical policy implications for university educators and administrators as well as government policy makers. First, the existence of strong entrepreneurial interest along with poor business knowledge implies a high potential impact of increasing the offering of entrepreneurship courses in polytechnics and universities, especially for engineering and computer science students, and postgraduate students. Their higher entrepreneurial interests and intentions despite having no significant difference in motivational attitudes and self-efficacy indicate higher potential of entrepreneurial behaviors if they can be trained with better business knowledge and are encouraged to develop stronger motivational attitudes (e.g., through greater exposure to successful role models). In particular, the higher entrepreneurial interest of postgraduate students suggests that public policy to encourage high tech spin-offs from university should concentrate on postgraduate students who are likely to have the specialized technical knowledge for viable commercialization in the marketplace. This is in contrast to polytechnic students who may have higher motivational attitudes, but lower intentions, due to the less advanced nature of their knowledge.

Secondly, our findings show that entrepreneurial desirability and feasibility are more influenced by attitude toward independence and self-efficacy compared to attitude toward achievement and risk. This suggests that future entrepreneurship training courses for students should emphasize more on imparting practical business knowledge and nurturing self-confidence and desire for independence, aspects that are often neglected and unintentionally suppressed under the current educational system emphasizing the accumulation of specialized disciplinary knowledge.

Thirdly, our findings show that business students may have higher motivational attitudes but not stronger entrepreneurial interests and intentions. We suspect that good prospects as corporate employees hinder their desire for entrepreneurship. Entrepreneurial education for this group should thus emphasize more on the entrepreneurial feasibility especially in nurturing their self-confidence for starting one own business. At the same time, the strong desire for entrepreneurship among students with technological background indicates the potential of entrepreneurship training to these non-business students. Especially under the knowledge-based economy, start-up entrepreneurs are expected to have good technological background and creative ideas, graduates from engineering or computer sciences have a greater potential for high-technology start-ups. With such a perspective, tertiary education should train students more on attitude and mindset beyond pure conceptual knowledge.

We believe that fruitful future research can build upon this study in several directions. Theoretically, we suggest that a more comprehensive entrepreneurship model can be developed by incorporating the consideration of alternative career prospects. Empirically, we believe that extending the current study on Singapore to other countries in Asia or elsewhere in the world where the environment may be different, may provide new comparative insights not obtainable in a single country focused study. In addition, a more disaggregated analysis of the effect of specific fields of specialization may also be useful in revealing more clearly the role of the nature of the technical education in predisposing exposure to entrepreneurial opportunities of a technological nature (e.g., computer engineering vs. mechanical engineering). Finally, given our findings that technical education may exert an independent influence on the entrepreneurial propensity of university students, we believe that it may be fruitful to extend the investigation of the independent influence of technological opportunities on entrepreneurial propensity in other settings. For example, to what extent do technical professionals belong to different technical disciplinary specialization exhibit different entrepreneurial propensities, after controlling for their individual characteristics?

ACKNOWLEDGMENT

The authors gratefully acknowledge the research support of the Centre for Management of Innovation and Technopreneurship (CMIT), NUS and the National Science and Technology Board (NSTB) in Singapore.

REFERENCES

Ajzen, I. (1985). From intentions to actions: A theory of planned behavior. In J. Kuhl & J. Beckmann (Eds.), *Action-control: From cognition to behavior* (pp. 11–39). Heidelberg: Springer.

Ajzen, I. (1987). Attitudes, traits and actions: Dispositional prediction of behavior in personality and social psychology. In L. Berkowitz (Ed.), *Advances in experimental and social psychology* (pp. 1–63). San Diego, CA: Academic Press.

Bird, B. (1988). Implementing entrepreneurial ideas: The case for intention. *Academy of Management Review, 13*, 442–453.

Black, B., & Gilson, R. (1998). Venture capital and the structure of capital markets: Banks versus stock markets. *Journal of Financial Economics, 47*, 243–277.

Boyd, N.G., & Vozikis, G.S. (1994). The influence of self-efficacy on the development of entrepreneurial intentions and actions. *Entrepreneurship Theory & Practice, 18*, 63–77.

Brenner, O.C., Pringle, C.D., & Greenhaus, J.H. (1991). Perceived fulfillment of organizational employment versus entrepreneurship: Work values and career intentions of business college graduates. *Journal of Small Business Management, 29*(3), 62–74.

Brockhaus, R.H., & Horwitz, P. (1986). The psychology of the entrepreneur. In D.L. Sexton & R.W. Smilor (Eds.), *The art and science of entrepreneurship.* Cambridge, MA: Ballinger.

Crant, J.M. (1996). The proactive personality scale as a predictor of entrepreneurial intentions. *Journal of Small Business Management, 34*(3), 42–49.

De Wit, G., & Van Winden, F.A. (1989). An empirical analysis of self-employment in the Netherlands. *Small Business Economics, 1*(4), 263–272.

Douglas, E.J., & Shepherd, D.A. (2000). Entrepreneurship as a utility maximizing response. *Journal of Business Venturing, 15*(3), 231–251.

Dyer, Jr. W.G. (1994). Toward a theory of entrepreneurial careers. *Entrepreneurship Theory and Practice, 19*(2), 7–21.

Evans, D.S., & Leighton, L.S. (1989). Some empirical aspects of entrepreneurship. *The American Economic Review, 59*(3), 519–535.

Fishbein, M., & Ajzen, I. (1975). *Belief, attitude, intention, and behavior: An introduction to theory and research.* New York: Addison-Wesley.

Furnham, A. (1992). *Personality at work: The role of individual differences in the working place.* London: Routledge.

Gartner, W.B. (1989). Some suggestions for research on entrepreneurial traits and characteristics. *Entrepreneurship Theory & Practice, 13*, 27–37.

Ghazali, A., Ghosh B.C., & Tay R.S.T. (1995). The determinants of self-employment choice among university graduates in Singapore. *International Journal of Management, 12*(1), 26–35.

Gorman, G., Hanlon, D., & King, W. (1997). Some research perspectives on entrepreneurship education and education for small business management: A ten-year literature review. *International Small Business Journal, 15*(3), 56–77.

Hisrich, R.D. (1986). The woman entrepreneur: Characteristics, skills, problems and prescriptions for success. In D.L. Sexton & R.W. Smilor (Eds.), *The art and science of entrepreneurship.* Cambridge, MA: Ballinger.

Johnson, B. (1990). Toward a multidimensional model of entrepreneurship: The case of achievement motivation and the entrepreneur. *Entrepreneurship Theory & Practice, 14*, 39–54.

Kolvereid, L. (1996). Organizational employment versus self-employment: Reasons for career choice intentions. *Entrepreneurship Theory and Practice, 20*(3), 23–31.

Kourilsky, M.L., & Walstad, W.B. (1998). Entrepreneurship and female youth: Knowledge, attitudes, gender differences, and educational practices. *Journal of Business Venturing, 13*(1), 77–88.

Krueger, N.F. (1993). The impact of prior entrepreneurial exposure on perceptions of new venture feasibility and desirability. *Entrepreneurship Theory and Practice, 18*(1), 5–21.

Krueger, N.F., & Carsrud, A.L. (1993). Entrepreneurial intentions: Applying the theory of planned behavior. *Entrepreneurial & Regional Development, 5*, 315–330.

Krueger, N.F., Reilly, M.D., & Carsrud, A.L. (2000). Competing models of entrepreneurial intentions. *Journal of Business Venturing, 15*(5/6), 411–432.

Matthews, C.H., & Moser, S.B. (1996). A longitudinal investigation of the impact of family background and gender on interest in small firm ownership. *Journal of Small Business Management, 34*(2), 29–43.

Mesch, G.S., & Czamanski, D. (1997). Occupational closure and immigrant entrepreneurship: Russian Jews in Israel. *Journal of Socio-economics, 26*(6), 597–610.

Robinson, P.B., Stimpson, D.V., Huefner, J.C., & Hunt, K.H. (1991). An attitude approach to the prediction of entrepreneurship. *Entrepreneurship Theory and Practice, 16*(4), 13–31.

Scherer, R., Adams, J., Carley, S., & Wiebe, F. (1989). Role model performance effects on development of entrepreneurial career preference. *Entrepreneurship Theory and Practice, 13*(3), 53–81.

Schiller, B.R., & Crewson, P.E. (1997). Entrepreneurial origins: A longitudinal inquiry. *Economic Inquiry, 35*(3), 523–531.

Scott, M.G., & Twomey, D.F. (1988). The long-term supply of entrepreneurs: Students' career aspirations in relation to entrepreneurship. *Journal of Small Business Management, 26*(4), 5–13.

Shane, S., & Venkataraman, S. (2000). The promise of entrepreneurship as a field of research. *Academy of Management Review, 25*(1), 217–226.

Shapero, A. (1982). Social dimensions of entrepreneurship. In C. Kent, D. Sexton, & K. Vesper (Eds.), *The encyclopedia of entrepreneurship* (pp. 72–90). Englewood Cliffs, NJ: Prentice-Hall.

Stevenson, H.H., & Jarillo, J.C. (1990). A paradigm of entrepreneurship: Entrepreneurial management. *Strategic Management Journal, 11*(Special Issue), 17–27.

Stewart, Jr., W.H., Watson, W., Carland, J.C., & Carland, J.W. (1999). A proclivity for entrepreneurship: A comparison of entrepreneurs, small business owners, and corporate managers. *Journal of Business Venturing, 14*(2), 189–214.

Taylor, M.P. (1996). Earnings, independence or unemployment: Why become self-employed? *Oxford Bulletin of Economics and Statistics, 58*(2), 253–266.

Van de Ven, A.H., & Schroeder, D.M. (1984). Designing new business startups: Entrepreneurial, organizational, and ecological considerations. *Journal of Management, 10*(1), 87–107.

CHAPTER 5

REGIONAL INNOVATION RESOURCES FOR ENVIRONMENTAL MANAGEMENT

Gregory Theyel

ABSTRACT

This paper presents research on the importance of regional sources of information and technical assistance for innovation in environmental management. Using data from U.S. chemical plants collected with a national survey, firm visits, and phone interviews, this research shows that local suppliers, customers, universities, and competitors are important for helping firms improve their environmental efforts. The paper also shows that relationships with local universities and customers help explain firm leadership in environmental management. Implications of this research are that firms can enhance their environmental efforts by leveraging regional resources, and regional institutions can enhance and help sustain the environmental efforts of local firms.

INTRODUCTION

Does firm location matter for leadership in environmental management? What is the importance of regional resources for assisting firms with their adoption of innovative environmental management practices and technology? A review of the literature on regional innovation systems suggests that firms located in regions with interconnected firms, specialized suppliers, service providers, firms in related industries, and associated institutions are more innovative than firms outside of these clusters (Porter, 1998). This literature describes how regional innovation systems or clusters create competitive advantages for the firms located there such as labor-force pooling, inter-firm collaboration, supplier networks, and technology spillovers (Audretsch, 1998; Feldman & Florida, 1994; Porter, 1998). Most of this literature on regions and innovation has focused on the development of new products and production processes in high technology industries. Few researchers have assessed how regional innovation systems can assist firms with innovation in environmental management.

This paper presents a test of the claims made by researchers studying regions to gauge the extent to which their claims can be extended to innovation in environmental management in the U.S. chemical industry. First, this paper tests whether or not the region (within 100 miles of a firm) is an important source of information and technical assistance for environmental management. Firms in regions with diverse economies may benefit from linkages with customers that share specialized information or suppliers that have expertise in aspects of their production processes. Firms may benefit from regional economies of scope and subcontract parts of the production process for which they do not have the most sophisticated knowledge or equipment to improve environmental performance. Regions can develop resources and a reputation for excellence in technological innovation in particular industries. Resources unique to a region can include: networks of skilled workers moving from one firm to another transferring tacit knowledge; local universities that provide a source of new employees and ideas; business associations that facilitate the exchange of ideas and technology; and government agencies who share information and assistance.

Second, this paper tests whether or not firm location matters for encouraging interaction with customers, suppliers, competitors, universities, governments, and consultants for improving environmental performance. Proximity to plants that are involved in related production processes can assist in addressing environmental problems during the entire life-cycle of products because firms that are located near each other can work together more closely to integrate their production systems in an effort to form closed production loops. Location in a regional network may facilitate collaborative technology development agreements among customers, suppliers, competitors, and other research institutions, which can result in the exchange of information and the process of team-building to pool expertise to solve pollution problems and develop technology for improving environmental performance. Concentrations of firms in the same industrial sectors may facilitate the development and transfer of technology and management practices through employees who move from one firm to another and through the informal transfer of information between employees at like firms.

The paper begins with a review of the literature on regional innovation systems and regional clusters. The paper then presents the results of a mailed questionnaire, firm visits, and telephone interviews that inquired about firms' adoption of environmental strategies, technology, and management practices and the sources of information and assistance. The results of this research partially support the claim that regional resources give firms an advantage in adopting innovative environmental management practices. Relationships with local universities and customers help explain firm leadership in environmental management. The findings of this research have implications for firm strategy, regional institutions, and regional economic development and environmental quality.

LITERATURE REVIEW

The regional studies and strategic management literatures identify numerous regional factors that are credited with enhancing the innovation potential of local firms. These literatures present an image of the firm among these factors capable of connecting with the regional factors as an extension of the firm. The overarching relationship is that regional resources aid technological innovation and create opportunities that encourage entrepreneurship. Location in a vibrant region can offer demand signals as well as resources leading to new business opportunities for start-up companies as well as within existing firms (Porter 1998). Regions can offer information about opportunities—new technologies, local markets, and access to needed assets. These regional offerings can enhance existing firms as well as offer opportunities for entrepreneurs. This literature review develops the relationship between resources, innovation, and opportunities by reviewing the contribution of regional resources to innovation and entrepreneurship.

Figure 1 shows some of the regional resources researchers have identified. Firms may not have access to or take advantage of all of these relationships, but instead these represent options for the firm to access and the number and quality of the firm's regional options reflect the strength of the firm's locational advantage. This research goes beyond identifying whether firms located in rich, option-laden regions have significant advantages to assess how firms value regional resources for enhancing their environmental efforts and how regional resources help firms lead in environmental management.

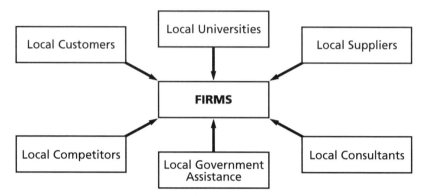

Figure 1.   Regional innovation resources.

Authors have long insisted that there are important locational dimensions in processes of innovation, technology development, and entrepreneurship (Best, 1990; Marshall, 1890; Piorre & Sabel 1984; Porter, 1990). In particular, researchers claim that there is a distinct territoriality to innovation, whereby manufacturing competence becomes embedded within a region allowing it to develop comparative advantage in specific production processes (Angel, 1994; Camagni, 1991; DeBresson & Amesse, 1989; Malecki, 1991). Angel (1994) claims that much of technological knowledge is tacit, which is embedded in the skills and experiences of workers, institutions, and communities, and not easily transferable across national and regional boundaries. Others claim that the opportunities for technological development and the capacity to pursue them are distinctly local and regional in character (Dosi, 1988; Krugman, 1991; Mowery et al., 1996).

The focus on regional resources and innovation systems is a refinement of earlier work on national systems of innovation. Nelson (1993) and Lundvall (1996) assessed the extent of convergence or divergence among national innovation systems. They found there are multiple models of national systems. However, they also found it difficult to make systemic claims for entire nations, especially large nations (Braczyk et al., 1998). Using the region as the unit of analysis has allowed researchers to compare regions within nations and distinguish the role regional entities play with national conditions such as tax and trade policy.

Firms located in proximity to their customers are better able to learn from their customers about their needs and co-develop knowledge through the give and take of providing goods and/or services (Angel, 1994; Harrison et al., 1996; Porter, 1998). Linkages with local customers can also lead to referrals to other local firms and reduced costs for acquiring new customers. Customer requirements can spur innovation and it is likely that proximity to demanding customers can enhance the learning process for both parties. Firms working with local customers can gain traditional benefits of collaboration such as risk and resource sharing, but they can also improve their communication and information flow with these local customers (Audretsch, 1998).

There are often regional advantages related to better access to suppliers and service providers. Just as local customers convey and create knowledge with their suppliers, second and third tier suppliers are often more closely linked when they are near one another. This proximity helps firms know their options when they are addressing a problem or developing new technology. Local suppliers can be a source of knowledge or help develop new knowledge. Proximity between firms and their suppliers can quicken this process and lower the cost (Porter, 1998). Local suppliers can improve just-in-time performance, recovery of packaging, implementation of Total Quality Management, and monitoring of supplier performance. Harrison (1992) and Porter (1990, 1998) connect inter-organizational collaboration and the formation of geographically concentrated clusters of producers by arguing that relative proximity promotes the exchange of information, the building of trust, and the pooling of resources of customers and suppliers to jointly design new specialized equipment and products.

Researchers also assert that firms in complementary industries benefit from locating in a region by sharing inputs. The presence of like producers attracts a greater number and variety of subcontractors than would be available had the firms been more geographically dispersed. As a result, all members of the region enjoy the cost-reducing and information-sharing benefits of economies of agglomeration (Feldman & Florida, 1994; Glasmeier, 1988; Harrison, 1992; Henderson, 1996; Krugman, 1991; Scott, 1988).

Regions populated with competitors may present a keener struggle for retaining customers. However, researchers credit proximity to competitors for quicker knowledge of evolving information and technology, availability of equipment, and new management concepts (Porter, 1998). In addition, there is greater pressure to differentiate products or services because competitors that are near each other share more things in common such as transportation costs and wage and utility rates (Porter, 1998). This increases the pressure on firms to be innovative and look for ways to improve their efficiency. Reducing waste and environmental compliance costs are ways to do this.

The movement of employees between competitors is encouraged by proximity. This is important for labor availability as well as the diffusion of information and technology (Angel, 1991). This is particularly relevant for environmental management because the technologies are often non-proprietary and the management practices are tacit and best transferred as the experience of individuals.

Suarez-Villa (1993) claims regions that are able to develop innovations are also likely to create new economic activities, markets, and technological applications. Regions with an innovation infrastructure may become favored destinations for highly skilled individuals and labor, reinforcing their knowledge and educational infrastructure by attracting skilled in-migration from other areas without incurring many of the long-term invest-ment and incubation costs. In addition to supply chain linkages and com-petitors, regional infrastructure can include universities, research laboratories, industry associations, and government assistance programs. Firms that are located outside of vibrant regions incur greater costs for hir-ing people and from having to generate knowledge internally (Audretsch & Feldman, 1996; Harrison et al., 1996; Jaffe et al., 1994; Porter, 2000).

Several authors have brought attention to the relationship between interregional technology transfer and the localization of technology link-ages and innovation for improved environmental performance (Cramer & Schot, 1993; Frosch, 1994; Frosch & Gallopoulos, 1992; Knight, 1990). These authors claim the integration of departments within the plant, sup-plier and producer networks, and networks between recyclers and manu-facturers facilitate the creation of closed systems of resource use. They also highlight the importance of proximity in the formation of industrial net-works for addressing environmental problems during the entire product life cycle. Companies that are located near each other can work together more closely to integrate their production systems. In addition, the pres-ence of local, industry-specific trade associations that advocate self-regula-tion rather than government requirements facilitate the development and transfer of environmental technology. Associations can facilitate the shar-ing of environmental information and cultivate a sense of regional identity. Empirical and theoretical investigation of the significance of region-spe-cific relationships in facilitating technical change for environmental per-formance is at an early stage. Based on a review of the literature, research is needed on how region-specific characteristics affect the ability of the firms in a region to improve their environmental strategy, management, and technology.

RESEARCH METHODOLOGY

The U.S. chemical industry is a significant industry to study for environ-mental performance because nearly half of the total volume of chemical pollution in the United States, as recorded by the U.S. Environmental Pro-tection Agency's Toxic Release Inventory, is released by plants in the chem-ical industry (Gottlieb, 1995). The U.S. chemical industry is also well suited for the study of the significance of firm location for environmental performance. There are more than 12,000 plants employing nearly one million people in the U.S. chemical industry, which includes several regional clusters. The largest agglomerations are in Texas and Louisiana. There are also significant clusters of plants in northern New Jersey; Illinois and Indiana along Lake Michigan; and in the Los Angeles area (U.S. Department of Commerce, 1993). Within these agglomerations, large, multinational companies are well represented. A second type of firm in these regional clusters is small, vertically disintegrated producers.

This research required detailed information on the environmental management activities and performance of U.S. chemical manufacturers. The research design involved three broad tasks of data collection. The first task was the development of an extensive data set on U.S. chemical plants. The second task involved conducting an in-depth, survey-based analysis of chemical plants to identify their environmental management practices and strategies and their environmental performance. The third task involved follow-up interviews with a sample of the plant managers responding to the mailed questionnaire survey that I used to further verify the results of the mailed questionnaire. Of the 650 surveys mailed, plant managers returned 188 for a response rate of 28.9%. The sample firms are located across the United States, in regional clusters and isolated from other chemical firms. I also conducted follow-up interviews with 20 chemical plant managers.

REGIONAL RESOURCES FOR
ENVIRONMENTAL MANAGEMENT

The literature on clusters and regional networks of innovators focuses on proximity as the vital ingredient for effective collaboration among suppliers, customers, and competitors. Harrison (1992) claims that proximity to business partners or like firms increases the likelihood of collaboration as frequent contact builds trust. Chemical firms answered questions about the importance of local suppliers, customers, and competitors as sources of ideas, information, and assistance for their environmental efforts. Table 1 shows the means and distribution of the responses. The firms rate the importance of local suppliers and customers highest. The mean rating for importance of local suppliers is the highest at 3.16 on a scale of 1 to 5, with 1 being not important and 5 being very important. Of the firms answering the question about local suppliers, 44% rated them a 4 or 5 for importance when dealing with environmental issues. Local customers are only slightly less important on average, rating at 3.14, with 41% of firms rating their local customers as a 4 or 5 for importance with help dealing with environmental issues. Local competitors, with a mean of 2.21, received the lowest rating for importance with environmental help. Only 15% rated their competitors as a 4 or 5, while 37% firms rated their competitors as not important (1). Follow-up interviews revealed that firms in the chemical industry are not highly trusting of their competitors, as there is a high level of rivalry in the industry.

Table 1.   Contribution of the Region for Pollution Prevention

	Mean	Not Important			Very Important		N
		(1)	(2)	(3)	(4)	(5)	
Local Suppliers	3.16	22	21	35	35	26	139
Local Customers	3.14	27	17	39	25	33	141
Local Government	3.14	23	25	32	30	30	140
Local Consultants	2.71	29	29	41	24	12	135
Local Universities	2.36	42	33	36	12	10	133
Local Competitors	2.21	50	34	30	12	8	134

Source: Mail Survey

Sample firms also answered questions about the importance of other sources of ideas, information, and assistance for their environmental efforts. These sources included local government, local consultants, and local universities. Of these three sources, local government received the highest mean rating with 3.14. Forty-three percent of firms rated the local government at 4 or 5 in importance. Local consultants received a mean rating of 2.71, and local universities received a mean rating of 2.36. These two sources may have received lower ratings because there may not be consultants or universities in the local area of some of the sample firms.

Table 1 also shows there are groups of sample firms that rate the importance of local sources of ideas, information, and assistance for their environmental efforts at both ends of the spectrum of importance. Table 1 shows that two nearly equal sized groups exist and that they differentially value local suppliers, customers, and the government. For local suppliers, 18.7% of the sample firms rate them very important, while 15.8% rate them not important. For local customers, 23.4% of the sample firms rate them very important, while 19.1% rate them not important. For the local government, 21.4% of the sample firms rate it very important, while 16.4% rate it not important. For local consultants, local universities, and local competitors, the scales are not as balanced with fewer firms rating these sources as very important compared to not important.

To learn more about the firms that value local resources for their environmental efforts, I conducted Pearson correlation analysis. In addition to the six local sources of environmental help, I added seven other variables. First, in order to assess firms' environmental management efforts, I used a composite score for each firm's adoption of 10 environmental management practices (Environmental Management). A "yes" answer to having adopted a practice equaled 1, and a "no" answer equaled zero. For the 10 practices, a score of 10 is the maximum and a score of zero is the minimum. The 10 management practices include waste audits, total quality management for pollution prevention, pollution prevention plans, employee training for pollution prevention, total cost accounting, designated environmental manager, R&D for pollution prevention, environmental standards for suppliers, life-cycle analysis, and employee incentive programs for environmental suggestions.

I also used plant employment (Employment) as a variable to represent the size of the firm at the location where the plant manager completed the survey. I used the organization of the firm (single-plant firm or part of a multi-plant firm) as a variable (Organization). I used whether the respondent was from different four-digit standard industrial classifications (SIC) within the chemical industry. I also used three location variables, the concentration of manufacturing in the county where the firm is located, the location quotient, which is the concentration of firms in the same industry in the county where the firm is located, and the type of metropolitan area where the firm is located.

Regions with large concentrations of industry have diverse economies and are more likely to offer linkages with firms that specialize in aspects of the sample plants' production processes. Firms located in agglomerations may benefit from regional economies of scope, and it is more likely that firms are able to establish and maintain partnerships with customers, suppliers, and competitors. I measured the size of the concentration of industry as the natural logarithm of total manufacturing in the county in which each sample plant is located (Manufacturing Concentration). Data on total manufacturing employment by county are from the U.S. Bureau of Census, County Business Patterns (1993).

Geographically concentrated clusters of firms in similar industrial sectors may exchange information and pool resources to share costs and jointly design new specialized equipment and products. I measured the concentration of specialized firms in each sample firm's region by calculating a location quotient for each county (Location Quotient). A location quotient is a measure of the proportion of a county's employment in an industrial sector divided by the proportion of the nation's employment in that sector. A location quotient of less than one for a particular sector indicates that the county is less specialized in that sector than the nation. A location quotient of greater than one indicates that the county is more specialized in that sector.

Plants located in large metropolitan regions are likely to have access to more information and technical assistance for environmental management. Large metropolitan areas are also likely to offer greatly opportunities to team with nearby customers, suppliers, and competitors (Harrison et al., 1996). I classified the counties where sample firms are located. I used population and established five categories (Metropolitan). I defined a large, metropolitan county as one with a population of one million people or more. I defined medium metropolitan counties as those with a population between 250,000 and one million people. I classified a small metropolitan county as having a population between 50,000 and 250,000 people, and I identified the counties with fewer than 50,000 people as rural.

The results of the Pearson correlation analysis with the 13 variables reveal several key findings. First, there is a significant relationship between firms' adoption of environmental management practices and the reliance on several local sources of ideas, information, and assistance with environmental efforts (see Table 2). Relations with local universities, customers, competitors, and suppliers are related to leadership in environmental management. This result supports the hypothesis that regional resources can assist firms with their environmental efforts and are likely to help them with their environmental performance. In many cases, firms can improve their environmental efforts by leveraging their supply chains. They can also take advantage of low cost or free resources from local universities and from competitors through university research centers and local industry associations and other day-to-day contacts that are facilitated by proximity.

This analysis also shows that firms that rely on their local suppliers also rely on their local customers for ideas, information, and assistance with their environmental matters. This indicates that firms have developed forward relations with customers and backward relations with suppliers for improving how they address environmental issues. These teams of customers and suppliers give firms resources beyond their boundaries helping them build capabilities and knowledge. Follow-up interviews confirmed the existence of these local supply chain relations. Several plant managers conveyed situations where their firms engaged local customers and suppliers in team efforts to solve environmental problems. These findings are significant for firm strategy and the management of value chains.

Next, I used multiple regression analysis to further clarify the relationships between firms' use of regional resources and their environmental efforts. I used the 13 variables that I described above and used for the Pearson correlation analysis. I used Environmental Management Performance as the dependent variable and the remaining 12 variables as independent variables. Table 3 shows the results of the regression analysis. The data

Table 2.   Pearson Correlation Coefficients

	1	2	3	4	5	6	7	8	9	10	11	12
1. Environmental Management												
2. Employment	.026											
3. Organization	-.154*	-.083										
4. SIC	-.091	-.426**	.113									
5. Location Quotient	.075	.269**	-.006	-.306**								
6. Metropolitan	.141	.162*	-.129	-.227**	.363**							
7. Manufacturing	-.088	-.127	.086	.250**	-.440**	-.827**						
8. Local Suppliers	.166*	-.025	-.024	.076	.030	-.191*	.146					
9. Local Customers	.269**	-.195*	-.033	.260**	-.115	-.115	.060	.597**				
10. Local Government	.106	-.113	-.030	.077	-.155	-.081	.097	.208*	.378**			
11. Local Consultants	.021	.090	-.100	-.335**	.094	.100	-.072	.197*	.059	.219*		
12. Local Universities	.295**	.093	-.109	-.113	.003	.163	-.085	.305**	.367**	.397**	.337**	
13. Local Competitors	.227**	-.056	-.128	.032	.032	-.185*	.095	.345**	.499**	.211*	.264**	.397**

$N = 141$
** = 0.01 Statistical Significance
* = 0.05 Statistical Significance
Source: Mail Survey

shown are regression estimates of the effects of the independent variables on the environmental management performance of the sample plants. The regression results presented in Table 3 are fully significant at the 0.02 level of confidence, though the amount of variation explained is low. Variables that may explain more of the variation include the regulations of the state, the age of the plant, ISO certification, etc. Using these and other variables was outside the scope of this study.

Table 3.   Multiple Regression Analysis of Environmental Management Performance

	Coefficient	p-value
Constant		0.68
Employment	−0.05	0.62
Organization	−0.01	0.92
SIC	−0.20	0.08
Location Quotient	0.02	0.87
Manufacturing Concentration	0.22	0.18
Metropolitan	0.13	0.10
Local Suppliers	−0.02	0.89
Local Customers	0.30	0.03
Local Government	−0.00	0.99
Local Consultants	−0.16	0.16
Local Universities	0.25	0.03
Local Competitors	−0.01	0.92

$N = 141$
Dependent variable: Environmental Management Performance
R squared (adjusted) = 0.11
$p = 0.02$
Source: Mail Survey

Two independent variables are significant at the 0.05 level—local universities and local customers. Of the five variables discussed above that are correlated with environmental performance (see Table 2), multiple regression shows the systemic relationship between firms' environmental management performance and the importance of local universities and customers. These two regional resources stand out as the most significant for firms improving their environmental performance (see Figure 2).

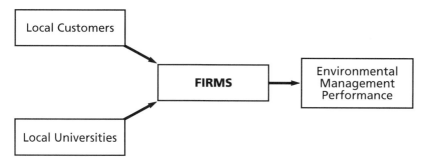

Figure 2.   Regional innovation resources and environmental management

CONCLUSIONS AND IMPLICATIONS

This paper shows that firms are using regional resources to assist them with their environmental efforts. Local suppliers are most important to the firms, followed by local customers. Some firms place a high value on local government, universities, and competitors as sources of ideas, information, and assistance with their environmental efforts. This paper also reveals a significant relationship between the adoption of environmental management practices and valuing local resources. Firms adopting a set of best management practices for environmental performance also place higher value on the contributions of local universities and customers for their environmental efforts.

These findings do not deny the advantages of improvements in communication and transportation and their influence on sourcing and plant location. However, this paper shows that the resources of the region where a firm is located can enhance a firm's environmental efforts. This finding is consistent with the argument presented by Porter (1998, 1990) that factor conditions (the cost and quality of inputs), demand conditions, rivalry, and related and supporting industries combine to produce a dynamic, stimulating, and intensely competitive business environment. Implications for firm strategy include plant location decisions that consider the business environment of a region as well as more traditional location factors such as the transportation infrastructure and the tax policies. In addition, firms need to take advantage and cultivate regional assets in order to maximize the competitive advantages regional resources can offer for environmental management.

This paper also provides a better understanding of the nature of the relationships between the firms studied and their customers and suppliers for enhancing environmental efforts. Firms that are most successful at implementing environmental practices are leveraging their value chain by collaborating with both their suppliers and their customers. This multi-tier teaming multiplies the opportunities for product and process innovations for improving environmental performance. These relationships are facilitated in part by the trust that is established from frequent contact and interaction that are more likely when firms are in proximity to each other (Harrison, 1992). Implications of multi-tier teaming with regional suppliers and customers for firm strategy exist for small and large firms. Small firms can expand their boundaries by taking advantage of free or low cost regional assets, thus allowing them to compete more effectively with larger firms. Large and small firms can reduce their transaction costs in the form of administrative costs and contracts by trusting their regional partners with whom they have developed relationships. Large and small firms can also gain from regional information sharing which may encourage innovation and a regional spirit of entreprenuership.

Multi-tier teaming for environmental management may also be an important contributor toward sustaining environmental improvement. The commitment and resources for environmental improvement by more than one entity are more likely to be sustainable compared to solo efforts of firms. In addition, regional efforts for environmental improvement are likely to be longer lasting because the local parties are likely to be more committed to efforts designed to improve the region where they are located.

REFERENCES

Acs, Z., & Audretsch, D. (Eds.). (1990). *The economics of small firms.* Boston: Kluwer Academic.

Angel, D. (1991). High-technology agglomeration and the labor market: The case of silicon valley. *Environment and Planning A, 23.*

Angel, D. (1994). Tighter bond? Customer-supplier linkages in semiconductors. *Regional Studies, 28.*

Audretsch, D.B. (1998). Agglomeration and the location of innovative activity. *Oxford Review of Economic Policy, 12,* 18–29.

Best, M. (1990). *The new competition.* Cambridge, MA: Harvard University Press.

Braczyk, H., Cooke, P., & Heidenreich, M. (Eds.). (1998). *Regional innovation systems: The role of governance in a globalized world.* London: UCL Press.

Camagni, R. (1991). *Innovation networks: A spatial perspective.* London: Pinter.

Cramer, J., & Schot, J. (1993). Environmental comakership among firms as a cornerstone in the striving for sustainable development. In K. Fischer & J. Schot (Eds.), *Environmental strategies for industry: International perspectives on research needs and policy implications.* Washington, DC: Island Press.

DeBresson, C., & Amesse, F. (1989). Networks of innovators: A review and introduction to the issue. *Research Policy, 20.*

Dosi, G. (1988). Sources, procedures, and microeconomic effects of innovation. *Journal of Economic Literature, 26*(4).

Feldman, M., & Florida, R. (1994). The geographic sources of innovation: Technological infrastructure and product innovation in the United States. *Annals of the Association of American Geographers, 84*(2).

Florida, R., & Kenney, M. (1990). High-technology restructuring in the USA and Japan. *Environment and Planning A, 22.*

Freeman, C. (1991). Networks of innovators: A synthesis of research issues. *Research Policy, 20.*

Frosch, R. (1994, November). Industrial ecology: Minimizing the impact of industrial waste. *Physics Today.*

Frosch, R., & Gallopoulos, N. (1992). Towards an industrial ecology, In A. Bradshaw et al. (Eds.), *The treatment and handling of wastes.* London: Chapman and Hall.

Glasmeier, A. (1988). Factors governing the development of high tech industry agglomerations: A tale of three cities. *Regional Studies, 22.*

Harrison, B. (1992). Industrial districts: Old wine in new bottles? *Regional Studies.*

Harrison, B. (1994). *Lean and mean.* New York: Basic Books.

Harrison, B., Kelley, M., & Gant, J. (1996). Innovative firm behavior and local milieu: Exploring the intersection of agglomeration, firm effects, and technological change. *Economic Geography, 72*(3).

Imai, K., & Baba, Y. (1989). *Systemic innovation and cross-border networks: Transcending markets and hierarchies to create a new techno-economic system.* **City:** OECD, Conference of Science Technology and Economic Growth.

Knight, P. (1990, November 14). A rebirth of the pioneering spirit. *Financial Times* (London).

Krugman, P. (1991). *Geography and trade.* Cambridge, MA: MIT Press.

Malecki, E. (1991). *Technology and economic development.* Harlow: Longman.

Mowery, D., Oxley, J., & Silvermann, B. (1996). Strategic alliances and interfirm knowledge transfer. *Strategic Management Journal, 17,* 77–91.

Piore, M., & Sabel, C. (1984). *The second industrial divide: Possibilities for prosperity.* New York: Basic Books.

Porter, M. (1985). *Competitive advantage: Creating and sustaining superior performance.* New York: Free Press.

Porter, M. (1990). *The competitive advantage of nations.* New York: The Free Press.

Porter, M. (1998). *On competition.* Boston: Harvard Business School Press.

Saxenian, A. (1989). *Regional networks and the resurgence of silicon valley* (Working Paper 508). Berkeley: Institute of Urban and Regional Development, University of California.

Saxenian, A. (1990, Fall). Regional networks and the resurgence of silicon valley. *California Management Review.*

Saxenian, A. (1991). The origin and dynamics of production networks in silicon valley. *Research Policy.*

Saxenian, A. (1995). *Regional networks.* Cambridge, MA: Harvard University Press.

Scott, A. (1988). *New industrial spaces.* London: Pion.

Storper, M., & Scott, A. (1989). The geographical foundations and social regulation of flexible production complexes. In J. Wolch & M. Dear (Eds.), *Territory and social reproduction*. Boston and London: Unwin and Hyman.

Storper, M., & Walker, R. (1989). *The capitalist imperative: Territory, technology, and industrial growth*. New York and Oxford: Basil Blackwell.

Suarez-Villa, L. (1993). The dynamics of regional invention and innovation: Innovative capacity and regional change in the twentieth century. *Geographical Analysis, 25*(2).

U.S. Department of Commerce. (1993). *County business patterns*. Washington, DC: U.S.Government Printing Office.

Part II

**VENTURE CAPITAL IN
TECHNOLOGICAL ENTREPRENEURSHIP:
GOVERNANCE IN TURBULENT ENVIRONMENTS**

CHAPTER 6

ALLOCATION OF ATTENTION WITHIN VENTURE CAPITAL FIRMS:

A Queuing Network Model

Dean A. Shepherd, Michael J. Armstrong, and Moren Lévesque

ABSTRACT

In this article we use a simple queuing network to model the process through which entrepreneurs receive venture capital funding. Our model focuses in particular on the allocation of venture capitalists' attention between pre- and post-investment activities, and on the degree of selectivity in deciding which ventures to fund. Based upon this model we develop expressions for the financial performance of the venture capital process, both overall and also from the perspectives of the investors, managers, and venture capitalists involved. For these financial measures we derive the optimal allocation of attention between pre- and post-investment activities, and the optimal proportion of venture proposals to accept. Further analysis shows how these different financial measures and optimal values respond to changes in the business climate. More interestingly, our analysis also shows where and to what extent the different parties could be expected to agree or disagree on how best to manage the process.

INTRODUCTION

There are more than 500 venture capital firms (VC firms) in the United States, which in aggregate manage approximately $35 billion invested in ventures (portfolio companies), with available capital currently reported to exceed $15 billion. In 1995, according to Boston Economics, VC firms invested $3.86 billion in 1,128 ventures. However, the amount invested by VC firms today is likely to be higher according to the National Venture Capital Association, which reported that more than $10 billion was invested in 1,502 deals in 1996. Venture capitalists (VCs) are the investment managers of these venture capital funds.

Not surprisingly, there has been considerable scholarly interest in VCs. The predominant perspective is that VCs are experts at predicting new venture success and therefore there is much to be gained by tapping into that expertise (Hall & Hofer, 1993; Muzyka, Birley, & Leleux, 1996; Sandberg, 1986; Sandberg & Hofer, 1987; Shepherd, 1999; Zacharakis & Meyer, 1998). Indeed there is evidence to suggest that VC backed firms perform better than non-VC backed firms (Dorsey, 1979; Sandberg & Hofer, 1987). However, these findings do not necessarily indicate VCs' superior selection abilities as the decision itself likely has an impact on the outcome—VCs' post-investment activities can also add value to the venture. Such non-financial value added includes help in finding and recruiting top quality management, finding other co-investors for immediate or follow up investment, introductions to important service providers such as specialized accountants, finding and developing necessary strategic alliances, and acting as sounding board for management, strategic and operational ideas (Lerner, 1994, 1995; Sweeting, 1991; Tyebjee & Bruno, 1984). Companies with VC backing are also seen as more legitimate than those that are not (Cable & Shane, 1997).

Sandberg (1986) argues persuasively that such non-financial benefits provided by the VC firm to the entrepreneur are not sufficient to account for VCs' success. From the findings discussed above it appears reasonable to assume that both VCs' ability to select ventures and their ability to assist in the ongoing management of these ventures are competencies that impact the performance of VC firms. Acknowledging the importance of both selection and assistance merely reinforces the major issues facing managers of VC firms. For example, VCs often face situations where they are flooded with entrepreneurs' requests for financing (often in the form of lengthy business plans) and simultaneously need to assist current portfolio ventures in improving performance. The more active VCs spend 35 hours per month per venture assisting the management team, while less active firms spend less than 7 hours per month per investment (Elango et al., 1995). Thus, the VC is faced with an important question: how should time, effort and/or resources within the VC firm be allocated?

Gifford (1998) proposes that the allocation of attention is analogous to a person that spins plates atop long sticks—how much time should the performer spend respinning existing plates and how much time spinning new plates. Gifford (1998) explores the allocation of a VC's attention between currently funded ventures (existing plates) and investing in new ventures (new plates) and contrasts the optimal outcome for the VC firm and the entrepreneur. But unlike the metaphorical plate-spinner, a VC firm is not a monolithic entity but rather it is made up of several important stakeholder groups, including investors, managers, and employees. It may well be that these stakeholders will have differing interests and therefore different views on how best to allocate attention within the firm.

The above discussion leads to this paper's two key research questions. What is the optimal allocation of a VC firm's attention (time, talent, and treasure) between pre-investment activities and post-investment activities? How and under what conditions is the allocation of attention that is optimal for the process overall (i.e. is best for the common good) different from that which might be preferred by the various stakeholders (investors, managers and employees)? We investigate these important questions by using a Jackson queuing network model. A queuing network is a system of queues (waiting lines) where the departures from one queue become the arrivals at another. Queuing networks are useful models of systems that involve some form of customer flow (e.g., of venture proposals) among various locations (e.g., stages in the venture capital process) where the inherent variability of the flow can lead to lineups and delays at a given location (e.g., an overflowing stack of proposals to review). Despite the usefulness of this approach to the investigation of the venture capital process it has yet to be used for this purpose, though it is often used to evaluate systems of machines in a factory (e.g., Papadopoulis et al., 1993) or the operations of health care service providers (e.g., Bretthauer & Cote, 1998).

By addressing these important issues facing VC firms, the present article makes a number of contributions to the literature. First, this study acknowledges that some scholars highlight the importance of a VC's role in selecting attractive investment ventures (Sandberg & Hofer, 1987) while other scholars emphasize VCs' assistance to portfolio ventures in order to improve new venture performance (Sweeting, 1991; Tyebjee & Bruno, 1984). Bringing together these two streams of VC research acknowledges that the role of the VC firm manager becomes one of allocating attention between the various and important tasks of the venture capital process. Second, a VC firm (as all firms) has a number of stakeholders each with different expectations and aspirations for the firm. This article provides a deeper understanding of the tradeoffs among these stakeholder groups.

Third, research on the VC process has made a significant contribution to the literature, in particular Tyebjee and Bruno (1984), although such process research is limited in number. This article builds on these primarily descriptive studies, to provide a decision model with prescriptive benefits. Such benefits are likely to have important practical implications for the managers of VC firms and may also benefit other entrepreneurial financing firms (e.g., the Small Business Development Corporation). The allocation of attention is an important issue as individual VCs have limited time and energy to allocate among the various tasks of the venture capital process. Each firm only has a limited number of VCs, a limited budget, etc., and thus limited attention to allocate between tasks.

The remainder of the paper proceeds as follows. We begin by reviewing the existing research on the VC process. We then describe our assumptions about the venture capital process in terms of operations and financing. Based upon these assumptions, we formulate models of financial performance for the VC process from the different viewpoints of the investors, managers, and VC employees. We analyze these different measures of performance to investigate how they would vary in response to changing business conditions, and more interestingly how the different entities involved would likely agree or disagree regarding the management of the process. We conclude with a discussion of the limitations of the model and suggest possible avenues for future research. An appendix contains the details of our mathematical analysis.

VENTURE CAPITAL PROCESS

The VC process can be thought of as a series of activities or stages that each new venture works through from the time the venture is first proposed, up until the time when the VC firm successfully exits from the venture and takes its profit. For example, Tyebjee and Bruno (1984) proposed a model of the venture capital process with five such stages: deal origination, deal screening, deal evaluation, deal structuring and post-investment. Because of our particular focus in this paper, we use a simpler classification with only two categories of VC activities: pre-investment and post-investment.

The first category, "pre-investment activities," refers to all VC tasks up to and including the signing of an investment contract: soliciting new venture proposals for submission to the VC firm, determining whether these proposals meet the firm's broad screening criteria, conducting due diligence (more extensive research to determine the likely success of the venture), and then negotiating and structuring a relationship with the entrepreneur. It should be noted that most proposals that the VC firm receives are referrals from third parties including other VCs and that VCs spend little time in searching for deals—this task is rather passive (Tyebjee & Bruno, 1984). Sweeting (1991) however points out that with greater competition between VC firms there is increasing proactiveness in this task. VCs differ in the screening criteria they use to select ventures including type of industry, industry stage of development, geographic location, and size of investment required. These are detailed in lists of VCs, for example *Pratt's Guide to Venture Capital Sources* (1998). There is considerable research on how VCs use the information gathered from due diligence to make their assessment of likely success; e.g., VCs typically use decision criteria such as entrepreneur/team characteristics, product/service characteristics, and market and financial characteristics (Zacharakis & Meyer, 1998). Eventually the relationship between the VC firm and the entrepreneur needs to be developed and formalized (i.e., the terms of the venture capital contract need to be negotiated and agreed upon) in order for the venture investment, and hence the "pre-investment activities," to be completed.

The second category, "post-investment activities," includes all actions by the VC firm after the initial investment deal has been signed. In general this involves providing guidance (and possibly additional funding) to help improve the performance of the venture. One of the most important benefits arising from a relationship with a VC is access to their extensive network. This is often utilized to find and recruit top quality management, to find other co-investors for immediate or follow up investment, to introduce the venture to important service providers such as specialized accountants, and to help find and develop necessary strategic alliances (Sandberg, 1986). Furthermore, VCs often serve in a role as sounding board for management ideas, and are a valuable source of strategic and operational advice (Lerner, 1994, 1995; Sweeting, 1991; Tyebjee & Bruno, 1984). Ultimately, the VC's final action is to exit from the venture. The VC can exit shortly after the venture goes for an initial public offering, through a trade sale, or through venture bankruptcy.

QUEUING NETWORK MODEL AND ASSUMPTIONS

VC Process—Operations

We begin by constructing a model of the operation of the VC process for a generic VC firm. For this purpose we have chosen to use an open queuing network with 3 nodes (labeled N1, N2, and N3; see Figure 1) through which ventures flow. Node N1 represents the involvement of the proposed venture and a VC firm in "pre-investment activities"; similarly, N3 represents the involvement of a funded venture and a VC firm in "post-invest-

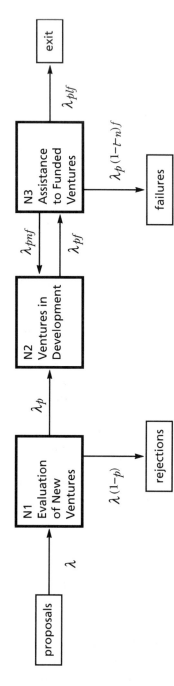

Figure 1. Venture capital process as an open queuing network.

ment activities." Node N2 represents the development efforts of a funded venture during periods that do not require the responsible VC firm to be actively involved.

Entrepreneurs with venture ideas that require financing submit their proposals on an unscheduled (i.e., random) basis to the VC firm for consideration; on average, we suppose that λ venture proposals arrive at node N1 ('evaluation of new ventures') each year. We will phrase our discussion in terms of years, but this choice of time units is unimportant (one could just as well use, e.g., months). The amount of time it takes a VC to perform all of the pre-investment activities (e.g., screening, evaluation, structuring) varies from one venture to another; we shall assume that on average the VC firm can deal with sa proposals per year. We use s to represent the proportion of VC attention (time, effort, etc.) devoted to pre-investment activities (so s takes values between 0 and 1), and a as the average number of ventures the VCs could handle per year if they devoted all of their attention to this category of activity. Note that depending on the rate at which proposals arrive and the amount of attention devoted to working with them, a given proposal may have to wait (queued-up in the VC's in-basket) before being looked at by the VC. We assume that the average capacity sa is larger than the average total proposal submission rate λ (otherwise work could pile up without end). Given these assumptions, we can model N1 as a single server queue with service rate sa. Once the VCs have finished processing a venture proposal at N1, the proposal has either successfully passed the screening and evaluation (with probability p) or it has failed (with probability $1-p$). Ventures which pass receive funding and proceed to N2; ventures which fail are rejected by the VC and leave the system.

Ventures at node N2 ("ventures in development") are in the firm's funded portfolio and are undergoing development. The entrepreneurs have their funding and are working to develop their new product or service with no significant assistance from the VC. We assume that a venture spends an average amount of time c in development before again requiring the VC's attention. Because no VC assistance is required here, there is never a line-up of idle ventures; they are all busy with development. We can therefore model N2 as an infinite server queue with service rate $1/c$.

Eventually a venture will again require the attention of a VC at the firm, for any of several possible reasons. The venture may be succeeding, so that the VC's attention is required to manage the exit process (IPO or trade sale); on the other hand, the venture may be failing, so that the VC may need to become involved in salvage efforts. It is also possible that the venture may have spent all of its previous round of capital and needs additional funding, or that the entrepreneur may simply require some management advice or other non-monetary assistance from the VC. Whatever the reason, at this point the venture will leave this node N2 and proceed to N3.

Ventures at N3 ("assistance to funded ventures") are still in the funded portfolio, but are either receiving assistance from the VC or are waiting their turn to do so; in either case, we suppose that their development efforts are temporarily on hold. We assume that the VCs can handle tb ventures per year at this node. We let t indicate the proportion of VC attention devoted to post-investment activities (e.g., providing advice, arranging extra funding, managing the exit process), and b indicate the average number of ventures the VCs could deal with in a year if they devoted all of their attention to post-investment work. Note that $s + t = 1$. Like N1, we can also model N3 as a single server queue with service rate tb; we again assume that the average work capacity tb is larger than the average workload (which we later show to be $\lambda p f$). A venture which completes service at N3 either continues with its development efforts (with probability n), achieves a successful exit (with probability l), or fails outright (with probability m); note that $l + m + n = 1$.

A venture that leaves N3 either due to a successful exit or because it has failed is no longer in the funded portfolio but rather has left the system. In contrast, a venture that leaves N3 to resume development returns to N2 and remains in the portfolio. The returning venture then carries on with its development efforts until it once again needs a VC's intervention. We refer to this return path as a "feedback loop," as a venture may cycle many times between development efforts (at N2) and obtaining assistance (at N3). For later calculations concerning this feedback of repeating ventures, it will be convenient to define a *feedback factor* $f = 1/(1-n)$. This f is the average number of times a funded venture engages in development efforts at N2: one initial visit, plus $(f - 1)$ repeat visits. Due to this feedback effect, at any point in time only some of the ventures at each of N2 and N3 are there for the first time. A smaller number are there for their first repeat visit, and still smaller numbers are there for their second, third, etc. repeat visits. These "multiple repeaters" can be thought to represent what other authors (e.g., Timmons, 1999) have referred to as "the living dead": ventures which spend a long time in the portfolio without ever seeming to either succeed or fail.

Defined in this way our model of the VC process forms a simple Jackson open queuing network with three nodes. This type of queuing network has a steady state distribution in *product form*, which means that the analysis of each node and the flow between nodes can be handled in a relatively simple manner (see, e.g., Gelenbe & Pujolle, 1987). The average flows on each arc of the network (in number of ventures per year) are derived in the appendix and are shown in Figure 1. These flow rates can in turn be used to derive the average number of ventures present at each node in system's steady state (see the Appendix for details). The expected number of ventures undergoing or awaiting VC pre-investment processing at N1 is $V_1 = \lambda / (sa-\lambda)$ while the expected total number of ventures undergoing or awaiting VC post-investment assistance at N3 is $V_3 = \lambda pf / (tb - \lambda pf)$. The expected number of ventures undergoing development (at N2) is given by $V_2 = \lambda pfc$; of this total, λpc are there for the first time, while the remaining $\lambda pc(f-1)$ are "repeaters," i.e., this is their second or subsequent period of development effort.

It is worth emphasizing that these expressions for network flows and queue status are all *long-run averages*; the *actual* number of ventures moving from N2 to N3 for example may vary greatly from year to year due to random variation in arrival and service times. It is this variation (or randomness) that causes lineups and delays at N1 and N3, in spite of the fact that each of these nodes has sufficient processing capacity to handle its average workload.

Although there is a fair amount of detail in this operating model of the VC firm and process, it is still of course a major simplification of reality. For example, we have not made any distinction among senior VCs (partners in the firm), junior VCs (associates), and support staff (such as administrative assistants) in regards to their productivity in working with ventures. Instead, we implicitly assume that the firm employs these three categories of workers in fixed proportions, so that our parameters a and b represent the weighted average productivity of the entire workforce.

VC Process—Revenues and Expenditures

We assume that each venture that successfully completes the pre-investment activities (N1) and commences development (at N2) receives an initial lump sum capital investment of an average of I dollars from the VC investment fund (this is a simplification: in practice the payment from the VC firm to the venture is often in the form of smaller amounts spread-out over time as milestones are met). Similarly, each time a venture recommences development (at N2) after receiving assistance from the VC during post-investment (N3) it receives an additional capital investment of an average of J dollars; we expect that typically $I \geq J \geq 0$. Note that this follow-on investment can occur many times (since a venture may visit N2 and N3 many times) and that J is simply the average amount; thus ventures that merely require management advice would not receive any additional money at this point.

A venture which successfully exits the portfolio (from N3) provides the VC investment fund with an average capital revenue of $R(p)$ dollars at time of exit. We treat this as a lump sum, since a VC's return comes primarily from the selling of equity in the venture; in some cases it may represent the present value of a future revenue stream. Here we assume that the average revenue per exit is a function of the quality controls that the VCs use when they perform their pre-investment activities. Generally speaking, we would expect that the higher the proportion p of proposals that are accepted, the lower the average quality of these ventures and thus the lower the average revenue from their eventual exit. To model this, we assume that the average revenue function $R(p)$ is decreasing in p at an accelerating rate, so $R(p)' \geq 0$ and $R(p)'' \geq 0$. This revenue is used to cover the VC firm's initial investment in the venture and other associated costs as well as provide a profit for the VC firm. Ventures which fail at N3 also leave the portfolio but provide zero revenue. Note that here and in the rest of this paper for convenience we assume that all payments are measured on an after-tax basis.

In addition to these investment revenues and expenditures, the VC process involves a number of other payments among participants. We assume that the investment fund (i.e., the limited partners or investors) pays the VC firm a bonus of proportion $x \in [0, 1]$ of the investment revenue $R(p)$ when each venture successfully exits, so that the investors are left with revenue of $(1 - x)R(p)$. The investment fund also pays the firm a yearly management fee of proportion $z \in [0, 1]$ of the fund's assets.

In turn, the firm must pay its VC employees a total of H dollars per year in salaries, benefits, and related variable expenses. In addition to this base salary cost, the firm rewards the VCs with a commission of proportion $y \in [0, x]$ of successful exit revenue $R(p)$, which comes out of the firm's own bonus share; thus the VC employees (as a group) get $yR(p)$ and leave the firm with $(x - y)R(p)$. Beyond paying its VCs, we assume that the firm also must pay a total of G dollars per year in overhead expenses; this could cover such things as rent, wages for a receptionist or accounting staff, etc. In the next section we combine these financial assumptions with our queuing network model of the VC process to construct several financial models of the VC process. The reader may find it helpful to refer to Table 1 for (among other things) a summary of the notation introduced.

Table 1.   Effect of Changing Parameters on Financial Models

		How is each of the following affected by a change in one parameter?			
Item	Brief Description	Investor ROI_I	Manager Earnings	Employee Pay	Angel ROI_A
λ	proposal arrival rate	–	+	+	quasi-concave
p	proposal acceptance probability	–	+[1]	concave	quasi-concave

Table 1.   Effect of Changing Parameters on Financial Models (Cont.)

		How is each of the following affected by a change in one parameter?			
Item	Brief Description	Investor ROI_I	Manager Earnings	Employee Pay	Angel ROI_A
t	VC attention: proportion post-investment	quasi-concave	quasi-convex	ne	quasi-concave
s	VC attention: proportion pre-investment	quasi-concave	quasi-convex	ne	quasi-concave
a	VC productivity: pre-investment	+	−	ne	+
b	VC productivity: post-investment	+	−	ne	+
c	development time	−	+	ne	−
G	firm overhead costs	ne	−	ne	−
H	employee salary	ne	−	+	ne
I	initial investment	−	+	ne	−
J	follow-on investment	−	+	ne	−
$R(\cdot)$	exit revenue function	+	+	+	+
x	exit bonus paid to firm	−	+	ne	ne
y	exit commission paid to employees	ne	−	+	ne
z	management fee paid to firm	−	+	ne	ne
l	probability of successful exit	+	+	+	+
n	probability of continued development	varies	+	+	varies

+	financial objective is increasing in that parameter
−	financial objective is decreasing in that parameter
ne	no effect, financial objective is independent of that parameter
varies	effect on financial objective varies depending on values of other parameters
1	When the decline in quality due to an increasing acceptance proportion is minimal (i.e. $\partial R(p)/\partial p \approx 0 \ \forall p$); otherwise, the relationship may depend on other parameters.

FINANCIAL OBJECTIVES

Although there may be many individuals involved in the VC process (aside from the entrepreneurs), for the purposes of this study we shall consider three main groups: investors, managers, and employees. Investors supply the funds to invest in ventures; depending on how the firm is structured, these may be limited partners in the firm or they may be purchasers of mutual fund units. By managers, we mean the general partners (if the VC firm is a partnership), or the major shareholders (if the firm is a corporation); these are the people who make the major decisions and benefit from any residual profit or loss by the company. By employees we mean the Venture Capitalists who actually do the pre- and post-investment work with the ventures; they may be junior associates or employees of the firm. In some cases, individual investors (often referred to as Business Angels) fill all three roles simultaneously: they provide the funds, manage the investment, and advise the ventures. In this section we consider what the objectives of these different groups might be, and how these objectives relate to the operation of the VC process.

Investors

The investors provide the funds to invest in ventures in exchange for a future return to their investment. They thus would clearly be interested in the performance of these venture investments, but presumably would be interested in the rest of the VC firm (the managers and employees) only to the extent that the firm is managing these investments on their behalf. We therefore shall assume that the goal of the investors is to maximize their Return On Investment (ROI_I) from the venture portfolio (Dean & Giglierano, 1990; Zacharakis & Meyer, 1998). ROI_I is calculated as an annual percentage ratio by taking the net income of the investment portfolio and dividing by the amount of money invested in that portfolio. Thus

$$ROI_I = [Net\ Income] / [Investment] \tag{1}$$

To derive the average amount invested in the portfolio, we need to know when money enters the portfolio and becomes available for investment. It is clear that funds have to be available at least some amount of time before they can be provided to a venture; thus any investment portfolio will consist partly of cash (awaiting investment) and partly of actual venture investments. This would be especially true for those VC firms that run their portfolios as mutual funds; cash could arrive (from the sale of fund units) and then sit idle for some time until it is invested. Rather than trying to directly model this fund-raising process and its time lags, we will simply choose a reasonable point in time as an approximation. We assume herein that money to invest in a venture becomes available (at least on average) at the moment that a venture proposal first arrives at the VC firm (i.e., at N1), even though the actual investment will not occur until after the venture successfully completes all pre-investment activities and enters the funded portfolio (at N2).

Having made this assumption about investment timing, we can calculate the average total portfolio investment by multiplying the average number of funded ventures at each node (or "to-be-funded" ventures, in the case of

N1) by the average amount invested in each one. This leads to an expression for the size of the investment portfolio (in dollars).

$$Investment = I\,[\,pV_1 + V_2 + V_3] + J\,(f\text{-}1)\,[\,V_2 + V_3] \tag{2}$$

$$= I\left[\frac{\lambda p}{sa - \lambda} + c\lambda pf + \frac{\lambda pf}{tb - \lambda pf}\right] + J(f-1)\left[c\lambda pf + \frac{\lambda pf}{tb - \lambda pf}\right] \tag{3}$$

To calculate the portfolio's average Net Income we take the annual revenue from successful venture exits (minus the portion paid as a bonus to the VC firm) and subtract the costs of the original and follow-up investments made, as well as the management fee paid to the firm. We can write this as

$$Net\ Income = (1 - x)\lambda plfRp) - I\lambda p - J\lambda phf - z[Investment]\,. \tag{4}$$

If the venture portfolio is profitable, then this expression will of course be positive; we shall assume this to be true in our later analysis.

We next divide Net Income by Investment to obtain an expression for the investor's ROI_I.

$$ROI_I = \frac{\lambda p[(1 - x)lfR(p) - I - Jnf]}{\lambda\left\{p[I]\left[\dfrac{1}{sa - \lambda}\right] + [I + Jnf]\left[cf + \dfrac{f}{tb - \lambda pf}\right]\right\}} - z\,. \tag{5}$$

The behavior of ROI_I with respect to changes in business conditions (i.e., individual parameters) is mostly straightforward; Table 1 lists a summary of sensitivity results for this and other financial expressions that we derive later. For example, we can see that ROI_I will increase if the VCs become more efficient at pre-investment activities (i.e., if a increases) but it will decrease if more venture proposals are submitted (i.e., if λ increases).

More interesting is the question of how investors will want the VC process to be managed so as to maximize their ROI_I. In other words, from their point of view what is the best allocation of attention t and acceptance proportion p?

Maximization of investor's ROI_I with respect to attention allocation t: ROI_I is quasi-concave in t, so there exists a unique optimal allocation of VC attention to post-investment activities t_{inv} such that

$$I\frac{a}{\langle a - at_{inv} - \lambda\rangle^2} = (I + Jnf)\frac{bf}{\langle t_{inv}b - \lambda pf\rangle^2}\,. \tag{6}$$

Maximization of investor's ROI_I with respect to acceptance proportion p: ROI_I is decreasing in p, so investors would prefer to have as small a proportion of ventures accepted as possible, i.e., $p_{inv} \to 0$.

Since the VC employees have only a fixed amount of attention (time, energy, etc.) to provide, the investor's ROI_I can be maximized primarily by choosing the best allocation of attention between pre-investment activities (at N1, via variable s) and post-investment activities (at N3, via variable t). Recall that since $s = (1 - t)$, by determining the best value of t we implicitly determine the corresponding value for s. The first result above shows that investors would like to see a "balanced" allocation of attention by the VCs between pre- and post-investment activities. This moderate approach allows for the fastest possible flow of ventures through the process, thus reducing the amount of capital tied-up in the investment pool at any one time. The second result indicates that investors would prefer to have only the highest quality ventures to invest in; our model implicitly assumes that investors are free to put their money elsewhere if desired, so they have no incentive to settle for anything but "the very best."

Management

By management, we mean the senior members of the firm who would share any residual profits. If the VC firm is structured as a partnership, then these would be the partners of the firm; in a corporate setting, these could instead include major shareholders and any senior managers who receive a significant portion of their remuneration through profit sharing or stock options. We assume that management is interested in maximizing the firm's annual Earnings. This is similar to the Net Revenue expression we obtained for investors, but the firm receives only a share (proportion x) of the revenue from successful exits, and does not invest any of its own funds in ventures; rather, it invests the investors' money on their behalf. On the other hand, it does receive a management fee of proportion z of the investments under management. Management must also pay the salaries and benefits H of the VC employees as well as their commission of proportion y of the revenue from successful exits. Thus, we derive the following expression.

$$Earnings = (x - y)\lambda p l f R(p) - G - H + z\lambda p \left\{ [I]\left[\frac{1}{sa - \lambda}\right] + [I + Jnf]\left[cf + \frac{f}{tb - \lambda pf}\right] \right\}. \quad (7)$$

As with the investors, we are interested in knowing management's view of an "optimal" VC process, i.e., one that would maximize their own gains.

Maximization of manager's Earnings with respect to attention allocation t:
Earnings is quasi-convex in t, so the worst possible value would be $t = t_{inv}$ as this
would minimize Earnings. Instead management would prefer to have t either as
small as possible or as large as possible, i.e., $t_{mgr} = t$ such that either $t \rightarrow (a-\lambda)/a$
or $t \rightarrow min\{\lambda pf/b, 1\}$.

Maximization of manager's Earnings with respect to acceptance proportion p:
except possibly when $R'(p)$ is very negative (i.e., the decline in exit revenue due to
venture quality is very steep), Earnings are increasing in p, so managers would
generally prefer to have as large a proportion of ventures accepted as possible, i.e.,
$p_{mgr} \rightarrow min\{tb/\lambda f, 1\}$.

The first result is due to management's desire to have a large pool of
investments upon which to charge the management fee. Through an
"unbalanced" allocation of attention, the VC firm could for example provide good pre-investment service to quickly admit ventures into the investment pool, but then provide minimal attention to post-investment activities
and thereby retard their exit. For similar reasons, the second result shows
that management would generally prefer to fund as many ventures as possible; only if venture quality were dropping-off drastically would management be inclined to refuse them funding.

Employees

By employees, we mean the venture capitalists who actually deal with
ventures during the pre- and post-investment activities but who would typically not share in any residual profits of the firm. If the firm is structured as
a partnership, then these would be the associates of the firm (i.e., the professional workers who had not yet been admitted into the partnership). We
assume that the employees as a group are interested in maximizing their
annual Pay. This is composed of a mix of fixed salaries and benefits H plus
the variable commissions calculated as proportion y of the revenue from
successful exits. This leads to the following simple expression.

$$Pay = H + y\lambda plfR(p). \tag{8}$$

The following results show how employees could be expected to view
the operation of the VC process.

Maximization of VC employee's Pay with respect to attention allocation t: Pay is
independent of t (except to the extent it limits p, see below), so employees would
not have a strong preference regarding the allocation of attention.

Maximization of VC employee's Pay with respect to acceptance proportion p: R(p) is concave in p, so there exists a unique optimum acceptance proportion p_{emp}:

(a) $p_{emp} \rightarrow \min\left\{\dfrac{tb}{\lambda f}, 1\right\}$ *if at p = tb/λ we have* $\left[R(p) + \dfrac{tb}{\lambda f}\dfrac{\partial}{\partial p}R(p)\right] > 0$; *otherwise*   (9)

(b) $p_{emp} = p$ *such that* $R(p) + p\dfrac{\partial}{\partial p}R(p) = 0$ *with* $0 < p < \min\left\{\dfrac{tb}{\lambda f}, 1\right\}$.   (10)

Note that this optimal acceptance proportion is independent of any parameters other than the revenue function R (except to the extent that t, b, λ, and f limit the range of p).

The first result follows from the VC employees being paid the same, regardless of how long it takes for a venture to make it through the VC process. The second result reflects a tradeoff by the employee: accepting more ventures leads to more eventual exits and so more commission checks; but accepting fewer ventures means the venture quality is higher and so the average commission check is larger. The optimal acceptance proportion provides a balance between these two influences.

Angels

In this section we consider the case of a "business angel": a single wealthy individual who invests in ventures and then provides them with management assistance and supervision. In terms of our model, this business angel is acting as investor, manager and VC employee all combined in a single economic entity. Beyond representing a wealthy individual's objectives, this case also allows us to consider how an "ideal" process would be run if the investors, managers, and VC employees were to work together for their common economic good, rather than for their individual interests.

Since we are considering a single entity (which for convenience we shall refer to as the angel), we can ignore any payments among its component members. Thus the financial model here can ignore salaries H, exit bonuses x and commissions y, and management fees z, because these represent transfers of wealth within the entity, not from the entity to an outside agent. Since the whole purpose of the VC process is to invest in new ventures, we shall assume that the goal of the angel (collectively, the investors, managers, and VCs) is to maximize the overall Return On Investment ROI_A. As in the case of the investor, this is derived as a ratio of Net Income to total Investment, with appropriate adjustments to eliminate the payments listed above.

$$ROI_A = \frac{\lambda p[Rlf - I - Jnf] - G}{\lambda p\left\{[I]\left[\dfrac{1}{sa-\lambda}\right] + [I+Jnf]\left[cf + \dfrac{f}{tb-\lambda pf}\right]\right\}}. \qquad (11)$$

The following results indicate how the VC process should be managed if it is to provide the best possible return overall, without regard to how that return might be shared among the investors, managers, and employees.

Maximization of angel's ROI_A with respect to attention allocation t: ROI_A is quasi-concave in t, so there exists a unique optimal allocation of VC attention to post-investment activities t* such that

$$I\frac{a}{\langle a - at^* - \lambda\rangle^2} = (I+Jnf)\frac{bf}{\langle t^*b - \lambda pf\rangle^2}. \qquad (12)$$

Thus, we have that t* = t_{inv}.

Maximization of angel's ROI_A with respect to acceptance proportion p: ROI_A is quasi-concave in p, so there exists a unique optimal probability of venture acceptance p*,

$$0 < p^* < min\left\{\frac{tb}{\lambda f},1\right\}, \text{ such that}$$

$$[\lambda^2(p^*)^2(Rlf - I - Jnf) - \lambda p^*G](I+Jnf)\frac{f^2}{\langle tb - \lambda^* f\rangle^2}$$

$$= [G - \lambda(p^*)^2 lf R']\left[I\frac{1}{a-at-\lambda} + (I+Jnf)\left(cf + \frac{f}{tb-\lambda p^* f}\right)\right]. \qquad (13)$$

These results show that an angel would seek a "balance" both in allocation of attention and in selecting ventures in which to invest. Note that for a particular situation the angel would need to find a *simultaneously* optimal pair of values for *t* and *p* using nonlinear optimization techniques, but this is beyond the scope of our discussion herein (see, e.g., Bazaraa et al., 1993). Table 2 illustrates how these optimal balances p^* and t^* (and also t_{inv}, since $t_{inv} = t^*$) will change as business conditions change. For example, an increase in the productivity of VC employees involved in pre-investment activities (i.e., an increase in *a*) would lend itself to an increase in attention allocated to post-investment activities (i.e., t^* would increase), since less effort would be required for pre-investment (recall that $s^* = 1 - t^*$). Note that we have restricted our sensitivity analysis in Table 2 to those optima (p^*, t^* and t_{inv}) that are interior solutions.

Table 2.   Effect of Changing Parameters on VC Process Optimization for Angels

Item	Brief Parameter Description	t^* and t_{inv}	p^*
λ	proposal arrival rate	varies	Varies
p	proposal acceptance probability	+	n/a
t	VC attention: proportion post-investment	n/a	Varies
s	VC attention: proportion pre-investment	n/a	Varies
a	VC productivity: pre-investment	+	–
b	VC productivity: post-investment	–	+
c	development time	ne	+
G	firm overhead costs	ne	+
I	initial investment	–	+
J	follow-on investment	+	Varies
$R(\cdot)$	exit revenue function	ne	–
l	probability of successful exit	ne	–
n	probability of continued development	+	Varies

+	strength of preference (like/dislike) is increasing in that parameter
–	strength of preference (like/dislike) is decreasing in that parameter
ne	no effect, strength of preference is independent of that parameter
	Note: for parameters not shown, there is also no effect.
n/a	not applicable

COMPARISON OF PREFERENCES

In the previous section, we determined how each of the various entities involved in the VC process would view decisions about allocation of attention (i.e., the best value for t) and acceptance control for venture proposals (i.e., the best value of p). In this section, we compare the extent to which they could be expected to agree or disagree with each other, and how these individual preferences might or might not lead to the best possible results for the overall system.

Let us consider first the allocation of VC attention (as described by t) between pre- and post-investment activities. In the previous section we found that an investor would prefer to see an allocation of attention t_{inv} which would coincide with the best allocation for the process as a whole t^* (i.e., from the angel's viewpoint). This "balanced" allocation of attention would lead to fewer delays in the flow of ventures through the portfolio (from investment to harvest) and consequently minimize the total investment tied-up in the venture portfolio. Conversely, we saw that this same allocation is the *worst* possible from the point of view of the firm's managers. Management could instead be expected to prefer a more "unbalanced" allocation of attention (i.e., a t_{mgr} very low or very high); this would cause ventures to spend more time in the portfolio and so result in a larger pool of assets in the fund on which to charge the management fee.

Therefore, we could expect investors and managers to have directly opposing opinions on what constitutes "best practice" for allocation of attention in the VC process. The strength of this disagreement will of course vary depending on the particular business situation; one aspect of this is illustrated in Table 3. For example, an increase in management fees z paid to the firm will cause managers to become more strongly opposed to allocating attention according to t^* (since they would have even more to gain if they could increase the portfolio size) and thus increase investor-management tensions. On the other hand, an increase in exit bonuses x paid to the firm will cause the investors to become less concerned about using allocation t^* (a higher bonus means less revenue leftover for them, so less to be concerned about) and so reduce tensions.

Table 3.   Effect of Changing Parameters on Investor/Manager Disagreement

Item	Brief Parameter Description	Investor preference in favor of t^*	Manager preference against t^*
λ	proposal arrival rate	+	+
p	proposal acceptance probability	–	+
a	VC productivity: pre-investment	+	ne
b	VC productivity: post-investment	+	ne
c	development time	–	ne
I	initial investment	–	ne
J	follow-on investment	–	ne
$R(\cdot)$	exit revenue function	+	ne
x	exit bonus paid to firm	–	ne
z	management fee paid to firm	ne	+
l	probability of successful exit	+	ne
n	probability of continued development	varies	ne

+   strength of preference (like/dislike) is increasing in that parameter
–   strength of preference (like/dislike) is decreasing in that parameter
ne no effect, strength of preference is independent of that parameter
    Note: for parameters not shown, there is also no effect.

We can also refer back to Table 1 in this regard. For example, an increase in either the overall revenue function $R(\beta)$ or the probability of successful exit l would lead to improvements in everyone's finances. On the other hand, an increase in the venture proposal rate λ would benefit the management and employees, but would be harmful for the investors; thus, we could expect such an increase to lead to more disagreements among these two sides. Note that the actual VC employees would not much care about how they are to allocate their attention, since (under our model's assumptions) they work and get paid the same total amount either way.

Now let us consider the parties' views regarding how strict the acceptance criteria should be for deciding which ventures will receive funding; i.e., what should be the proportion of venture proposals p to accept for funding. We showed that for the process as a whole there is an optimal proportion of proposals to accept p^* which gives the best balance between accepting too many and too few proposals. We showed as well that VC employees would also like to see a "balanced" approach to setting the acceptance controls, but that their idea of a perfect balance p_{emp} could be quite different from the p^* preferred by the angel.

The divergence between investors and managers is even more pronounced. We found that investors would prefer to accept only the best ventures for funding (thus p_{inv} approaching zero), so that their money could earn the highest possible return. By contrast we saw that managers would typically like to accept a large proportion of proposals (p_{mgr} perhaps approaching 100%), so as to create a large portfolio upon which to charge management fees. The following result summarizes the relative preferences of these different groups.

Preferences for venture proposal acceptance (a.k.a. "quality control standards"): for a given VC process, managers would prefer a higher acceptance proportion than would employees, employees would prefer a higher acceptance proportion than would angels, and angels would prefer a higher acceptance proportion than would investors. Thus, we have

$$1 \geq p_{mgr} > p_{emp} > p^* > p_{inv} \geq 0. \qquad (14)$$

Overall these comparative results suggest that there may be significant potential for disagreements about the proper operation of the VC process, as each entity tries to maximize its own rewards at the possible expense of each other and of the "greater good." This may suggest a need to change the way that VC firms and employees are paid, so as to reduce the potential for this kind of principal-agent disagreement.

DISCUSSION

Summary of Results

In this article we examined the venture capital process by which new ventures obtain investor funding via venture capital firms. To do this, we constructed a simple Jackson queuing network with two key management parameters: the allocation of VC attention between pre- and post-investment involvement with the ventures; and the proportion of venture proposals that would be accepted for funding. Using this queuing network along with a number of simple assumptions concerning the financial aspects of the VC process, we developed a set of expressions to describe the financial performance of the process. These expressions allowed us to consider how to best manage the VC process in order to optimize the process overall ("What's best for the common good?") and also from the differing viewpoints of the investors, VC firm managers, and VC workers ("What's best for me?"). Our sensitivity analysis showed how these "best practice" results would be affected by changes in the business environment. More interestingly, our comparative analysis showed how the different parties could rationally be expected to disagree in several respects over what would in fact constitute "best practice." With regards to the allocation of VC attention between pre- and post-investment activities, we found that while investors would typically support a "balanced" allocation that would also be in the best interests of the process overall, the managers of the VC firm would likely be diametrically opposed to this allocation. With regards to the acceptance of proposed ventures to fund, we found that each of these three groups would have a differing view as to how selective the process ought to be, and that none of these views would coincide exactly with the overall process optimum.

Limitations

In our financial modeling we deliberately chose a single financial measure (out of many possible ones) to represent the motivation of each of the parties involved in the VC process. Our model's results therefore could be criticized as mere artifacts of the particular choices we made. We would reply that although our choices of measures are to some extent arbitrary, they are nonetheless reasonable and are at least representative of the way these parties actually evaluate performance. Thus we believe that while our conclusions may not be definitive, they would at least be indicative of actual behavior.

To keep the model tractable and relatively easy-to-follow, we have ignored some of the higher-order interdependencies among parameters.

For example, while our revenue function R does take into account the selectivity of the VC firm in accepting proposals, it does not directly consider the time lag between the moment of investment and the moment of successful exit, or the amount invested in any particular venture, etc. We would argue that this sort of simplification is a necessary feature of modeling work (one cannot include everything) and that we have included the most important relationships; thus we believe that our modeling simplification does not detract from the value of the analysis.

We also note that there are several technical assumptions inherent in our queuing model that we have made in order to keep the mathematics relatively simple. For example, we have assumed that the work done by the VCs with the ventures can be appropriately represented by single server Markovian queues; while these are rarely exact representations of reality, they are often approximately correct and are a standard assumption in the absence of detailed data. We have also made a somewhat arbitrary division of VC labor between pre- and post-investment activities. This assumption may not be true in reality (these two types of work may well be blended together in the course of the day), but it greatly simplifies the mathematical treatment without (we believe) adversely affecting the validity of the results.

CONCLUSION

There are a number of tasks that venture capitalists must perform well within the venture capital process in order to maximize the profitability of the process. In this article we have proposed a simple operating model of the venture capital process that gives us some insight as to how the process might best be managed and why there may be disagreements about what "best" actually means. Each factor that requires consideration in our model is readily operationalized and therefore the model proposed here could (and hopefully will) be of practical assistance to VC firms, and will furthermore provide a basis for empirical testing.

Our work complements previous studies which have tended to concentrate more on what VCs do at each stage of the process (thus describing the elements of current practices), rather than on how these stages fit together and should best be managed (thus suggesting the development of better practices). These descriptive studies have made a substantial contribution to the literature, but we believe that more research is required into the means of improving/increasing the efficiency of the venture capital process. We believe that we have taken a small but important step in this direction and hope that other scholars will also focus on improving (over and above describing) the VC process.

APPENDIX: MATHEMATICAL DERIVATIONS

Flow of Ventures through the System

Derivation of the average rate of venture flow through each arc of the network is mostly a straightforward process; begin with rate λ of new proposals arriving at N1 and proceed from left to right through the network. For the "feedback loop" between N2 and N3 the flows are derived by simultaneous solution of 2 flow balance equations:

$$Flow_{2 \to 3} = \lambda p + Flow_{3 \to 2} \text{ and } Flow_{3 \to 2} = n\, Flow_{2 \to 3}$$

The solutions of these flows are shown along with the flows on the other arcs on Figure 1.

System Steady State

We model nodes N1 and N3 as M/M/1 queues; thus we implicitly assume that the group of VCs working at each node can reasonably be represented as a single server, and that the times between arrivals and the times for service both follow exponential distributions. Given these assumptions, the expected number of ventures at each node i (either being helped or awaiting service) is calculated as $V_i =$ (arrival rate) / [(service rate) − (arrival rate)]. Node N2 is modeled as an M/M/∞ queue (hence no line-ups and no waiting), so the expected number of ventures at that node undergoing development is simply $V_2 =$ (arrival rate)(average stay).

Results for the Investors

For optimization of ROI_I with respect to t, replace s by $1-t$ and take the first derivative to obtain

$$\frac{\partial}{\partial t} ROI_I = -\frac{\lambda^2 p^2}{D(t,p)^2}\left\{[(1-x)lfR(p) - I - Jnf]\left[I - \frac{a}{\langle a - at - \lambda\rangle^2} + (I + Jnf)\frac{-bf}{\langle tb - \lambda pf\rangle^2}\right]\right\}, \quad \text{(A1)}$$

where $D(t,p)$ ($\text{Æ}0$) represents the denominator of the original ROI_I expression. When this equals zero we have an extreme point. To verify that this is a maximum, take the second derivative at such a point (where $\partial ROI_I / \partial t = 0$) to obtain

$$\frac{\partial^2}{\partial t^2} ROI_I = -\frac{\lambda^2 p^2}{D(t,p)^2}\left\{[(1-x)lfR(p) - I - Jnf]\left[I - \frac{2a^2}{\langle a - at - \lambda\rangle^3} + (I + Jnf)\frac{2b^2 f}{\langle tb\ \ \lambda pf\rangle^3}\right]\right\}. \quad \text{(A2)}$$

Since this is negative at any such point (at least so long as the VC process is profitable with a positive net income), we know that the point must be a unique maximum t^* and thus that ROI_I is strongly quasi-concave in t.

Regarding acceptance probability p, we obtain a first derivative of

$$\frac{\partial}{\partial p}ROI_I = \frac{\lambda^2 p^2}{D(t,p)^2} \left\{ \begin{array}{l} (1-x)lfR(p)'\left\{ [I]\left[\frac{1}{a-at-\lambda}\right] + [I+Jnf]\left[cf + \frac{f}{tb-\lambda pf}\right] \right\} \\ \\ -[(1-x)lfR(p) - I - Jnf]\left\{ [I+Jnf]\left[\frac{\lambda f^2}{\langle tb - \lambda pf \rangle^2}\right] \right\} \end{array} \right\}. \quad \text{(A3)}$$

This is negative so long as the firm is profitable, so we have that ROI_I is decreasing in p.

Results for the Managers

For optimization of Earnings with respect to t, substitute $s = 1 - t$ and take the first derivative to obtain

$$\frac{\partial}{\partial t}Earnings = z\lambda p\left\{ [I]\left[\frac{a}{\langle a-at-\lambda \rangle^2}\right] + [I+Jnf]\left[\frac{-bf}{\langle tb-\lambda pf \rangle^2}\right] \right\} \quad \text{(A4)}$$

(note the similarity between this and $\partial ROI_I / \partial t$. The second derivative is

$$\frac{\partial^2}{\partial t^2}Earnings = z\lambda p\left\{ [I]\left[\frac{2a^2}{\langle a-at-\lambda \rangle^3}\right] + [I+Jnf]\left[\frac{2b^2 f}{\langle tb-\lambda pf \rangle^3}\right] \right\}. \quad \text{(A5)}$$

Since this is always positive, Earnings must be strongly quasi-*convex* in t with a unique *minimum* at t^*; thus either very high or very low values should be selected to maximize Earnings. The stated range for t is a consequence of the M/M/1 queue assumption that the service rates at each of N1 and N3 must exceed the arrival rates.

With respect to p, the derivative $\partial Earnings / \partial p$ is

$$\begin{array}{l} (x-y)\lambda lf[R(p) + pR(p)'] + z\lambda\left\{ [I]\left[\frac{1}{sa-\lambda}\right] + [I+Jnf]\left[cf + \frac{f}{tb-\lambda pf}\right] \right\} \\ \\ + z\lambda p[I+Jnf]\left[\frac{\lambda f^2}{\langle tb-\lambda pf \rangle^2}\right] \end{array} \quad \text{(A6)}$$

Note that this expression is positive except (perhaps) for the $[R(p) + pR(p)']$ term. If the drop-off in revenue due to looser acceptance control is minimal (i.e. $R(p)' \approx 0 \ \forall \ p$), then this term will also be positive and thus Earnings would be increasing in p; even if the term is slightly negative, this would still be true. If the drop-off in revenue is quite steep, then the sign of the whole expression could possibly go negative for some parameter values.

Results for the Employees

With respect to p, take the first and second derivatives as follows:

$$\frac{\partial}{\partial p}Pay = \lambda ylf[R(p) + pR(p)'] \text{ and } \frac{\partial^2}{\partial p^2}Pay = \lambda ylf[2R(p)' + pR(p)''] . \quad \text{(A7)}$$

The second derivative is always negative, so Pay is concave in p with a unique maximum at p_{emp}.

Results for the Angels

For optimization with respect to t, replace s by $1-t$ and take the first derivative to obtain

$$\frac{\partial}{\partial t}ROI_A = \frac{-1}{D(t,p)^2}\left\{ [\lambda p(R(p)lf - I - Jnf) - G]\lambda p \left[I\frac{a}{\langle a - at - \lambda\rangle^2} + (I + Jnf)\frac{-bf}{\langle tb - \lambda pf\rangle^2} \right] \right\}, \quad \text{(A8)}$$

with $D(t,p)$ as before. When this equals zero we have an extreme point. To verify that this is a maximum, take the second derivative at such a point (where $\partial ROI_A / \partial t = 0$) to obtain

$$\frac{\partial^2}{\partial t^2}ROI_A = \frac{-1}{D(t,p)^2}\left\{ [\lambda p(R(p)lf - I - Jnf) - G]\lambda p \left[I\frac{2a^2}{\langle a - at - \lambda\rangle^3} + (I + Jnf)\frac{2b^2 f}{\langle tb - \lambda pf\rangle^3} \right] \right\}. \quad \text{(A9)}$$

Since this is negative at any such point (at least so long as the VC process is profitable with a positive net income), we know that the point must be a unique maximum t^* and thus that ROI is strongly quasi-concave in t. The stated range for t is a consequence of the M/M/1 queue assumption that the service rates at each of N1 and N3 must exceed the arrival rates.

For optimization with respect to p, find the first derivative and rearrange to obtain

$$\frac{\partial}{\partial p}ROI_A = \frac{1}{D(t,p)^2}\left\{ \begin{array}{l} -\lambda^2 p[\lambda p(R(p)lf - I - Jnf) - G](I + Jnf)\dfrac{f^2}{\langle tb - \lambda pf\rangle^2} \\ + \lambda[G + \lambda p^2 lfR(p)']\left[I\dfrac{1}{\langle a - at - \lambda\rangle} + (I + Jnf)\left(cf + \dfrac{f}{\langle tb - \lambda pf\rangle} \right) \right] \end{array} \right\}. \quad \text{(A10)}$$

When this is zero, the second derivative is

$$\frac{\partial^2}{\partial p^2}ROI_A =$$

$$\frac{1}{D(t,p)^2}\left\{\begin{array}{l} -2\lambda^2[\lambda p(R(p)lf - I - Jnf) - G](I + Jnf)\dfrac{f^2}{\langle tb - \lambda pf\rangle^2} \\[2ex] -\lambda^2 p[\lambda p(R(p)lf - I - Jnf) - G](I + Jnf)\dfrac{2\lambda f^3}{\langle tb - \lambda pf\rangle^3} \\[2ex] + \lambda^2 p[2lfR(p)' + plfR(p)'']\left[I\dfrac{1}{\langle a - at - \lambda\rangle} + (I + Jnf)\left(cf + \dfrac{f}{\langle tb - \lambda pf\rangle}\right)\right] \end{array}\right\}, \quad (A11)$$

which is negative so long as the process is profitable and $R(p)' \le 0$, $R(p)'' \le 0$. Thus ROI_A is strongly quasi-concave in p with a maximum at p^*.

Results for Comparing Preferences

The ordering of acceptance probability preferences follows from a comparison of the various derivatives with respect to p. Note that at the employee optimum p_{emp} we have $R(p) = -pR(p)'$ and so $R(p)' = -R(p)/p$. On the other hand, at the angel optimum p^* Eq. (A10) yields

$$\begin{array}{l} [G + \lambda p^2 lfR(p)']\left[I\dfrac{1}{\langle a - at - \lambda\rangle} + (I + Jnf)\left(cf + \dfrac{f}{tb - \lambda pf}\right)\right] \\[2ex] - \lambda p[\lambda p(R(p)lf - I - Jnf) - G](I + Jnf)\dfrac{f^2}{\langle tb - \lambda pf\rangle^2} = 0 \end{array}, \quad (A12)$$

which implies that (for a profitable VC process) the first term $[G + \lambda p^2 lfR(p)']$ is positive. If we substitute $R(p)' = -R(p)/p$ to get $[G - \lambda plfR(p)]$, then (for a profitable VC process) this term would be negative, and thus the entire derivative $\partial ROI_A/\partial p$ would be negative rather than zero. Thus, it must be that $p^* < p_{emp}$.

Next consider managers' preferences. When $\partial Earnings/\partial p$ [Eq. (A6)] is evaluated at p_{emp}, we make the same substitution $R(p)' = -R(p)/p$ as above and cancel terms to obtain

$$z\lambda\left\{[I]\left[\frac{1}{sa - \lambda}\right] + [I + Jnf]\left[cf + \frac{f}{tb - \lambda pf}\right]\right\} + z\lambda p[I + Jnf]\left[\frac{\lambda f^2}{\langle tb - \lambda pf\rangle^2}\right]. \quad (A13)$$

This derivative would be positive, so management's optimal value for p must be higher than p_{emp}.

Finally, $\partial ROI_I/\partial p$ is negative for all p, including at p^*. Thus investors would prefer a value of p less than p^*.

Results for Tables

The sensitivity results in Table 1 are obtained by examining the sign of the derivative of each financial equation with respect to that parameter. For example, to find the effect of a change in the proposal arrival rate λ on ROI_I [Eq. (5)], take the derivative

$$\frac{\partial}{\partial \lambda} ROI_I =$$

$$\frac{-\lambda^2 p^2}{D(t,p)^2}\left\{[(1-x)lfR(p)-I-Jnf]\left\{[I]\left[\frac{1}{\langle sa-\lambda\rangle^2}\right]+[I+Jnf]\left[cf+\frac{pf^2}{\langle tb-\lambda pf\rangle^2}\right]\right\}\right\}. \quad (A14)$$

Since this is negative we know that ROI_I must be decreasing in λ. The other listed results are obtained in similar manner, starting with Eqs. (5), (7), (8) or (11) as appropriate. For the effect of changes in revenue function $R(p)$, we take derivatives with respect to R as if it were a parameter rather than a function; i.e., as if $R(p)$ were increasing by the same percentage for all p.

The sensitivity results in Table 2 are obtained by examining the sign of the partial derivative of the first derivative of each financial equation with respect to that parameter at the original optimum. For example, to find the effect of a change in the proposal acceptance probability p on the optimal t_{inv}, begin with the derivative $\partial ROI_I/\partial t$ [Eq. (A1)]. At $t=t_{inv}$ (so $\partial ROI_I/\partial t=0$) take the partial derivative with respect to p to obtain

$$\frac{\partial}{\partial p}\frac{\partial}{\partial t} ROI_I = \frac{-\lambda^2 p^2}{D(t,p)^2}\left\{\begin{array}{l}[1-x)lfR(p)']\left[I\dfrac{a}{\langle a-at-\lambda\rangle^2}+(I+Jnf)\dfrac{-bf}{\langle tb-\lambda pf\rangle^2}\right] \\[2em] +[(1-x)lfR(p)-I-Jnf]\left[(I+Jnf)\dfrac{-2\lambda bf^2}{\langle tb-\lambda pf\rangle^3}\right]\end{array}\right\}. \quad (A15)$$

Since this is always positive, we know that $\partial ROI_I/\partial t$ is increasing in p. Thus at the original t_{inv} $\partial ROI_I/\partial t$ would become positive (rather than zero); and since ROI_I is concave in t, this means that (new t_{inv}) > (original t_{inv}). The other listed results are obtained in similar manner, starting with Eq. (A1) (equivalently, A8) or (A10) as appropriate.

For Table 3 we work with Eqs. (A1) and (A4). Note that in both cases the location of the extreme point t^* (maximum ROI_I, minimum Earnings) is determined by the expression

$$\left[I \frac{a}{\langle a - at - \lambda \rangle^2} + (I + Jnf) \frac{-bf}{\langle tb - \lambda pf \rangle^2} \right].$$ (A16)

When this equals zero, the derivatives are zero. When this is not zero, then the magnitude of each derivative (i.e. the marginal cost or benefit) is determined by the "multipliers" $[z\lambda p]$ for $\partial Earnings/\partial t$ and

$$\frac{\lambda^2 p^2 [(1-x)lfR(p) - I - Jnf]}{D(t,p)^2}$$ (A17)

for $\partial ROI_I /\partial t$. The results in Table 3 are obtained by taking the partial derivative of each multiplier with respect to each parameter. For example, the effect of an increase in p follows from $\partial [z\lambda p]/\partial p = z\lambda > 0$ and

$$\frac{\partial}{\partial p}\left[\frac{\lambda^2 p^2 [(1-x)lfR(p) - I - Jnf]}{D(t,p)^2} \right]$$

$$= \frac{\lambda^3 p^3}{D(t,p)^3}\left\{ (1-x)lfR(p)'\frac{D(t,p)}{\lambda p} - 2[(1-x)lfR(p) - I - Jnf](I + Jnf)\frac{\lambda f^2}{\langle tb - \lambda pf \rangle^2} \right\} < 0.$$ (A18)

REFERENCES

Bazaraa, M.S., Sherali, H.D., & Shetty, C.M. (1993). *Nonlinear programming: Theory and algorithms.* New York: John Wiley and Sons.
Bretthauer, K.M., & Cote, M.J. (1998). A model for planning resource requirements in health care organizations. *Decision Sciences, 29,* 243–270.
Cable, D.M., & Shane, S. (1997). A prisoner's dilemma approach to entrepreneur-venture capitalist relationships. *Academy of Management Review, 22,* 142–176.
Dean, B.V., & Giglierano, J.J. (1990). Multistage financing of technical start-up companies in Silicon Valley. *Journal of Business Venturing, 5,* 375–389.
Dorsey, T. (1979). *Operating guidelines for effective venture capital funds management* (#3 in a Technical Series). Austin: University of Texas.
Elango, B., Fried, V.H., Hisrich, R.D., & Polonchek, A. (1995). How venture capital firms differ. *Journal of Business Venturing, 10,* 157–179.
Gelenbe, E., & Pujolle, G. (1987). *Introduction to queuing networks.* New York: John Wiley and Sons.
Gifford, S. (1998). *The allocation of limited entrepreneurial attention.* Boston: Kluwer Academic.
Hall, J., & Hofer, C.W. (1993). Venture capitalists' decision criteria in new venture evaluation. *Journal of Business Venturing, 8,* 25–42.

Lerner, J. (1994). Venture capitalists and the decision to go public. *Journal of Financial Economics, 35*, 293–316.

Lerner, J. (1995). Venture capitalists and the oversight of private firms. *Journal of Finance, 50*, 301–318.

Muzyka, D., Birley, S., & Leleux, B. (1996). Trade-offs in the investment decisions of European venture capitalists. *Journal of Business Venturing, 11*, 273–287.

Papadopoulos, H.T., Heavey, C., & Browne, J. (1993). *Queuing theory in manufacturing systems analysis and design.* London: Chapman and Hall.

Pratt, S.E. (1998). *Pratt's guide to venture capital sources.* New York: Securities Data Publishing.

Sandberg, W.R. (1986). *New venture performance: The role of strategy, industry structure, and the entrepreneur.* Lexington, MA: Lexington Books.

Sandberg, W.R., & Hofer, C.W. (1987). Improving new venture performance: The role of strategy, industry structure and the entrepreneur. *Journal of Business Venturing, 2*, 5–28.

Shepherd, D.A. (1999). Venture capitalists' assessment of new venture survival. *Management Science, 45*, 621–632.

Sweeting, R.C. (1991). UK venture capital funds and the funding of new technology-based businesses: Process and relationships. *Journal of Management Studies, 28*, 601–622.

Timmons, J.A. (1999). *New venture creation: Entrepreneurship for the 21st century.* Homewood, IL: Irwin McGraw Hill.

Tyebjee, T.T., & Bruno, A.V. (1984). A model of venture capitalist investment activity. *Management Science, 30*, 1051–1066.

Zacharakis, A.L., & Meyer, G.D. (1998). A lack of insight: Do venture capitalists really understand their own decision processes? *Journal of Business Venturing, 13*, 57–76.

CHAPTER 7

VENTURE CAPITAL FIRMS AND THE MONITORING OF ENTREPRENEURIAL FIRMS

The Case of Japan

Toru Yoshikawa

ABSTRACT

This study investigated the effects of VC firms' affiliations, investment amount per portfolio firm, the number of portfolio firms per investment manager, performance-based compensation, and managerial ownership on the monitoring of their portfolio firms in Japan. It was found that the affiliated VC firms are less likely to send outside directors to their portfolio firms and are less likely to use the hands-on investment approach. Those VC firms that are more active in monitoring through board representation tend to invest a greater amount per portfolio firm on average and their management are shareowners of their VC firms. Those that monitor their portfolio firms through staged investment tend to use performance-based compensation for their investment managers. These findings are generally consistent with the agency theory rationale.

INTRODUCTION

Many Japanese venture capital (VC) firms have over 20 years of history having been established in the 1970s and 1980s. However, they have been operating rather differently from VC firms in the United States. Since many of them were founded as subsidiaries of banks and securities companies, they often have objectives other than the maximization of investment returns, such as the generation of underwriting and loan businesses from small and medium-sized companies for their parent firms. In the past few years, however, an increasing number of independent VC firms have been founded because the recent establishment of the stock markets for venture firms, MOTHERS (Market of the High-growth and Emerging Stocks) and NASDAQ Japan, now provide exits for private equity investments. In addition, some affiliated VC firms have also started to focus on investment returns through active involvement in management of their portfolio firms. Further, the long recession in Japan since the early 1990s raised interest in venture business, which is often seen as the catalyst for change, and venture capital business has started to attract more talent. Thus, we have begun to see some changes in the investment practices of Japanese VC firms.

The focus of this paper is the monitoring of entrepreneurial firms by Japanese VC firms. VC firms' monitoring practices are becoming increasingly important in Japan because investment by VC firms in early-stage and technology-oriented firms has recently started to increase. For example, investment in IT-related firms (computers, internet, communications, and electronics) by Japanese VC firms accounted for only about 16% of the total investment of VC firms in 1995. However, during the 1999–2000 period, these investments increased to almost 60%, although they have recently declined to about 50% after the burst of the IT bubble (Venture Enterprise Center, 2001). Also, investment in relatively early-stage firms (younger than 5 years) increased from less than 50% in 1997 to 62% in 2000 (Venture Enterprise Center, 2001). Firms in early stages or with high levels of investment in research and development, such as those in IT industries, should pose greater agency problems. Since early-stage firms have very short histories, they are difficult to evaluate. It is also difficult to evaluate technologies and to observe the R&D efforts of technology-oriented firms. Thus, VC firms need to closely monitor such firms (Gompers, 1995). As Japanese VC firms shift their investments to early-stage and technology-oriented firms, it is expected that they will need to emphasize the monitoring of their portfolio firms.

One of the objectives of this paper is to examine the impact of VC firms' affiliations with banks, securities companies, insurance companies, and non-financial firms on their practices in the monitoring of their portfolio firms. I theorize that, notwithstanding the recent changes, the affiliated VC firms are still less likely to pay much attention to the monitoring of venture firms in which they invest, for the following reasons. First, since they are often expected to promote the interests of their parent organizations, higher investment returns may not be their sole objective. In other words, the selection and monitoring process of their portfolio firms may be distorted due to their affiliations (Gompers & Lerner, 1998; Siegel, Siegel, & MacMillan, 1988). Second, many investment managers of these VC firms were transferred from the parent organizations and thus do not have much experience or expertise in venture capital investment or venture business management (Osano, 2001). Thus, investment managers of the affiliated VC firms tend to have neither a strong incentive nor expertise to enhance investment returns. Because of these reasons, the affiliated VC firms are less likely to monitor their portfolio firms.

The second objective of this paper is to investigate the effects of investment practices of VC firms, such as the investment amount per portfolio firm, the number of portfolio firms per investment manager, compensation schemes for investment managers, and managerial ownership of VC firms on their firms' monitoring of their portfolio firms. From these investigations, I attempt to show the relationships between VC firms' characteristics and their monitoring practices.

To examine these issues, the paper proceeds as follows. First, theory is reviewed to present the relationships between VC firms and their portfolio firms' management from a theoretical perspective. Then, the background of Japanese VC industry and the characteristics of VC firms in Japan are briefly discussed. In the following sections, I develop hypotheses and present the data and analysis of this study. I show the results of the analysis in the next section. The last section presents discussion and conclusions.

THEORY

Agency theory attempts to explain the problems that arise between the principal and the agent who usually has complete control over the transaction specific assets of the principal and when the goals of both parties conflict (Eisenhardt, 1989; Fama, 1980; Jensen & Meckling, 1976). In the relationship between a VC firm (investor) and management of a firm in which the VC firm invests, the separation of ownership and management is not always a major problem because management of the portfolio firm often holds large equity positions in the firm. However, the interests of outside investors or VC firms do not always coincide with those of the management of the portfolio firm (Gompers & Lerner, 1999; Kaplan & Stromberg, 2001). For example, even if a top executive of a venture firm is a shareholder, he or she may want to spend the firm's capital for personal interests, such as generous company benefits and excessive managerial compensation. VC investors, on the other hand, prefer a more prudent use of capital.

In addition, there is a problem of information asymmetries between outside investors and management, because managers have more inside information than external owners. The problem of information asymmetries becomes even more important for investments in technology-oriented firms (Gompers, 1995). External owners face a difficulty in assessing R&D efforts by those venture firms. Such owners therefore face a moral hazard problem since the value of managerial decisions and R&D efforts may be difficult to determine (Jensen & Meckling, 1976; Myers & Majluf, 1984). Further, it is often difficult to predict investment returns from technology-oriented firms because of the inherent uncertainty in technology development. Thus, even when the venture managers hold shares in a firm which they manage, there are problems of potentially conflicting interests and information asymmetries between venture managers and VC investors.

VC firms usually have various mechanisms to solve these problems. They include staging of investment (Bergemann & Hege, 1998; Gompers, 1995), active monitoring and advise through board representations (Lerner, 1995), and structuring of investment that allows venture capitalists to keep firm control (Sahlman, 1990). Using these mechanisms, venture capitalists in the United States attempt to monitor and control venture firms in which they invest.

In Japan, however, since VC industry has developed and VC firms are organized quite differently from the United States, VC firms have not always used such mechanisms to mitigate the agency problem. The next section briefly presents the background of VC industry and the characteristics of VC firms in Japan.

VENTURE CAPITAL FIRMS IN JAPAN

Many of Japan's large VC firms have been operating for more than 20 years. However, there are some important differences between VC firms in the United States and Japan. One of the major differences is that because VC firms could not legally adopt limited partnerships in Japan, many VC firms were established as subsidiaries or affiliated firms of large securities companies, banks, and other financial institutions. Thus, while limited partnerships are common in VC industry in the United States, many Japanese VC firms were founded as stock companies in which the parent firms hold the majority ownership. Because of the relationships with the parent organizations, many investment managers of Japanese VC firms were transferred from the parent companies, often for a limited term. These managers are, therefore, often employees of the parent firms who work for the VC subsidiaries only for several years. Thus, they are not professional venture investors (Muraguchi's commentary in Harmon, 2000).

In terms of investment amount, these affiliated VC firms still dominate the industry today. For example, JAFCO, the largest VC firm in Japan, was established by Nomura Securities, Sanwa Bank, and Nippon Life in 1973. Nomura Securities' group companies still hold large equity stakes in the firm and also send many directors to sit on the board, although there are not many investment managers who have been transferred from the parent company anymore. Among the top 100 Japanese VC firms, over 70% of them are subsidiaries of securities companies, banks, insurance companies, or non-financial firms (calculated from the data in the *Nikkei Financial Journal*, July 7, 2000). Thus, many VC firms in Japan are quite different from American VC firms in terms of their background and organizational structure.

Another difference is that many Japanese VC firms tended to focus on relatively well-established small and medium-sized firms rather than venture firms in the start-up or early stages. This is because there were no IPO markets, such as NASDAQ in the United States, into which venture firms could issue their shares in Japan until quite recently. As it usually takes a long time for a company to list its shares on a stock exchange in Japan due to the stringent listing requirements, VC firms could not afford to invest in firms in the start-up or early stages (Hata & Higashide, 2000). In addition, small and medium-sized firms were traditionally financed by banks in Japan, and thus there was not much risk capital for VC firms to invest in early-stage firms in the past (Hata & Higashide, 2000; Prowse, 1996). Since established small and medium-sized firms that accept investment funds from VC firms simply do not require much management advice, Japanese VC firms had not been actively involved in management of firms in which they invest. Thus, unlike American VC firms, Japanese VC firms had not often used the "hands-on" investment approach in which they in effect acted as a management consultant and a member of the management team (Hamada, 1999).

Since the late 1990s, however, VC industry in Japan has begun to change because of the establishment of MOTHERS in the Tokyo Stock Exchange in 1999, NASDAQ Japan in 2000, and the rise of IT-related venture firms in Japan. These new markets were founded specifically for venture firms and thus the listing requirements are not as stringent, although information disclosure requirements are strict (Hata & Higashide, 2000). These markets now provide venture firms with access to IPO markets in a much shorter period of time. At the same time, they provide investment exits for VC firms, which imply that VC firms can more quickly gain returns from their investments. Because of this new opportunity, many investment managers of the established large VC firms have left their firms and set up their own VC firms. In addition, foreign VC firms have begun to establish Japanese subsidiaries. Thus, there has been an explosive increase of VC firms in Japan in the last few years, and many of them are independent from any large domestic financial institutions and non-financial firms.

Further, Japanese VC firms have recently started to invest in more early-stage and technology-oriented firms, especially those in IT-related sectors. This is an important shift from their traditional investment practices that focused on relatively well-established small and mid-sized firms. This change is leading many Japanese VC firms to emphasize the monitoring of their portfolio firms by using the hands-on investment approach. Thus, it appears that the role of VC firms in Japan has started to change.

MODEL AND HYPOTHESES

As shown in Figure 1, it is theorized that a VC firm's affiliation, investment amount per portfolio firm, the number of portfolio firms per investment manager, performance-based compensation, and managerial ownership affect the monitoring practices of the VC firm. Since the investment amount, the number of portfolio firms for each investment manager, performance-based pay, and managerial ownership indicate the degree of incentive for a VC firm and investment managers to monitor their portfolio firms, these factors are expected to have some impacts on the monitoring practices. These factors are treated as the incentive alignment mechanisms. The affiliation of a VC firm also suggests the degree of incentive, because it can affect the VC firm's monitoring practices when the parent firm has non-investment objectives in its VC subsidiary. Thus, all these factors are chosen to measure a VC firm's monitoring incentive.

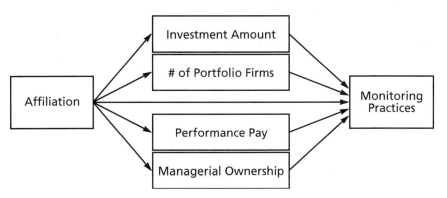

Figure 1.   Model of the relationships between VC and the monitoring.

Affiliation

The traditional corporate structure in Japan is a network form based on the *keiretsu*, and organized around main banks or industrial firms such as Matsushita and Hitachi. These banks and firms usually act as stable shareholders that own shares of other firms primarily for the purpose of cementing and growing stable business relationships rather than to earn returns on their equity investments (Clark, 1979; Gerlach, 1992; Kester, 1991). The majority of shares in Japanese firms have been held by stable investors, such as *keiretsu* firms, main banks, insurance companies, and sometimes the parent firms. Since a large portion of Japanese shares is still held by these stable investors,[1] Japanese firms do not always act to maximize profitability or shareholder value. This implies that Japanese firms, whose major shareholders are affiliated firms or financial institutions, are less likely to achieve superior economic performance compared to those without such ownership structure (Caves & Uekusa, 1976; Hundley & Jacobson, 1998; Nakatani, 1984).

This logic applies even more strongly to subsidiary firms since many Japanese firms set up their subsidiaries to promote their interests or to pursue their own objectives. For example, when a bank wants to provide loans to high-risk borrowers, it can book such loans with its subsidiaries so that the parent bank can shield itself from potential losses.[2] Banks can also use private equity investments to generate lending business from firms in which their VC subsidiaries invest. Similarly, securities companies may be able to earn underwriting business through their VC subsidiaries' investments in private firms. Non-financial firms might be interested in investing in venture firms that fit with their strategic goals (Gompers & Lerner, 1998; Prowse, 1996). Thus, subsidiaries often function to complement the parent firms' business goals and strategy, which in turn implies that they are not always expected to maximize profitability.

As many Japanese VC firms are subsidiaries, their strategies are often heavily influenced by their parent organizations. This implies that they do not always seek the maximization of investment returns. Even if these affiliated VC firms seek to generate financial returns, they may also be expected to accomplish other incompatible objectives, which lead to a lack of investment focus (Siegel, Siegel, & MacMillan, 1988). Thus, it is expected that these subsidiary or affiliated VC firms are less likely to be interested in the monitoring of firms in which they invest and less inclined to get involved with management of such firms.

On the other hand, independent VC firms usually have no close associations with other firms through ownership structure or staff transfer. Therefore, they are likely to be more focused on investment returns and more interested in monitoring and supporting their portfolio firms. In short, the structure of these independent VC firms is quite similar to that of U.S. VC firms. Their monitoring practices are, therefore, expected to be quite different from those of the affiliated VC firms.

H1. The affiliated VC firms are less likely to monitor firms in which they invest and to get involved with management of such firms.

Investment Amount per Portfolio Firm

The amount invested in a single firm represents the degree of a VC firm's commitment and exposure to that firm. A greater investment means that a VC firm is exposed to a potentially larger investment loss, which in turn gives a motivation for an investment manager of the VC firm to closely monitor a firm in which she made a large investment. Thus, it is expected that the investment amount and a VC firm's or an investment manager's monitoring incentive are closely related.

Further, a larger investment amount implies a VC's greater power to influence a portfolio firm's management, for example, through board representation. This view is supported by previous corporate governance research which concluded that ownership concentration or block positions would confer an ability to influence management decisions and firm strategies (Hill & Snell, 1989; Baysinger, Kosnik, & Turk, 1991; Shleifer & Vishny, 1997). Thus, it is expected that the larger the investment amount in a single firm, the more likely it is that a VC firm has an incentive to monitor and to get involved with management of the firm in which it invests.

H2. The larger the investment amount, the more likely it is that a VC firm monitors firms in which it invests and gets involved with management of such firms.

Number of Portfolio Firms per Investment Manager

When a VC firm's investment policy is to allocate its investment funds to a large number of firms with relatively a small amount so that it can diversify the portfolio risk, each investment manager has a large number of firms in his or her portfolio. This kind of investment practice will lead to less monitoring of the portfolio firms by VC managers for the following reasons. First, one of the advantages of portfolio diversification is that an investor can avoid a high monitoring cost. By spreading the investment exposure to a large number of firms, an investor can reduce the potential negative impact of firm specific risk in his or her portfolio. Thus, this investment practice is a less costly means to reduce the portfolio risk because it makes the close monitoring of each portfolio firm unnecessary.

Second, when a VC firm has such an investment policy, its investment managers are not motivated to monitor each portfolio firm closely. Based on CAPM theory that predicts a linear relationship between risk and return, it can be argued that a VC firm that diversifies its portfolio has chosen lower risk rather than higher return as its primary goal. Investment managers of such a firm are expected to reduce the investment risk by diversifying their portfolios rather than by monitoring their portfolio firms. It is therefore likely that they are not rewarded for superior performance through their monitoring practices. Thus, the number of portfolio firms for each investment manager is expected to be negatively associated with the monitoring of her portfolio firms.

H3. The larger the number of portfolio firms each investment manager is responsible for, the less likely it is that he or she monitors those firms closely and gets involved with management of such firms.

PERFORMANCE PAY

Performance pay, on the other hand, naturally motivates investment managers to monitor and get more involved with management of the firms in which they invest. As many Japanese VC firms are subsidiaries of other firms, they often use the same compensation schemes as their parent organizations. Although performance factors have increasingly been adopted in the compensation schemes in Japan, many Japanese firms still heavily rely on seniority to determine pay. Thus, investment managers of many VC firms, especially those from the parent firms, are not compensated by capital gains from successful IPO of venture firms in which they invest. This is similar to U.S. venture capital organizations that are corporate subsidiaries. It is suggested that these organizations have much lower incentive-based compensation compared to independent venture capital organizations and therefore tend to be less successful (Block & Ornati, 1987; Gompers & Lerner, 1998). Those VC firms that do not provide performance-based or incentive-based compensation to their investment managers are, therefore, less likely to monitor and to get involved with management of the portfolio firms because they are not motivated to do so.

H4. VC firms with performance pay are more likely to monitor the portfolio firms closely and to get involved with management of such firms.

Managerial Ownership

It is argued that firm managers have an incentive to adopt policies consistent with shareholder wealth maximization when they own shares (Hill & Snell, 1989; Jensen & Meckling, 1976; McConnell & Servaes, 1990). Managerial ownership of a VC firm is expected to align the interests of management and investment managers and the VC firm itself. When a VC firm's senior executives and investment managers hold shares in the firm, their compensations or investment returns are affected by how well the portfolio firms perform and successfully issue their stocks to the public. In other words, shareholdings provide a motivation to these executives and managers. This case presents a clear contrast to the case of investment managers of the VC firms where compensation schemes are not always based on performance or capital gains. It is expected that these managers would not be as motivated as owner-managers would be. Since an owner-manager of a VC firm has high stakes in the performance of the portfolio firms, he or she has a strong incentive to get involved with the monitoring of these firms.

H5. VC firms in which senior executives hold shares are more likely to monitor the portfolio firms closely and to get involved with management of such firms.

SAMPLE AND DATA

Sample

All data of Japanese VC firms were collected by structured interviews of investment managers and from several business journals. The interviews were conducted during the three-month period between December 2000 and February 2001. Sample firms were chosen from the top 106 VC list in terms of outstanding investment amounts on the *Nikkei Kinyu Shimbun* (*Nikkei Financial Journal*) in July 2000. From this list, I first segmented VC firms by their affiliations, such as securities company-affiliated, bank-affiliated, and independent, based on the ownership structure. Then I contacted the top four to five VC firms in each category with their head office in Tokyo. I was able to visit 41 VC firms in Tokyo and one VC firm in Kyoto, and thus collected the data from 42 VC firms in total. There are 63 VC firms among the top 106 that have their offices in Tokyo. Thus, these 41 VC firms represent about 65% of the Tokyo-based VC firms among the top 106 list.

There are more than 200 VC firms in Japan but the exact number cannot be confirmed as there is no official data. The 42 sample firms are among the top 106 VC firms on the *Nikkei Financial Journal* list, and 29 out of the 42 samples firms are in the top 50, and the remaining 13 firms are in the top 51–106.

Variables

There are three dependent variables in this study: outside director (*Director*), staged investment (*Staged*), and "hands-on" ratio (*Handson*). All these data were collected from the interviews. *Director* is the ratio of the number of firms to which a VC firm sends an outside director to the total number of the portfolio firms. This variable measures the degree to which each VC firm monitors its portfolio firms through outside directors. Board representation is one of the direct means of control of portfolio firms by VC firms (Lerner, 1995; Prowse, 1996). Another dependent variable is staged investment. This is a dummy variable: 1 for a VC that often uses this investment approach and 0 for a VC that does not or rarely uses this approach. This is another direct means of control by VC firms (Gompers, 1995; Sahlman, 1990). *Handson* is the degree to which a VC firm takes the "hands-on" approach. "Hands-on" is defined here as the active involvement in management, often as management consultants, of firms in which a VC firm invests. This is also a direct means to keep control of portfolio firms (Sahlman, 1990). The degree of the hands-on control was assessed and classified into the following four categories by the respondents of the interviews: 1 = weak hands-on, 2 = hands-on for less than 10% of the portfolio firms, 3 = hands-on for 10%–30% of the portfolio firms, 4 = hands-on for more than 30% of the portfolio firms.

Sample firms were categorized into affiliated VC, independent VC, and mixed ownership VC. The affiliated VC firms are those in which a majority owner is a securities company, bank, insurance company, or non-financial firm. The independent VC firms are those without any affiliations with other firms. The mixed ownership VC firms include government-affiliated venture finance companies and VC firms that have mixed ownership in which several firms are large shareholders but none of them holds the majority ownership. Those data were collected from the interviews and from the *Venture Club.*

Amount/Firm (*Amtfirm*) is the average investment amount per portfolio firm. A larger amount indicates a higher financial exposure to each portfolio firm. Firm/Staff (*Firmstaff*) measures the number of portfolio firms per investment manager or officer. A larger number suggests greater constraints on each investment manager to monitor each portfolio firm closely. Performance pay (*Pay*) indicates whether a VC firm uses a performance-based compensation scheme using capital gains to compensate its investment managers. These variables are chosen to measure the motivation of investment managers of each VC firm. These data were culled from the interviews, *Venture Club*, and *Nikkei Financial Journal.*

Managerial Ownership (*Mgtown*) is the ratio of shares senior executives and other investment managers hold in a VC firm. A higher ratio indicates a greater alignment of interests between management and a VC firm. The data was collected from the *Venture Club* and information materials of each VC firm. In addition, lead investor ratio and the age of the firm were included. Lead investor ratio (*Lead*) measures a ratio in the number of the portfolio firms in which a VC firm acts as a lead investor. Since a lead investor usually has a higher commitment in a firm in which it invests, it is expected that a higher ratio is associated with greater attention to the monitoring of the portfolio firms. *Age* of the firm suggests whether a longer track record in venture business investment has any effects. These data were collected from the interviews.

Analysis

First, *t*-test was conducted to examine whether there were significant differences between various characteristics and the monitoring practices between the affiliated VC and the independent VC. This study examined the means differences in amount/firm (*Amtfirm*), firm/staff (*Firmstaff*), performance pay (*Pay*), managerial ownership (*Mgtown*), age of the firm (*Age*), lead investor ratio (*Lead*), as well as outside director (*Director*), staged investment (*Staged*), and "hands-on" ratio (*Handson*) between the affiliated VC and the independent VC. In this analysis, I compared 25 affiliated firms and 12 independent firms. Five mixed ownership VC firms were excluded.

In the next step, the relationships between the characteristics of VC firms and the three dependent variables are analyzed with the 42 sample firms by regression. I have chosen *Amtfirm*, *Firmstaff*, *Pay*, *Mgtown*, and *Age* as independent variables, and excluded *Lead* because this variable is highly correlated with *pay* (.611). Table 1 shows Pearson correlations of the data.

Table 1. Pearson Correlations of the Data

	Mean	S.D.	1	2	3	4	5	6
1.Amtfirm	.8838	1.0836	1.000					
2.Firmstaff	17.6667	16.3329	$-.333^*$	1.000				
3.Pay	.4762	.5055	.291	$-.521^{**}$	1.000			
4.Mgtown	19.1905	33.7323	$.309^*$	$-.466^{**}$	$.548^{**}$	1.000		
5.Age	10.4762	9.0047	$-.086$	.298	$-.169$	$-.463^{**}$	1.000	
6.Lead	30.3333	31.3708	$.367^*$	$-.535^{**}$	$.611^{**}$	$.564^{**}$	-0.16	1.000

Two-tailed
*p<.05
**p<.01

RESULTS

The results of *t*-test are presented in Table 2. It is shown that there are significant differences in means in *Firmstaff, Pay, Mgtown, Age, Lead, Director,* and *Handson* between the affiliated VC and the independent VC. These findings suggest that compared with the independent VC firms, the affiliated or subsidiary VC firms are more likely to have a greater number of portfolio firms per investment manager, less likely to have performance-based compensation, and their management is less likely to have shareholdings. They are also less likely to act as a lead investor and tend to be older. Further, these VC firms tend not to send outside directors to a firm in which they invest and are less likely to use the "hands-on" investment approach. The results suggest that the affiliated VC firms' monitoring practices are quite different from those of the independent VC firms, which lend support to Hypothesis 1.

Table 2.   Results of t-Test

	N	Mean	S.D.	t-value	Sig. (2-tailed)
Amtfirm	25	.7240	.6030	−1.202	.252
	12	1.3600	1.7842		
Firmstaff	25	24.0000	17.7928	5.108	.000
	12	5.0833	3.5537		
Pay	25	.2800	.4583	−5.140	.000
	12	.9167	.2887		
Mgtown	25	.0000	.0000	−8.637	.000
	12	67.1667	26.9405		
Age	25	13.0000	8.0208	4.835	.000
	12	3.5833	3.8248		
Lead	25	16.3200	20.0992	−4.028	.001
	12	56.7500	31.8637		
Director	25	1.6800	2.2725	−4.766	.001
	12	42.1667	29.3872		
Staged	25	.4800	.5099	−.573	.572
	12	.5833	.5149		
Handson	25	2.1600	1.0677	−5.295	.000
	12	3.6667	.6513		

Only variables for which I could not find significant differences are *Amtfirm* and *Staged*. Contrary to expectations, there was no significant difference in *Staged* between the affiliated VC and the independent VC. However, the independent VC firms have a much larger investment amount per portfolio firm on average (.7240 vs. 1.3600).

Table 3.   Results of Regression Analysis

	Model 1 Dir			Model 2 Staged Investment			Model 3 Hands-on		
	Beta	T	Sig.	Beta	t	Sig.	Beta	t	Sig.
(Constant)		−.338	.738		1.329	.192		8.089	.000
Amtfirm	.339	3.478	.001	−.027	−.189	.851	.144	1.615	.115
Firmstaff	−.025	−.224	.824	−.085	−.507	.615	−.302	−2.936	.006
Pay	.023	.198	.844	.640	3.675	.001	.510	4.768	.000
Mgtown	.644	5.232	.000	−.223	−1.216	.232	.144	1.275	.210
Age	−.004	−.038	.970	.153	.994	.327	.005	.056	.956
	$R^2 = .711$ Adj. $R^2 = .671$ $F = 17.699^{***}$			$R^2 = .356$ Adj. $R^2 = .267$ $F = 3.983^{**}$			$R^2 = .757$ Adj. $R^2 = .723$ $F = 22.376^{***}$		

Table 3 shows the results of regression analysis. Model 1 indicates that investment amount per portfolio firm and management share ownership are statistically positively associated with outside directors. These findings support Hypotheses 2 and 5. However, there was no support for Hypotheses 3 and 4. Also, the age of the firm was not related to a firm's propensity to send outside directors. Model 2 provides support for only hypothesis 4, which predicts a positive relationship between performance-based pay and the monitoring and control.

Model 3 shows that the number of portfolio firms per investment manager and performance-based pay are statistically positively associated with the hands-on investment approach. These findings are consistent with Hypotheses 3 and 4. However, Hypotheses 2 and 5 were not supported in this model. The findings are summarized in Table 4.

Table 4.   Summary of Findings

	Expected Result	Director	Staged Investment	Hands-on
H1 (Affiliation)	−	Support	No	Support
H2 (Amtfirm)	+	Support	No	No
H3 (Firmstaff)	−	No	No	Support
H4 (Pay)	+	No	Support	Support
H5 (Mgtown)	+	Support	No	No

DISCUSSION AND CONCLUSIONS

This study investigated the effects of VC firms' affiliations, investment amount per portfolio firm, the number of portfolio firms per investment manager, compensation schemes for investment managers, and managerial ownership of VC firms on their monitoring practices. It was found that the affiliated VC firms are less likely to send outside directors and not to use the hands-on investment approach as much as the independent VC firms, although there was no significant difference in the propensity to use staged investment.

These findings generally support the view that affiliated VC firms are often used to promote the interests and strategic objectives of their parent firms. The results are also consistent with the argument that since many investment managers of the affiliated VC firms are employees transferred from the parent firms, they lack the expertise in investment and monitoring of private firms. Another interpretation of these results is that as the independent VC firms are relatively new compared to the affiliated VC firms (3.58 years vs. 13 years), they lack the extensive business networks to gather information on their portfolio firms and thus need to pay greater attention to monitoring of these firms. Similarly, since the independent VC firms tend to be new, they may be compelled to differentiate from the established and affiliated VC firms by using the hands-on investment approach in order to attract investment funds. Thus, the differences between the affiliated and independent VC firms may stem from the structure of the affiliated VC firms as well as the competitive position of the independent VC firms.

In terms of the effects of investment amount per portfolio firm, the number of portfolio firms per investment manager, compensation schemes of investment managers, and managerial ownership of VC firms on VC firms' practices in the monitoring of their portfolio firms, the findings suggest that these variables do have some effect. Those VC firms that are more active in monitoring through board representation tend to invest a greater amount per portfolio firm on average and their management is also share-owners of their VC firms. Those that monitor their portfolio firms through staged investment tend to use performance-based compensation for their investment managers. When an investment manager is compensated by investment performance of a small number of portfolio firms, he or she has a greater leeway and motivation to get involved with management of those firms.

These results are consistent with the agency theory rationale. Large investment exposure to the portfolio firms and equity stakes in a VC firm itself by management provide a greater motivation to monitor the portfolio firms. Similarly, investment managers whose compensation is tied to investment returns are more motivated to monitor their portfolio firms. Thus, agency theory provides a useful framework to examine investment behaviors of VC firms and investment managers in Japan.

While this paper examined an unexplored area, i.e., monitoring of venture firms by VC firms in Japan, there are some limitations. First, the number of sample firms in this study was too small to generalize the findings, although it covers almost 20% of the VC population in Japan. Second, most of the sample VC firms are Tokyo-based, which might have given some bias. Third, the degree of the "hands-on" that I used in the study might not be highly reliable as I relied on subjective assessments of "hands-on" by investment managers of the sample firms. Future study should deal with these problems by increasing the size and geographic coverage of the sample and by using a more objective assessment of "hands-on."

It is also worthwhile for future research to examine the effect of monitoring practices on investment performance of VC firms. Many Japanese VC firms, however, do not disclose performance data and others, especially independent VC firms, are relatively new and therefore have recorded no capital gains so far. Thus, in order to investigate the relationship between the monitoring practices and performance of VC firms, we need to give more time to the newly established VC firms and wait for better information disclosure by VC firms in general in the future.

Another research direction is to investigate the relationships between the characteristics of venture firms that tend to present greater agency problems and the monitoring practices of VC firms in Japan. For example, start-up firms and technology-oriented or high technology firms are likely to pose greater agency problems because these firms present a high degree of uncertainty and information asymmetry. Theoretically, VC firms should monitor such firms more closely (Gompers, 1995). This line of research on Japanese VC firms will give us better insight on the applicability of agency theory to the Japanese context.

Finally, it is interesting to compare the monitoring practices of VC firms in two or more countries. Especially, given that VC industry is growing rapidly outside the United States, for example in many parts of Asia, it is interesting to see whether similar factors determine the investment behavior of VC firms across countries. Such a study can test the applicability of the agency theory framework to the monitoring practices of VC firms in different socioeconomic contexts.

NOTES

1. According to a study by NLI Research Institute, "stable" shareholdings accounted for 38% of all Japanese stocks, by value, in 1999, down from 48% in 1992.
2. Due to the recent accounting change, the parent company can no longer shield itself from its subsidiaries' losses easily.

REFERENCES

Baysinger, B., Kosnik, R., & Turk, TA. (1991). Effects of board and ownership structure on corporate R&D strategy. *Academy of Management Journal, 34,* 205–214.

Bergemann, D., & Hege, U. (1998). Dynamic venture capital financing, learning, and moral hazard. *Journal of Banking and Finance, 22,* 703–735.

Block, Z., & Ornati, OA. (1987). Compensating corporate venture managers. *Journal of Business Venturing, 2,* 41–52.

Caves, R., & Uekusa, M. (1976). *Industrial organization in Japan.* Washington, DC: Brookings Institution:.

Clark R. (1979). *The Japanese company.* New Heaven, CT: Yale University Press.

Eisenhardt, K.M. (1989). Agency theory: An assessment and review. *Academy of Management Review, 14,* 57–74.

Fama, E. (1980). Agency problems and the theory of the firm. *Journal of Political Economy, 88,* 288–307.

Gerlach, M.L. (1992). *Alliance capitalism: The social organization of Japanese business.* Berkeley: University of California Press.

Gompers, P.A. (1995). Optimal investment, monitoring, and the staging of venture capital. *Journal of Finance, 50,* 1461–149.

Gompers, P.A., & Lerner, J. (1998). *The determinants of corporate venture capital success: Organizational structure, incentives, and complementarities.* NBER Working Paper Series, No. 6725.

Gompers, P.A., & Lerner, J. (1999). *The venture capital cycle.* Cambridge, MA: The MIT Press.

Hamada, Y. (1998). *Nihon no Bencha Kyapitaru (Venture capital in Japan,* 2nd ed.). Tokyo: Nihon Keizai Shimbunsha.

Harmon, S. (2000). *Zero gravity: Riding venture capital from high-tech start-up to break out IPO.* [Japanese version translated and commentary inserted by K. Muraguchi.] Tokyo: Soft Bank Publishing.

Hata, N., & Higashide, H. (2000), Bencha fainansu no genjo to VC no yakuwari (The current state of venture finance and the role of VC). In Waseda University Entrepreneur Research Group (Ed.), *Venture Kigyo no Keiei to Shien* (pp. 135–168). Tokyo: Nihon Keizai Shimbunsha.

Hill, C.W., & Snell, S. (1989). The effects of ownership structure and control on corporate productivity. *Academy of Management Journal, 32,* 25–46.

Hudley, G., & Jacobson, CK. (1998). The effects of the keiretsu on the export performance of Japanese companies: Help or hindrance? *Strategic Management Journal, 19*(10), 927–937.

Jensen M., & Meckling, W. (1976). Theory of the firm: Managerial behavior, agency costs and ownership structure. *Journal of Financial Economics, 3*, 305–360.

Kaplan, S.N., & Stromberg, P. (2001). *Venture capitalists as principals: Contracting, screening, and monitoring.* NBER Working Paper Series, No.8202.

Kester, W.C. (1991). *Japanese takeovers: The global contest for corporate control.* Boston: Harvard Business School Press.

Lerner, J. (1995). Venture capitalists and the oversight of private firms. *Journal of Finance, 50*, 301–318.

McConnell, W.L., & Servaes, H. (1990). Additional evidence on equity ownership and corporate value. *Journal of Financial Economics, 27*, 595–612.

Myers, S.C., & Majluf, N.S. (1984). Corporate financing and investment decisions when firms have information that investors do not have. *Journal of Financial Economics, 13*, 187–221.

Nakatani, I. (1984). The economic role of financial corporate grouping. In M. Aoki (Ed.), *The economic analysis of the Japanese firm* (pp. 227–258). Amsterdam: North-Holland.

Osano, H. (2001). *Koporeito Gabanansu no Keizaigaku (Economics of corporate governance)*. Tokyo: Nihon Keizai Shimbunsha.

Prowse, S.D. (1996). The economics of private equity market. *Economic Review,* 3rd Quarter, 21–34, Federal Reserve Bank of Dallas.

Sahlman, W.A. (1990). The structure and governance of venture-capital organizations. *Journal of Financial Economics, 27*, 473–521.

Shleifer, A., & Vishny, R.W. (1997). A survey of corporate governance. *Journal of Finance, 52*, 737–783.

Siegel, R., Siegel, E., & MacMillan, I.C. (1988). Corporate venture capitalists: Autonomy, obstacles, and performance. *Journal of Business Venturing, 3*, 233–247.

CHAPTER 8

VENTURE CAPITAL FIRM INTERNATIONALIZATION AND MONITORING HIGH TECH ENTREPRENEURSHIP

The Case of India

Mike Wright, Sarika Pruthi, and Andy Lockett

ABSTRACT

This paper provides the first detailed analysis of venture capital firm monitoring activities in India, a major emerging market in Asia. The behavior of foreign and domestic venture capital firms is compared in terms of the range of monitoring and other services provided by venture capitalists together with issues concerning the identification and nature of resolution of performance problems in clients. Personal interviews were conducted with executives in 31 venture capital firms in India (84% response rate).

INTRODUCTION

The emergence of high technology entrepreneurs adds a crucial dimension to wealth creation in the developing countries of Asia. Venture capital markets are now developing in Asia to fund the growth of new entrepreneurial businesses. Venture capital finance in these countries can be provided either by domestically based firms or by foreign-based venture capital firms that have entered a particular market. Indeed, the globalization of venture capital has been marked by substantial cross-border entry into emerging markets (Aylward, 1998).

New entrepreneurial businesses require high levels of monitoring as well as equity finance, which raises issues of how venture capital firms deal with the agency problems that arise between themselves and the entrepreneur. While these agency problems exist in developed venture capital markets, they pose particular difficulties in emerging markets with weak institutional support. With the presence of domestic and foreign venture capital firms in these markets, a key research question concerns the extent to which these firms adopt different approaches to addressing monitoring problems.

This paper provides an exploratory extension of previous research in two respects. First, it examines the monitoring of venture capital investments in India, a major emerging market in Asia. Apart from Bruton et al. (1999, 2000), previous studies of the behavior of venture capital firms in Asia have generally focused on the screening stage in a developed economy like Japan (Ray & Turpin, 1993) as well as in newly industrialized economies such as Korea (Rah et al., 1994) and Singapore (Knight, 1994; Ray, 1991; Zutshi et al., 1999). Second, previous studies of venture capital monitoring do not distinguish the behavior of domestic from foreign firms within a particular market. Given the recent development of cross-border venture capital investment, this is an important general omission in the literature. For, while there may be some degree of commonality of venture capitalists' functions (Sapienza, Manigart, & Vermeir, 1996), firms may seek to obtain competitive advantage by adopting different approaches to monitoring than their competitors.

This paper is structured as follows. The first section outlines the context of venture capital in India. In the second section, propositions regarding differences between foreign and domestic venture capital firms operating in India are developed in respect of the different approaches to monitoring adopted by foreign firms versus domestic firms; their differing value adding services; their different perceptions about the causes of problems; and their approaches to taking action when problems arise. To derive these propositions we develop agency-based approaches to venture capitalists' monitoring with an understanding of the difficulties arising from weak institutional infrastructures in emerging markets. The third section provides an outline of the data and describes the method used in the study. This is followed by an analysis of the findings. In the final section, some conclusions are drawn and implications for researchers and practitioners discussed.

VENTURE CAPITAL ENVIRONMENT IN INDIA

Aylward (1998) has recently shown that the very different regulatory and legal frameworks in developing countries pose special challenges for the development of a venture capital market. In addition, different economic and fiscal environments can lead to very different patterns of fund-raising and investment in developing and U.S./Western European markets (Boocock & Presley, 1993).

The growth of venture capital in India was stimulated in the late 1980s with a series of measures to establish government-sponsored risk capital corporations and capital gains tax concessions for venture capital investments (Verma, 1997). The venture capital industry in India has subsequently witnessed increased activity with a rise in the number as well as the pool of funds for investment (IVCA Venture Activity, 1997). By 1998 total investment funds under management amounted to approximately $1.1 billions (AVCJ, 1999). In 1998 foreign institutional investors contributed 51% of the total pool of funds as compared to 26% contributed by Indian financial institutions. The balance of funds is provided by a mixture of multinational agencies, commercial banks (nationalized and others), insurance companies, corporate sector mutual funds, nonresident Indians, other public sector providers, etc. The venture capital industry is dominated by early stage investments (59.2% of value and 66.2% of numbers of investments, IVCA, 1999) while the largest industrial sector in the Indian market is industrial products (23.5% of investment value). Computer software is second largest, followed by computer hardware accounting for a further 5.9% and biotechnology and tele & data communications 5.4% of the value of investments in 1998.

The software industry in India has witnessed spontaneous growth, with "pockets of excellence" spreading rapidly from Bangalore and Bombay to cities like Madras and Pune (Leung, 1996). Having grown at an average rate of 50% a year over the last few years, exports totaled about U.S. $ 700 million in 1995 and are further expected to grow at the rate of $ 1.4 billion per annum over the next few years. The pool of 130,000 software engineers in India is probably the single most important factor responsible for the success of the industry. The Small Industries Development Bank of India (SIDBI) has set up an IT fund of Rs. 1000 million for exploiting this potential and another fund of Rs. 250 million has been proposed primarily for the students of the Indian Institute of Technology (IIT) to enable them to commercialize their research findings [Securities and Exchange Board of India (SEBI), 1999].

Until recently, prevailing conditions in India have not been conducive to the growth of entrepreneurship and risk capital. There are few incentives for individuals to invest in risk capital (Chitale, 1989). Companies find it difficult to raise loans but venture capital has yet to replace bank credit for early stage ventures (SEBI, 1999). The Securities and Exchange Board of India (SEBI) has introduced notional listing on the Over-the-Counter Exchange of India (OTCEI) to enable unlisted companies to trade on the stock exchange (SEBI, 1999). However, the proposal to relax the earlier norm of a minimum 25% public offering is still in its initial stages.

The legal and regulatory framework in India also poses problems. The present SEBI guidelines, requiring prospective investees to invest a minimum of Rs. 0.5 million, are a major deterrent for small investors (SEBI, 1999). Another stipulation, requiring 80% of the fund to be invested in early-stage investments or in listed securities in the case of financially sick or weak companies, is also restrictive. The guidelines of the Central Board of Direct Taxes (CBDT) and the Government of India are even more stringent. A venture fund is neither permitted to hold more than 40% equity stake in the investee company, nor can it invest more than 20% of the fund in any one company. Investment cannot be undertaken without registration both with the SEBI and the CBDT. Venture funds, being regulated by the Government of India, the SEBI, and the CBDT, need to adhere to three different sets of guidelines that are mutually contradictory (SEBI, 1999).

Although there has been some relaxation of government policy concerning multinational companies (Venkata Ratnam, 1998), different regulations apply to domestic and foreign venture capital funds operating in India (SEBI, 1999). Domestic funds are required to register with the SEBI but overseas funds are not. In addition, domestic funds need to apply to the CBDT to seek tax exemptions, whereas foreign funds need the approval of the Government. Moreover, whereas the overseas funds operating in India but registered in Mauritius, are only subject to minimal taxation, the Indian funds are not similarly exempted. This suggests that foreign funds face relatively lower pressure to conform to local conditions.

There are notable similarities and distinctions between India and other countries in Asia (Table 1). Even among the emerging markets of Asia, India has one of the lowest GNP/capita ratios and also fares poorly in terms of Foreign Direct Investment (FDI) in relation to national income (Hoskisson et al., 2000). La Porta et al. (1997) show that India has an English common law based legal system in common with Malaysia, Singapore, Thailand and Sri Lanka. In contrast, Japan, Korea and Taiwan have legal systems of Germanic origin, while Indonesia and the Philippines have French civil code based systems. Although the Indian venture capital market has been experiencing significant development, it remains sixth largest in Asia. The Hong Kong/China venture capital market has grown to be the largest in Asia, recently surpassing that of Japan. Total funds under management were $15.4 billion in 1998, compared to $12.5 billion in Japan.

Table 1. Comparisons of Selected Asian Venture Capital Markets

Country	GNP/Capita (US$, 1997)	FDI/GDP (%, 1997)	Venture Capital Under Management (US$m, 1998)	New Venture Capital Funds Raised (US$m, 1998)	Venture capital funds/Cos. (No.)	Base of Legal System
Hong Kong/ China	25,280/860	n.a.	15,442	3,218	129	English
India	370	0.2	1,053	60	41	English
Indonesia	1,110	0.7	328	38	46	French
Japan	37,850	n.a.	12,513	1,242	231	German
Korea	10,550	1.2	2,995	551	123	German
Malaysia	4,530	2.9	460	55	20	English
Philippines	1,200	0.5	224	52	10	French
Singapore	32,940	2.1	5,258	620	64	English
Taiwan	13,198	n.a.	3,598	1,096	124	German
Thailand	2,740	1.0	242	n.a.	8	English

Source: Asian Venture Capital Journal (1999) and La Porta et al. (1997)

153

The Singapore venture capital market as third largest had cumulative funds under management of $5.3billion. Singaporean venture capitalists, in contrast to those in India, invest significant funds outside the country. Of funds invested within Singapore, about two fifths are in start-up ventures, with approximately three tenths invested in the IT and communications sector and a fifth in Electronics. In contrast, the Malaysian venture capital market is about half the size of that in India and comprised 20 venture capital firms, with the government having an important role in the majority and almost all the remainder being captives. Only one venture capital firm is majority foreign owned. Total capital under management was $460 million in 1998, with about half of funds invested for expansion stage investments, with 13% for seed and start-ups, 28% for mezzanine and the balance for others.

DERIVATION OF PROPOSITIONS

Evidence suggests that monitoring approaches adopted by venture capital firms are conscious choices dependent on such factors as the stage of investment, degree of technological innovation and sector of venture, experience of CEO, performance of the company (Elango et al., 1995; Lerner, 1995; Sapienza et al., 1994) as well as the nature of the venture capital firm and the resources of the venture capital firms embodied in the specific skills of its executives (Beecroft, 1994; Rosenstein et al., 1993; Sweeting & Wong, 1997).

However, the institutional infrastructure in emerging markets may constrain venture capital firms' choices of behavior (Hoskisson et al., 2000). Previous studies have highlighted the similarities and differences between venture capital markets across differing countries (Manigart, 1994; Sapienza et al., 1994; Sapienza et al., 1996) but have not considered differences between foreign and domestic firms within the same market. Evidence from the general management literature suggests that these differences may be important.

Amba-Rao et al. (2000) show that within India foreign and domestic manufacturing firms have significantly different approaches to certain aspects of management. These differences may involve different degrees of emphasis of the same techniques with Indian firms using a more personalized style while Western firms adopt a more institutionalized approach (Virmani & Guptan, 1991).

In the remainder of this section, we utilize the agency cost perspective from the venture capital monitoring literature together with an understanding of the institutional and cultural environment in India to develop exploratory propositions about differences in approaches to the aspects of monitoring outlined above between domestic and foreign venture capital firms in India. To the extent that differences exist between domestic and foreign venture capital firms there may be important implications for the monitoring expertise available to aid entrepreneurs in high growth and technology ventures in emerging markets.

Our approach to analyzing the monitoring of venture capital investments builds on the stages in the process examined by Gorman and Sahlman (1989). First, as the corporate governance literature emphasizes that governance is both about ensuring accountability and enabling enterprise (Short et al., 1999), we address both these aspects of the monitoring process. Hence our starting point is to recognize that venture capitalists are involved both in monitoring investees by putting in place mechanisms to manage potential conflicts of interest between the entrepreneur and the venture capitalist resulting from opportunistic behavior by the entrepreneur (Barney et al., 1994; Sahlman, 1990; Wright & Robbie, 1998) as well as in providing services that add value to the enterprises through their role as active investors (Gorman & Sahlman, 1989; MacMillan et al., 1989; Sahlman, 1990). Second, notwithstanding these mechanisms and processes, problems may still develop as the venture operates in an uncertain environment. Hence, we develop the potential causes of problems identified by Gorman and Sahlman (1989) to include financial related issues. Third, venture capitalists are then responsible for taking actions to rectify these problems. To reflect the options open to venture capitalists (Sweeting, 1991) we extend the courses of action to include a range of options from less to more informal or relationship oriented.

Monitoring Mechanisms

In developed Western markets, venture capital firm monitoring of investees is typically viewed as an agency relationship (Bruton, Fried, & Hisrich, 1998). The nature and intensity of venture capital firm monitoring varies as the need dictates and increases with early stage investments, inexperienced entrepreneurs, where there are disagreements between venture capitalists and entrepreneurs, and in problem cases (Lerner, 1995; Sahlman, 1990; Sapienza & Gupta, 1994). Monitoring mechanisms may include both formal mechanisms such as requirements for the provision of detailed and regular accounting information and restrictions on management's actions encoded in an enterprise's Articles of Association/Corporate Charter as well as more informal mechanisms deriving from board representation and regular meetings between the venture capitalist and the entrepreneur (Mitchell et al., 1995). Fiet (1995) argues that venture capital firms generally view market risk as more important than agency risk as they can deal with the latter by contractual arrangements. This indicates a norm of venture capital behavior that transcends market environments. It might thus be expected that both domestic and foreign venture capital firms place high emphasis on formal mechanisms such as the regular provision of accounting information, restrictive covenants, etc. Hence:

> **Proposition 1a.** Similar to domestic venture capital firms, foreign venture capital firms in India are likely to emphasize formal monitoring mechanisms.

Asian culture, however, emphasizes shared responsibilities (Boisot & Child, 1996; Hofstede, 1984; Hofstede & Bond, 1988), suggesting a different emphasis to monitoring by incumbent domestic firms than by foreign firms. There is evidence that domestic firms in India adopt a more personalized approach in the use of management techniques while Western firms in India adopt a more formal, institutionalized approach (Amba-Rao et al., 2000). There is also some evidence that U.S. management practices in particular are aggressively market-oriented, inflexible, impersonal and lacking in empathy with the Indian ethos, in contrast to UK companies where there has been a long association under colonialism (Amba-Rao, 1994; Venkata Ratnam, 1998). This may be important given that the majority of foreign venture capital firms in India are of U.S. origin. Bruton et al. (1999) argue that venture capital firms in Asia view the relationship with entrepreneurs not as an arm's length agency one but as part of a unified network. As such, they may perceive less need to control agency risks. Rather, domestic venture capital firms in India may be more aware of the importance of networks (Amba-Rao et al., 2000; Ramachandran & Ramnarayan, 1993) and thus place significantly more emphasis on more informal monitoring. Hence:

> **Proposition 1b.** Foreign venture capital firms in India are significantly less likely to adopt informal monitoring mechanisms than domestic venture capital firms.

The regulatory environment can influence firm behavior. Weak institutional support, such poor legal enforcement, weak capital markets, undeveloped takeover markets and an absence of robust bankruptcy procedures, may be particularly problematical in emerging markets. One of the key aspects of the institutional support framework concerns the regulation of financial reporting, which has major implications for the nature and reliability of the information made available to venture capital firms for monitoring purposes. Differences in institutional frameworks have been identified as important in differentiating between venture capital markets, with consequent implications for the entry of foreign venture capital firms (Wright et al., 1992). The actual operation of local financial reporting frameworks in emerging markets in particular may not correspond to the developed market codes enacted in legislation (Hoskisson et al., 2000). Because of asymmetric information, domestic venture capital firms may be more aware of these problems, while foreign entrants may pay insufficient attention to developing an understanding of these differences (Murray, 1995; Wright & Robbie, 1998). In India, requirements for disclosure have been made more stringent with a view to enforcing strict standards of corporate governance (SEBI, 1999). More readily available financial data, improved regulatory structures, and increased transparency help promote better monitoring and surveillance. However, Indian accounting standards are still not on a par with practices in developed countries, there being notable differences between the quality of financial reporting in India and the United States (La Porta et al., 1998). In India, there continues to be debate as to whether to adopt the IAOSCO model, which is based on the standards of the major accounting firms, or to abide by the accounting standards of the GAAP. Moreover, it needs to be borne in mind that accounting standards for public firms may be better than those for private firms (Jeng & Wells, 2000). While both groups of venture capital firms may place emphasis on regular provision of financial reports, domestic venture capital firms may be more aware of the scope for deviation from prescribed standards leading to an expectation that they will be more likely to require certain accounting policies to be adopted. Hence:

Proposition 1c.   Domestic venture capital firms in India are significantly more likely to require specified accounting policies foreign venture capital firms.

Value Adding Services Provided by Venture Capital Firms

Evidence indicates that venture capitalists generally tend to emphasize their involvement in strategic and financial activities such as acting as a sounding board for management, monitoring financial performance and obtaining alternative sources of equity finance. They appear to be less involved in operational activities such as formulating marketing plans, developing products and soliciting customers (MacMillan et al., 1989). Sapienza et al. (1994) show that, in general the strategic role was viewed by venture capitalists to be more important than their operational role, irrespective of country. This suggests that the strategic roles of venture capitalists are likely to be scored more highly than operational roles for both foreign and domestic venture capitalists.

Proposition 2a.   Foreign venture capital firms in India are likely to place similar emphasis to domestic venture capital firms in India on strategic level value adding services.

However, there may be differences between venture capitalists from different countries within the same market in the relative importance they attach to strategic versus operational involvement. U.S. venture capital firms have been shown to place relatively more importance on strategic factors than their counterparts in Continental Europe (Sapienza et al., 1994). This approach may also be adopted by foreign venture capital firms in India, which are predominantly U.S. owned.

Cultural issues may also influence the manner in which domestic venture capital firms in India handle agency problems differently from foreign firms. Peng and Luo (2000) identify the importance of managerial network ties for organizational performance in an Asian environment but stress there is also a need for strategic capabilities. Domestic venture capital firms in India may, therefore, place more emphasis on providing inputs that will build capabilities and relationships, including such actions as becoming more involved in operational activities, motivating personnel, etc.

The U.S. business model, emphasizing efficiency with a focus on minimizing the inputs required to generate capital gains (Sahlman, 1990), suggests a relatively high ratio of fund size to number of executives. Sweeting (1991) also considers that venture capital firms constrained by time pressures are less likely to be involved in functional areas. In entering foreign markets, the within venture capital firm agency problems associated with the monitoring subsidiaries at a distance reinforces these points. In addition, since as noted above U.S. management practices in India have been seen as market-oriented and impersonal (Amba-Rao, 1994), foreign venture capital firms may be expected to have fewer resources and be less predisposed to intervention at an operational level, particularly where this involves relationship oriented activities. Hence:

Proposition 2b.   Foreign venture capital firms in India are likely to place significantly less emphasis than domestic venture capital firms in India on operational level value adding services.

Potential Causes of Problems in Investments

While venture capital firms can adopt various solutions to deal with the agency problem in monitoring investees, performance problems may still arise. Potential causes of problems may broadly relate to the nature of the management, the nature of the market and the firm and financial issues.

In India, new business opportunities and market niches may emerge in deregulating industries but the transfer of technologies and marketing of ideas already tested in developed countries may offer fresh avenues for investment (Sagari & Guidotti, 1992). In India, the post 1990 period has seen increased competition and reduced margins with problems compounded by the limited purchasing power of consumers and the lack of distribution channels (Daneels, 1998). International Country Risk Guide assessments indicate that the risks associated with undertaking contracts in India, such as contract repudiation and corruption are markedly higher than in the United States (La Porta et al., 1998).

The liberalization and deregulation of the Indian economy since 1991 has provided greater flexibility for entrepreneurs to act in the face of rising competition, changing technology and shifting consumer preferences (Das, 1996). The ability of entrepreneurs in India to adapt to such new found circumstances may be particularly important in such a dynamic environment, where not only is there a need to overcome earlier attitudes of complacency, but stringent demands are imposed on entrepreneurs to make an objective assessment of the direction and long term impact of changing markets. International evidence indicates that management and the nature of the product market are rated very highly across countries in assessing the riskiness of proposals (Karsai et al., 1999; Manigart et al., 2000; Wright & Robbie, 1996). In such a scenario, product market and management factors may be crucial areas for potential problems.

In general, experienced foreign venture capital firms in India may be more skilled at investment selection than domestic firms. Although market risk would appear to pose greater problems for foreign venture capital firms, their greater skills may mean they are more able to judge the risks associated with a particular market. Hence, market risk may in fact be a greater problem for domestic venture capital firms. Similarly, with respect to financial issues, foreign venture capital firms in India may be more skilled at scrutinizing expected costs and efficiencies, and more realistic about exit opportunities. In contrast, foreign venture capital firms may be less familiar with the management "culture" in an emerging market like India (Ramachandran & Ramnarayan, 1993) and may thus be more likely to misjudge management quality and their ability to work with management. This suggests, firstly, that a more contractual approach to monitoring management may be difficult given the weak institutional environment in India. Second, a formal contractual approach may in any case be less effective than informal monitoring that takes into account the managerial culture. Thus, the formal contractual solutions to dealing with agency problems may not work as well in India. Hence:

Proposition 3a.   Domestic venture capital firms in India are significantly more likely than foreign venture capital firms to cite market related issues as causes of problems.

Proposition 3a.   Domestic venture capital firms in India are significantly more likely than foreign venture capital firms to cite finance related issues as causes of problems.

Proposition 3c.   Foreign venture capital firms in India are significantly more likely than domestic venture capital firms to cite management related issues as causes of problems.

Course of Action to Improve Investee Performance

Venture capital investors have various options in dealing with problems, ranging from keeping the position under review to force an investee into receivership. Major interventions such as replacing management may only occur when things go seriously wrong, since to act precipitously may bring its own problems such as committing the investor to unknown amounts of time to rectify problems, destroying informal relationships which may be important conduits for obtaining information (Fried & Hisrich, 1995; Sweeting & Wong, 1997) as well as the problems arising from the absence of skills and resources to run the business directly. In the uncertain environment that venture capital investees typically operate, deviations from expectations may also be the result of changed circumstances (Hatherly et al., 1994). As such, courses of action may be more likely to involve discussion and exchanges of further information rather than action to renegotiate finance, sell the business, etc.

Given the expected closer and more operational involvement of Indian venture capital firms in monitoring, it follows that they may also be expected to be more informal/relationship oriented in their actions to improve performance. Evidence from Asia suggests less frequent removal of CEOs than is the case in Western developed markets (Bruton et al., 1999). Hence:

Proposition 4.   Foreign venture capital firms in India are significantly less likely than domestic venture capital firms to be informal/relationship oriented in taking action to deal with problems.

DATA AND METHODOLOGY

In order to examine the above propositions, a questionnaire, based on recent research elsewhere, was designed as the main research instrument. The ten-page long questionnaire included questions based on key aspects of monitoring mechanisms, the value-added services provided, potential causes of problems and courses of action to improve investee performance. Items were required to be scored on a scale of 1 to 5, with 1 meaning "irrelevant" and 5 meaning "essential."

Given the prevalence of U.S.-based firms among the foreign venture capital firms in India, the variables relating to these areas were based, as far as possible on scales previously used in U.S. studies. Variables relating to the range of monitoring options available were designed to capture both contractual financial reporting arrangements as well as those involving relationship-based monitoring (Sahlman, 1990). Barney et al. (1994) identify a number of contractual monitoring covenants including limits on capital expenditure, restrictions on remuneration, restrictions on obtaining further funds, etc. Venture capitalist monitoring also includes access to information systems, regular financial reporting, influences on accounting policies and audit, etc. (Mitchell et al., 1997). This list was extended by examining actual mechanisms used in venture capital firms' investees' articles of association (corporate charters) (see, e.g., Robbie & Wright, 1990 for a case example). Informal aspects were operationalized by variables relating to board representation, frequency of board meetings, requirements for regular meetings/contacts outside board meetings and board membership by specialists.

Gorman and Sahlman (1989) first surveyed the relative importance of the value adding services offered by venture capital firms, their variables subsequently being developed by MacMillan et al. (1989). Neither of these studies divided the variables into strategic and operational categories. In general, strategic variables can be defined as relating to issues concerning the overall scope and direction of the firm, whereas operational variables cover aspects of how the firm's strategy is implemented (Grant, 1998). Sapienza et al. (1994) define the strategic role of venture capitalists to combine roles such as financier, business consultant and sounding board, while the operational role combines roles such as sources of industry contacts, sources of professional contacts and managerial recruiter. Sweeting (1991) emphasizes the role of venture capital firms in developing the strategies of their investees, noting their role in appointing people to boards of directors. Sweeting also suggests that venture capital firms are more likely to require a qualified accountant to be employed in the business and to call on the assistance of specialist consultants experienced in dealing with the problems that can arise in new technology based firms. Mitchell et al. (1997) distinguish venture capitalists' monitoring of strategic and operational aspects of financial performance. On this basis, we categorized as strategic variables: developing new strategies to meet changing circumstances, evaluating acquisitions, helping to form and manage the board, monitoring financial performance, seeking additional equity finance and acting as a sounding board. We categorized as operational variables: services relating to assisting with operational planning and marketing plans, the monitoring of operational performance, making introductions to potential customers, suppliers and service providers, motivating personnel, recruiting management and resolving remuneration issues.

Variables relating to potential causes of problems in investee companies covered aspects relating to management, markets, products, internal efficiency, financing and exit, and relationships between entrepreneurs and the venture capital firm. Gorman and Sahlman (1989) provide some indicators of management, market and product related problems with respect to U.S. investees. But finance related factors may also be a cause of problems. Hence, we added finance related variables to cover trading through structuring and monitoring to exiting (raw material cost escalation, inappropriate financial structure, efficiencies failing to be realized and exit potential).

Courses of action to improve investee performance were captured with variables designed to cover the range of options from the most informal/ relationship oriented (keeping the position under review) to the most formal (forcing liquidation).

Given the nascent state of the Indian market, we were concerned that respondent apprehension about research of this nature may require further reassurance and clarification that could not be achieved through a mailed questionnaire. Therefore, it was decided to conduct personal interviews (May 1997). In the event, respondents had no problems comprehending the questionnaire. The face-to-face interviews lasted an hour on average. Except for two respondents, all others permitted the conversations to be tape-recorded. Verbatim transcriptions of the tapes were made after each interview.

The *Asia Pacific Private Equity Bulletin,* a directory of venture capital sources in the Asian region, was used as the primary source to identify the population of venture capital firms in India and the senior venture capital executives to contact. However, since the population of venture capital firms is constantly changing in India and directories can quickly become dated, snowball sampling was used to access a larger sample. On this basis, 47 venture capital firms were initially identified.

A covering letter, stating the purpose and significance of the study, and promising confidentiality of responses, was faxed to each of the venture capital firms in July 1999. They were subsequently contacted by telephone to arrange a convenient meeting time for the interview. This process established that 10 of the firms identified were not providing venture capital (typically advisers), had closed down or were not active. A further four firms were not contactable. In total, 23 face-to-face interviews were successfully conducted in India in July 1999 in Delhi, Bangalore and Bombay. These cities were selected because of the concentration of main venture capital firms.

Due to delays in contacting appropriate executives and arranging face-to-face interviews, a further eight respondents were interviewed by telephone in August and September 1999. In terms of the number of contactable venture capitalists, the 31 completed interviews represent a response rate of approximately 84% among the 37 active venture capitalists in India. The sample of 31 firms accounts for approximately £9.9 billion out of a total Indian market of (37 firms) approximately £10.6 billion (IVCA, 1998); this is approximately 94% of the total value of the Indian venture capital industry. This response is particularly encouraging in view of the difficulty of conducting survey research of this kind in India given the general tradition of secrecy.

The final sample comprised 13 captives, 14 independents and 4 public-sector firms. There were 18 foreign and 13 Indian firms. In terms of investment stage focus, 13 firms were exclusively late-stage investors, 3 were exclusively early stage investors and the rest were prepared to invest across all stages. The funds had been established for an average of 4.9 years, with the oldest being 11 years old and the youngest being less than a year old at the time of the interviews. There were on average 5.6 investment executives per firm with seniority varying from presidents, chairpersons, fund managers, portfolio managers, analysts and chartered accountants. Of the sample, 47% had an investment pool exceeding $50 m, while 20% invested between $21 and $50 million. Some 31% of firms had 10 or more industries represented in their portfolio, while 62% of the total had less than six industries. On the basis of the data, it is concluded that the sample is representative of the Indian venture capital industry. Follow-up telephone interviews were conducted in November 2000.

There are some notable differences between foreign and domestic venture capital firms in India in terms of their investment activity (Table 2). Foreign venture capital firms are on average smaller than domestic ones in terms of numbers of executives but tend to be larger in terms of the size of funds managed. Hence the amount of funds managed per investment executive is also significantly larger for foreign venture capital firms. Foreign venture capital firms tend to be more specialized in terms of the number of industries represented in their portfolios. However, there is no difference between the proportion of firms' portfolios invested in high technology-based industries, with both foreign and domestic firms being largely dominated by high technology investments. Finally, both foreign and domestic firms have multistage investment preferences.

Table 2.   Firm Characteristics—Domestic v Foreign

Firm Level Characteristics	Categories	Domestic	Foreign
Ownership (n)	Captive	3	5
	Independent	5	9
	Affiliated	–	4
	Public Sector	2	–
	Other	2	–
Number of years involved in venture capital		16.3 (5)	18.7 (3)
Number of investment executives		8.4 (4)	4.6 (3)
Fund size/No. execs		0.79	1.32**
Size of funds managed	0–$10m	6	–
	$11–20m	–	1
	$21–30m	1	4
	$31–40m	–	2
	$41–50m	–	2
	>$50m	5	9
Number of industries represented in portfolio	1–3	3	6
	4–6	1	8
	7–9	1	1
	10+	7	3*
Proportion of firm's portfolio in high technology based sectors	0–25% = 1; 26–50% = 2; 51–75% = 3; 76–100% = 4	Mean = 3.22	Mean = 3.33
Preferred stage of investment[a]	Start-Up/ Early stage	9	6
	Expansion/ Development	9	17
	Late stage	3	2

[a] A number of firms indicated that they had a preference for more than one stage of invest-ment. In such cases the both preferences have been included.

Figures in brackets are mode scores as a small number of venture capital firms have a much greater longevity than all others. Fund size/no.execs based on scores 1–6 for fund size where 1= <$10m through 6 = >$50m

Asterisks relate to results of Mann-Whitney U-test for differences between the two types of firm, where ** indicates $p < 0.05$ level of significance for difference regarding Fund size/No. execs and * indicates $p<0.10$ for difference regarding number of industries represented in portfolio.

With respect to executives' background, there was weak statistical evidence of more non-Indian nationals in foreign venture capital firms in India (at 10% level) than in domestic venture capital firms in India (Table 3). Surprisingly, an average of only 8.9% of the executives in foreign venture capital firms are foreign nationals. Some 31.2% of the foreign firms' executives have experience in the domestic market (i.e., the United States) of the firm's parent. Foreign venture capital firms generally have some discretion in their ability to make investment decisions (Table 4). Foreign venture capital firms in India are more likely to have most discretion when it comes to considering deals in unusual sectors (mean = 4.07) and less discretion when it comes to making decisions up to a specific size (mean = 3.53). With respect to specific dimensions of monitoring, foreign venture capital firms are generally found to take decisions in consultation with their foreign parent, but have some discretion regarding restrictions on management in articles of association. However, the standard deviation on these variables indicates considerable variations in firm strategies.

Table 3.   Investment Executives Background and Skills

	Domestic Mean	Foreign Mean	Domestic Std. Dev.	Foreign Std. Dev.	Mann-Whitney Test Statistic
Percentage of executives that are non-Indian nationals	0.00	8.93	0.00	13.87	45.0*
Percentage of executives with venture capital experience outside India	17.90	32.27	20.80	29.90	54.5

Asterisks relate to results of Mann-Whitney U-test for differences between the two types of firm, where *p < 0.1 level of significance.

Table 4.   Foreign Firms' Discretion in Decision Making and Monitoring

What is the nature of the policy you adopt towards potential investees? Please rate each item on a scale from 5 = have full discretion ... 3 = policy set in discussion with parent ... 1 = company sets a company-wide policy	Mean	Median	Std. Deviation
Discretion to make decisions up to a specified size	3.53	4.0	1.30
Need to seek approval for deals in unusual sectors	4.07	4.5	1.14
Venture capitalist board representation	3.33	3.5	1.46
Extent of financial reporting mechanisms	3.28	3.0	1.41
Restrictions on management in articles of association	3.83	4.0	0.99
Use of equity ratchets on management equity	3.65	3.0	0.86

Potential differences between the foreign and domestic venture capital firms operating in India with respect to the variables relating to the propositions developed earlier were analyzed using Mann-Whitney non-parametric tests. These tests were preferred as they have less restrictive data assumptions than parametric tests (De Vaus, 1991). The Mann-Whitney approach can be used with smaller samples and does not rely on assumptions of normality of the distribution. Given the size of the population of venture capital firms in India, and hence of the sample (notwithstanding our high response rate), it was considered appropriate to adopt this approach. The significance levels reported in the text below and in the tables relate to the results of these tests.

RESULTS AND ANALYSIS

Monitoring Mechanisms

The data relating to the monitoring mechanisms used by domestic and foreign venture capitalists are presented in Table 5. Both domestic and foreign venture capital firms score and rank audited annual accounts, restrictions on changes in ownership and board membership by the venture capital firm most highly. However, foreign venture capital firms then rank the provision of monthly management accounts, approval of capital expenditure and restrictions on additional borrowings more highly than domestic venture capital firms do. However, there were no significant differences between the two groups of venture capital firms on these variables. These findings provide some support for Proposition 1a.

Compared to their Indian counterparts, the foreign venture capitalists place significantly less importance on the board membership of the industry specialist at the investee company (significant at the 5% level) and the frequency of full board meetings (significant at the 5% level). Domestic firms report a higher score than foreign firms in the requirement for regular meetings with the venture capitalist and for the VC to be a member of the audit committee; but the differences are not statistically significant. These findings provide some support for Proposition 1b.

The only significant difference between the two groups with respect to more formal mechanisms was the requirement for the use of certain accounting policies (significant at the 5% level). This difference with regard to the use of certain accounting policies may reflect domestic firms' greater awareness of regulatory issues leading to reporting difficulties in an emerging economy and provides support for Proposition 1c.

Table 5. Monitoring Mechanisms

How important are each of the following as a means of monitoring investees?
Please rate each factor on a scale from 5 = essential, 4 = important, 3 = moderately
important, 2 = slightly important, 1 = irrelevant.

	Domestic Mean	Foreign Mean	Domestic Std. Dev.	Foreign Std. Dev.	Mann-Whitney test statistic
Formal					
Audited annual accounts	4.92 (1)	4.78 (1=)	0.28	0.43	100.0
Restrictions on changes in ownership	4.77 (2=)	4.78 (1=)	0.60	0.55	116.0
Requirement for certain accounting policies	4.69 (4)	4.03 (10)	0.63	0.85	60.5**
Restrictions on mergers & acquisitions	4.54 (7)	4.39 (6)	0.66	0.61	99.5
Provision of monthly management accounts	4.38 (8=)	4.67 (4)	0.77	0.69	91.0
Provision of evaluation of monthly performance	4.38 (8=)	4.38 (7)	0.65	0.94	114.5
No capital expenditure beyond certain limits without approval	4.38 (8=)	4.61 (5)	0.77	0.50	101.5
Restrictions on asset disposals	4.38(8=)	3.94 (12)	0.77	0.87	83.0
Restrictions on additional borrowings	3.69 (13=)	4.06 (8=)	0.95	0.70	92.0
Requirement for direct access to investee's accounting system	3.69 (13=)	3.31 (16)	1.11	1.51	103.5
Requirement to use a particular auditing firm	3.54 (16)	3.97 (11)	1.27	1.14	93.0
Restrictions on director's remuneration	3.46 (17)	3.50 (14)	1.05	1.06	117.0
Restrictions on senior management's remuneration	2.92 (18)	3.08 (18)	1.26	0.94	108.5
Informal					
Board membership of venture capitalist at the investee company	4.77 (2=)	4.77 (3)	0.44	0.43	116.0
Frequency of full board meetings	4.67 (5)	3.81 (13)	0.65	0.99	52.5**
Regular meetings with venture capitalist	4.62 (6)	4.06 (8=)	0.65	1.43	99.5
Industry specialist's board membership	3.92 (12)	3.14 (17)	0.86	1.14	67.0**
Venture capitalist membership of investee's audit committee	3.67 (15)	3.44 (15)	1.07	1.25	98.5

Asterisks relate to results of Mann-Whitney U-test for differences between the two types of firm, where **p < 0.05 level of significance. Figures in parentheses are ranks

Value Adding Services Provided by Venture Capital Firms

Table 6 presents findings of differences between the two groups of venture capital firm with respect to the strategic and operational variables described earlier. In terms of the added value services provided by domestic and foreign venture capital firm's differences were found for only four out of the 18 variables: three operational aspects and one strategic aspect (Table 6).

Generally, variables relating to strategic services received the highest scores and the highest ranks for both groups of venture capital firms, except for monitoring of investments of portfolio firms and, to a lesser extent, seeking further external finance. There were some differences between domestic and foreign venture capital firms in the rankings of the services provided. For foreign venture capital firms, assisting with strategic planning ranks first but for domestic firms this item ranks only fourth. In contrast, while serving as a sounding board for new ideas ranks first for domestic venture capital firms it ranks only fifth for foreign firms. Developing new strategies to meet changing circumstances and monitoring financial performance also rank slightly higher for domestic venture capital firms. The other notable difference relating to strategic issues concerned evaluating acquisitions (fourth for foreign, fourteenth equal for domestic). At the strategic level, the only significant difference was that foreign venture capital firms are significantly more likely to be involved in evaluating acquisitions of investees than are domestic venture capital firms (significant at the 10% level). These findings indicate general support for Proposition 2a except for this last difference.

At the operational level, compared to their foreign counterparts, the Indian venture capitalists are significantly more active in assisting investees only with respect to operational planning (significant at the 5% level), in motivating personnel (significant at the 10% level) and in managing crises and problems (significant at the 5% level). With respect to the other operational variables, domestic Indian venture capitalists generally gave higher scores but the differences were not significant. Interestingly, foreign venture capital firms gave scores averaging around 4 to monitoring operational performance and making introductions to customers and suppliers. The latter is perhaps a reflection of the ability of foreign venture capital firms to provide access to international markets. These differences provide only limited support for Proposition 2b.

Table 6. Value Adding Services Provided by Venture Capital Firms

How important is each of the following services provided by your venture capital fund? Please rate each factor on a scale from 5 = essential, 4 = important, 3 = moderately important, 2 = slightly important, 1 = irrelevant.

	Domestic Mean	Foreign Mean	Domestic Std. Dev.	Foreign Std. Dev..	Mann-Whitney test statistic
Strategic services					
Assist with strategic planning	4.50 (4=)	4.61 (1)	0.52	0.61	93.0
Development of new strategy to meet changing circumstances	4.58 (1=)	4.53 (2)	0.51	0.61	105.0
Evaluate acquisitions	3.75 (14=)	4.44 (4)	1.14	0.70	67.0*
Help form and manage board	4.25 (7)	3.78 (9)	0.97	1.15	79.5
Monitor financial performance	4.58 (1=)	4.50 (3)	0.67	0.79	103.0
Monitor investments of portfolio firm	3.50 (16=)	2.83 (15=)	1.38	1.25	78.0
Seek additional equity financing	3.83 (10=)	3.64 (11)	1.03	1.16	98.5
Serve as sounding board for new ideas	4.58 (1=)	4.25 (5)	0.90	0.81	77.0
Operational services					
Assist in operational planning	3.50 (16=)	2.69 (17)	0.80	1.25	63.0**
Assist with marketing plans	3.75 (15=)	3.17 (14)	0.62	1.26	76.5
Control of portfolio management	3.91 (9)	3.41 (13)	1.22	1.50	75.0
Make introductions to potential customers and suppliers	4.08 (8)	3.97 (7)	1.00	1.14	104.0
Make introductions to potential service providers	3.83 (10=)	3.86 (8)	1.11	0.97	107.0
Manage crises and problems	4.50 (4=)	3.68 (10)	1.19	0.34	48.9***
Monitor operational performance	4.50 (4=)	4.00 (6)	0.80	1.16	73.9
Motivate personnel	3.83 (10=)	2.56 (18)	1.19	1.12	41.0***
Resolve remuneration issues	3.00 (18)	2.83 (15=)	1.21	1.04	99.5
Search / recruit management	3.83 (10=)	3.56 (12)	1.27	1.39	96

Asterisks relate to results of Mann-Whitney U-test for differences between the two types of firm, where *p < 0.1 level, and **p < 0.05, ***p<0.01 level of significance. Figures in parentheses are ranks

Potential Causes of Problems in Investments

Table 7 highlights the potential causes of problems in investments for domestic and foreign firms. The results indicate that domestic Indian rather than foreign venture capital firms are significantly more likely to see market and some finance-related issues as important causes of problems. This difference is particularly evident in end-user market failing to develop as expected (significant at the 10% level), investees failing to capture market share (significant at the 5% level) and competitors taking advantage of the financially weakened state of the investee company (significant at the 5% level). With respect to financial issues, limited exit potential (significant at the 10% level), raw material cost escalation (significant at the 10% level) and assumptions of post deal efficiency improvements failing to be met (significant at the 5% level) are also a significantly greater cause of concern for domestic Indian venture capital firms. While ineffective senior management is the most serious cause of problems for foreign venture firms in India, market-related problems in terms of the end-user market failing to develop is ranked first for domestic venture capital firms. Limited exit potential ranks highly for both foreign and domestic venture capital firms.

A notable difference between the rankings of the two sets of venture capital firms concerns disputes within the management team. This scores more highly for foreign venture capital firms, but the difference with domestic venture capital firms is not statistically significant. For foreign venture capital firms this problem is second in importance while for domestic firms it ranks only eighth. Failure of the company to capture market share and assumptions of post deal efficiency improvements failing to be met both rank more highly for domestic venture capital firms. In contrast, inappropriate financial structures are more likely to be causes of problems for foreign venture capital firms. These findings provide support for Proposition 3a and 3b but not for Proposition 3c. The lack of support for Proposition 3c suggests that both domestic and foreign venture capital firms face similar problems with management.

Table 7. Potential Causes of Problems

How important is each of the following as a potential cause of problems in your investments. Please rate each factor on a scale from 5 = essential, 4 = important, 3 = moderately important, 2 = slightly important, 1 = irrelevant.

	Domestic Mean	Foreign Mean	Domestic Std. dev.	Foreign Std. Dev.	Mann-Whitney test statistic
Management					
Ineffective senior management	4.54 (2)	4.47 (1)	0.66	1.04	111.5
Ineffective functional management	3.92 (6=)	3.64 (6)	1.12	1.08	94.5
Disputes within the management team	3.78 (8)	4.19 (2)	1.54	1.05	109.5
Divergence in goals with venture capital investors	3.62 (10=)	3.28 (9)	1.33	1.41	100.5
Market					
Company fails to capture market share	4.31 (4)	3.50 (7)	0.63	0.99	60.0**
End user market fails to develop as expected	4.62 (1)	4.00 (3)	0.51	0.86	67.5*
Competitors take advantage of financially weakened state of investee company	3.69 (9)	3.00 (11)	1.03	1.03	70.0**
Financial					
Assumptions of post deal efficiency improvements failing to be met	3.92 (6=)	3.12 (10)	0.67	0.91	53.0**
Raw material cost escalation	3.62 (10=)	2.86 (12)	0.96	1.00	73.0*
Inappropriate financial structure	3.54 (12)	3.31 (8)	0.97	1.27	104.0
Limited exit potential	4.50 (3)	3.94 (4)	0.67	0.83	63.5*
Product problems	4.08 (5)	3.78 (5)	0.76	1.00	99.5

Asterisks relate to results of Mann-Whitney U-test for differences between the two types of firm, where *p < 0.1 level, and **p < 0.05 level of significance. Figures in parentheses are ranks

Courses of Action to Improve Investee Performance

The courses of action to improve investee performance are presented in Table 8. Consistent with the importance of relationship issues, the results indicate that domestic venture capital firms in India are significantly more likely than foreign venture capital firms to negotiate with management to take the necessary steps (significant at the 5% level). Neither of the groups of firm rate more severe formal actions such as renegotiating finance, seeking a buyer for the company or forcing liquidation as essential or important actions, indicating that they are less commonly used. In terms of the rankings, foreign venture capital firms rank keeping the position under review as highest in importance while this is third most important for domestic firms. Domestic venture capital firms rank negotiating with management to take the necessary steps first in importance while for foreign firms this is third highest. Requesting more in-depth information from management ranks second in importance for both sets of firms. These actions indicate that domestic venture capital firms are somewhat more informal/relationship oriented in dealing with problems than foreign venture capital firms and provide support for Proposition 4.

DISCUSSION AND CONCLUSIONS

This exploratory paper provides the first detailed analysis of the monitoring activity of venture capital firms in India. The paper combined the agency literature regarding venture capital firm monitoring with an understanding of the institutional context to obtain insights into the behavior of foreign and domestic venture capital firms in the Indian market, as follows.

The results of the study showed similarities in domestic and foreign venture capitalists' perceptions of their behavior in respect of a number of monitoring mechanisms and value-added services. There were similarities between the two groups of firms with respect to the importance attached to formal monitoring mechanisms and strategic level value adding services, suggesting a commonality of approach in some aspects of venture capital monitoring. Significant differences between domestic and foreign venture capital firms operating in India in a number of operational areas, suggest that domestic venture capital firms were significantly more likely to attempt to address agency problems by being involved in monitoring at a more informal level. There were some indications that domestic venture capital firms placed more stress on developing relationships and capabilities. Significant differences were found between the two groups with respect to the frequency of full board meetings and managing crises and problems, as well as higher scores (though not significant) with respect to

Table 8. Courses of Action to Improve Investee Performance

How much importance do you attach to each of the following courses of action to improve investee performance? Please rate each factor on a scale from 5 = essential, 4 = important, 3 = moderately important, 2 = slightly important, 1 = irrelevant.	Domestic Mean	Foreign Mean	*Domestic Std. dev.*	*Foreign Std. Dev.*	*Mann-Whitney test statistic*
Negotiate with management to take necessary steps	4.77 (1)	4.22 (3)	0.44	0.71	64.5***
Request management to provide more in-depth information	4.54 (2)	4.36 (2)	0.52	0.68	103.0
Keep position under review	4.35 (3)	4.50 (1)	0.65	0.86	97.5
Seek to find buyer for company	3.92 (4)	3.58 (5)	1.12	1.31	100.5
Seek to renegotiate financial issues (find additional financial partners)	3.85 (5)	3.64 (4)	0.99	1.03	97.5
Force receiverships / liquidation of investee	2.00 (6)	1.97 (6)	1.00	0.92	98.5

Asterisks relate to results of Mann-Whitney U-test for differences between the two types of firm, where **p < 0.05 level of significance. Figures in parentheses are ranks regularity of meetings and serving as a sounding board for ideas. As compared to their foreign counterparts, the Indian venture capitalists are significantly more active in providing some operational services, notably assisting investees with operational planning in motivating personnel and in managing crises and problems. However, at the strategic level, foreign venture capital firms are only significantly more likely to be involved in evaluating acquisitions of investees than are domestic venture capital firms. This difference may arise partly because of the lesser involvement at the operational level by foreign firms (see below) and because assistance in evaluating acquisitions may be a more familiar strategy in developed western markets where build-up strategies are more common.

Domestic Indian rather than foreign venture capital firms are significantly more likely to see market-related and some financial issues as important causes of problems, especially in the end-user market failing to develop as expected, investees failing to capture market share and competitors taking advantage of the financially weakened state of the investee company. Both domestic and foreign venture capital firms face similar problems with management, while financing structure problems are more likely for foreign venture capital firms. Domestic venture capital firms in India are more relationship-oriented in dealing with problems than foreign venture capital firms.

Our findings that foreign venture capital firms have significantly less operational and informal level involvement in some areas than domestic firms is interesting in the context of our sample, where foreign venture capital firms employ a high level of local Indian nationals as investment executives. This might be expected to contribute to overcoming problems relating to asymmetric information concerning the local environment. In addition, it was also evident that foreign venture capital firm parents tend to set policy after discussion with the local subsidiary. Therefore, rather than constraining the discretion of the subsidiary to make decisions and monitor investments, the foreign parent firms may attempt to institutionalize local executives into their way of conducting business. But strategies appear to differ. Some foreign firms have a significant percentage of executives in India with experience in the foreign parent's domestic market, suggesting a degree of inpatriation where host-country nationals spend some time in the organization's head office in order to provide a link between the head office and its foreign subsidiaries (Harvey et al., 1999). Further detailed case study analysis involving executives from both the foreign parent and the activity based in India is required to examination this issue.

The analysis in this paper suggests a number of implications for practitioners and researchers. For practitioners, the findings suggest that different approaches to monitoring may be appropriate in the different markets in which venture capital firms seek to operate. However, the differences in the level of operational and relational involvement between foreign and domestic venture capitalists introduces questions about their relative abilities to offer technological entrepreneurs the inputs they typically need. Domestic venture capital firms may be better placed to offer closer involvement to enable such entrepreneurs to establish their businesses. Foreign venture capital firms may be better positioned to provide more strategic growth assistance once the business has become established, such as through identifying potential acquisitions. These differences have clear implications for entrepreneurs in technology-based ventures since this heterogeneity of provision suggests a need for care in selecting venture capital partners whose style of involvement meet their needs. There may be a significant role for intermediaries in aiding entrepreneurs in this search process.

For researchers, the results of the study provide further evidence of differences between venture capital markets and highlight the dangers of over-generalization both from one market to another and within markets. These differences apply not just to comparisons between developed and undeveloped economies, but also within broader geographical areas. The findings highlight the need to consider the behavior of different types of venture capital firms, especially with respect to foreign and domestic players within a particular country.

This study has focused solely upon India. The small size of the Indian venture capital firm population means that, although the study obtained a high response rate, the findings need to be seen as exploratory. Nevertheless, the results do suggest a number of opportunities for further research. Further research might usefully test whether these findings are generalizable to other developing and developing markets. As seen earlier, there are significant differences between the countries of Asia with respect to GDP per capita, stock and venture capital market development and legal and financial systems. These differences suggest that it would be useful to explore whether different approaches to monitoring occur in countries of Asia according to whether they have English, Germanic or French-based governance systems (La Porta et al., 1997, 1998) and more or less developed venture capital markets.

The aim of this study was to provide preliminary analysis of the extent and nature of the differences in monitoring behavior between domestic and foreign venture capital firms in a particular market. Further research might usefully examine in greater depth the causes of the differences in approaches. The size of the venture capital industry in India prevented multivariate analysis that would have enabled us to take into account other factors influencing the monitoring approaches adopted by foreign and domestic venture capital firms in India, such as venture capital firm type and investee stage, sector and size. This analysis might also usefully examine the extent of any impact of differences in monitoring approach on the performance of investee firms. There is some debate about the impact of venture capital firms on investee performance, although recent work has suggested that venture capital firms do contribute positively to performance (Hellmann, 1998; Hellmann & Puri, 2000). There is a general absence, however, of evidence on the performance impact of foreign versus domestic venture capital firms. In order to examine these issues it would be necessary to extend the analysis to other countries so as to generate the requisite larger data set.

This paper also focused solely on the perspective of the venture capital firms. Further research might usefully consider the perspectives of the entrepreneurs who demand venture capital finance. What factors influence their decision to obtain finance from a foreign rather than a domestic venture capital firm. For example, are firms that use foreign venture capital firms more likely to expand in international markets?

This paper has focused upon differences in monitoring behavior between domestic and foreign venture capital firms within a particular market. Internationalization evidence from the general manufacturing sector indicates that, in entering new markets, foreign firms may either seek to work to the same "recipes" used in their home markets or may adapt to local market conditions (Rosenzweig & Singh, 1991). There are some indications that this may also be the case for venture capital firms. A coarse comparison between the foreign venture capital firms in India in this study and Gorman and Sahlman's (1989) and MacMillan et al.'s (1989) studies of U.S. venture capital firms in the United States suggests that, with respect to comparable variables between the studies, while there are some similarities there are a number of factors where behavior differs between the two environments. For example, seeking additional equity financing appears to be a more important value-added service by U.S. firms in the U.S. market than for foreign firms in India. In contrast, making introductions to potential customers and suppliers appears to be a more important value-added service by foreign firms in India than it is for U.S. firms in the United States. Additionally, while ineffective senior management is likely to be the major cause of post-deal problems in both cases, ineffective functional management appears to be identified as more problematical for U.S. firms in the United States. However, whether a venture capital firm adapts or replicates its domestic behavior when entering a foreign market may depend on its strategic choice. We interviewed the parent firms of two foreign venture capital firms operating in India as a follow-up to the survey.[1] One adapted its monitoring approach to be more formal in the Indian market than in its home market while the other pursued a very similar approach to its home market. Further research might examine more systematically the extent to which, and the reasons why, foreign venture capital firms adapt their behavior when they enter an international market compared to the way they behave in their own domestic market.

Further research is also required to examine potential differences between these two groups with respect to screening and valuing potential investees. To what extent do foreign venture capital firms adapt their approaches to local market conditions? How do they adapt their approaches to deal with different asymmetric information problems? Previous studies have identified both similarities and differences in screening (Ray, 1991; Zutshi et al., 1999) and valuation (Manigart et al., 2000, 2001) behavior between countries. However, potential differences in approach between foreign and domestic firms within countries and between foreign firms abroad and in their domestic markets have been neglected. Again, examination of these issues may have important implications for successful entry by foreign firms into emerging venture capital markets as well as for the development of competitive advantages by incumbent domestic firms.

There is an extensive literature on entry mode strategies by both manufacturing (Leonidou & Katsikeas, 1996) and service sector firms (Erramilli & Rao, 1993), but so far modes of internationalization by venture capital firms has been largely neglected in the academic literature. Examination of this issue was beyond the scope of this chapter but would be especially pertinent given the developing cross-border activity of venture capital firms both into and within Europe and into less developed markets elsewhere (Bygrave & Timmons, 1999). Moreover, given the evidence presented in this paper, the mode of entry may have important implications for developing an approach to monitoring investees that is appropriate to local market conditions.

ACKNOWLEDGMENTS

The constructive and helpful comments of the editor, two anonymous reviewers and Deniz Ucbasaran are acknowledged with thanks.

NOTE

1.   We attempted to contact all the parent firms of the foreign venture capital firms operating in India in September 2001. We obtained responses in two cases. In the remaining cases, the VC had either closed, was not a functioning VC in the domestic market where it raised funds or was affected by the events of September 11 and was unable to participate.

REFERENCES

Amba-Rao, S. (1994). US HRM principles cross-country comparisons and two case applications in India. *International Journal of Human Resource Management, 5*(3),755–778.

Amba-Rao, S., Petrick, J., Gupta, J., & Von der Embse, T. (2000). Comparative performance appraisal practices and management values among foreign and domestic firms in India. *International Journal of Human Resource Management, 11*(1), 60–89.

Asian Venture Capital Journal. (1999). The 2000 guide to venture capital in Asia (11th ed.).

Aylward, A. (1998). Trends in venture capital financing in developing countries. *IFC Discussion Paper No. 36.* Washington, DC: World Bank.

Barney, J., Busenitz, L., Fiet, J., & Moesel, D. (1994). The relationship between venture capitalists and managers in new firms: Determinants of contractual covenants. *Managerial Finance, 20*(1), 19–30.

Beecroft, A. (1994). The role of the venture capital industry in the UK. In N. Dimsdale & M. Prevezer (Eds.), *Capital markets and corporate governance.* Oxford:Oxford University Press.

Black, B., & Gilson, R. (1998). Venture capital and the structure of capital markets: Banks versus stock markets. *Journal of Financial Economics, 47*(3), 243–278.

Bliss, R. (1999). A venture capital model for transitioning economies: The case of Poland. *Venture Capital, 1*(3), 241–258.

Boisot, M., & Child, J. (1996). From fiefs to clans and network capitalism: Explaining China's emerging economic order. *Administrative Science Quarterly, 41,* 600–628.

Boocock, G., & Presley, J. (1993). Equity capital for small and medium sized enterprises in Malaysia: Venture capital or Islamic finance? *Managerial Finance, 19,* 82–95.

Bruton, G., Fried, V., & Hisrich, R. (1998). Venture capitalists and CEO dismissal. *Entrepreneurship Theory and Practice, 21,* 41–54.

Bruton, G., Dattani, M., Fung, M., Chow, C., & Ahlstrom. D. (1999, Winter). Private equity in China: Differences and similarities with the western model. *Journal of Private Equity, 2,* 7–13.

Bruton, G., Fried, V., & Manigart, S. (2000). *An institutional view of the development of venture capital in the U.S., Europe and Asia* (Working Paper). Texas Christian University.

Bygrave, W., & Timmons, J. (1999). Venture capital: Predictions and outcomes. Venture capital at the crossroads and realizing investment value revisited. In M. Wright & K. Robbie (Eds.). *Management buy-outs and venture capital: Into the next millennium* (Ch. 2, pp. 38–56). Cheltenham:Edward Elgar.

Calori, R., Lubatkin, M., & Very, P. (1994). Control mechanisms in cross-border acquisitions: An international comparison. *Organization Studies 15*(3), 361–379.

Chandler, G.N. (1996). Business similarity as a moderator of the relationship between pre-ownership experience and venture performance. *Entrepreneurship Theory and Practice 20,* 51–65.

Chitale, R.P. (1989, November 25). Risk capital for medium and small industries: Weaknesses in fiscal and monetary policies. *Economic and Political Weekly*, M-150-M-156.

De Vaus, D.A (1991). *Surveys in social research* (3rd ed.). London: Allen & Unwin.

Elango, B., Fried, V., Hisrich, R., & Polonchek, A. (1995). How venture capital firms differ. *Journal of Business Venturing, 10*, 157–179.

Erramilli, M.K., & Rao, C.P. (1993). "Service firms" international entry mode choice: A modified transaction-cost analysis approach. *Journal of Marketing, 57*, 19–38.

EVCA. (2000). *EVCA 2000 yearbook*. EVCA: Zaventem.

Fiet, J. (1995). Risk avoidance strategies in venture capital markets. *Journal of Management Studies, 32*, 51–74.

Fried, V.H., & Hisrich, R.D. (1995). The venture capitalist: A relationship investor. *California Management Review, 37*(2), 101–113.

Gorman, M., & Sahlman, W. (1989). What do venture capitalists do? *Journal of Business Venturing, 4*, 231–248.

Grant, R. (1998). *Contemporary strategy analysis* (3rd ed.). Oxford: Blackwell.

Harvey, M., Speier, C., & Novicevic, M. (1999). The role of inpatriation in global staffing. *International Journal of Human Resource Management, 10*(3), 459–476.

Hatherly, D., Innes, J., MacAndrew, J., & Mitchell, F. (1994). An exploration of the MBO-financier relationship. *Corporate Governance, 2*(1), 20–29.

Hellmann, T. (1998). The allocation of control rights in venture capital contracts. *Rand Journal of Economics, 29*(1), 57–76.

Hellmann, T., & Puri, M. (2000). The interaction between product market and financing strategy. *Review of Financial Studies, 13*(4), 959–984.

Hofstede, G. (1984). *Culture's consequences: International differences in work-related values*. Beverly Hills, CA: Sage.

Hofstede, G., & Bond, M. (1988). Confucius and economic growth: New trends in cultural consequences. *Organizational Dynamics, 16*(4), 4–21.

Hoskisson, R., Eden, L., Lau, C-M., & Wright, M. (2000). Strategies in emerging markets. *Academy of Management Journal, 43*(3), 249–267.

Indian Venture Capital Association *(IVCA) 1999. Venture Activity*, 1998. Delhi.

Jeng, L., & Wells, P. (2000). The determinants of venture capital funding: Evidence across countries. *Journal of Corporate Finance, 6*, 241–289.

Karsai, J., Wright, M., Dudzinskiand, Z., & Morovic, J. (1999). Screening and valuing venture capital investments: Evidence from Hungary, Poland and Slovakia. *Entrepreneurship and Regional Development, 10*, 203–224.

Knight, R. (1994). Criteria used by venture capitalists: A cross-cultural study. *International Small Business Journal, 13*(1), 1–21.

Kostova, T. (1997). Country institutional profiles: Concept and measurement. *Academy of Management Best Paper Proceedings*, 180–189.

La Porta, R., Lopez-De-Silanes, F., Shleifer, A., & Vishny, R. (1997). Legal determinants of external finance. *Journal of Finance, 52*(3), 1131–1150.

La Porta, R., Lopez-De-Silanes, F., Shleifer, A., & Vishny, R. (1998). Law and finance. *Journal of Political Economy, 106*, 1113–1155.

La Porta, R., Lopez-De-Silanes, F., Shleifer, A., & Vishny, R. (1999). Corporate ownership around the world. *Journal of Finance, 54*, 471–517.

Lawler, J., Jain, H., Venkata Ratnam, C., & Atmiyananda, V. (1995). Human resource management in developing economies: A comparison of India and Thailand. *International Journal of Human Resource Management, 6*, 319–346.

Leonidou, L.C., & Katsikeas, C.S. (1996). The export development process: an integrative review of empirical models. *Journal of International Business Studies, 27*(3), 517–552.

Lerner, J. (1995). Venture capitalists and the oversight of private firms. *Journal of Finance, 50*(1), 301–318.

Leung, J. (1996, June). Indian success story. *Asian Business,* 28–34.

MacMillan, I., Kulow, D., & Khoylian, R. (1989). Venture capitalists involvement in their investments: Extent and performance. *Journal of Business Venturing, 4*(1), 27–47.

Manigart, S. (1994). The founding rates of venture capital firms in three European countries (1970–1990). *Journal of Business Venturing, 9*(6), 525–541.

Manigart, S., De Waele, K., Wright, M., Robbie, K., Desbrieres, P., Sapienza, H., & Beekman, A. (2000). Venture capitalists, investment appraisal and accounting information: A comparative study of the USA, UK, France, Belgium and Holland. *European Financial Management, 6*(3), 389–404.

McDougall, P.P., Shane, S., & Oviatt, B.M. (1994). Explaining the formation of international new ventures: The limits of theories from international business research. *Journal of Business Venturing, 9*, 469–487.

McDougall, P., & Oviatt, B. (2000). International entrepreneurship: The intersection of two research paths. *Academy of Management Journal, 43*(5), 902–908.

Mitchell, F., Reid, G., & Terry, N. (1995). Post investment demand for accounting information by venture capitalists. *Accounting and Business Research, 25*(99), 186–196.

Mitchell, F., Reid, G., & Terry, N. (1997). Venture capital supply and accounting information system development. *Entrepreneurship Theory and Practice, 21*(4), 45–62.

Murray, G. (1995). The UK venture capital industry. *Journal of Business Finance and Accounting, 22*(8), 1077–1106.

Peng, M., & Luo, Y. (2000). Managerial ties and firm pebrformance in a transition economy: The nature of the micro-macro link. *Academy of Management Journal, 43*(3), 486–501.

Rah, J., Jung, K., & Lee, J. (1994). Validation of the venture evaluation model in Korea. *Journal of Business Venturing, 9*, 509–524.

Ramachandran, K., & Ramnarayan, S. (1993). Entrepreneurial orientation and networking: Some Indian evidence. *Journal of Business Venturing, 8*, 513–524.

Ray, D. (1991). Venture capital and entrepreneurial developments in Singapore. *International Small Business Journal, 10*(1), 11–26.

Ray, D., & Turpin, D. (1993). Venture capital in Japan. *International Small Business Journal, 11*(4), 39–56.

Robbie, K., & Wright, M. (1990). The case of Maccess. In S. Taylor & S. Turley (Eds.), *Cases in financial reporting.* Deddington: Philip Allan.

Rosenstein, J., Bruno, A., Bygrave, W., & Taylor, N. (1993). The CEO, venture capitalists and the board. *Journal of Business Venturing, 8*, 99–113.

Rosenzweig, P., & Singh, J. (1991). Organizational environments and the multinational enterprise. *Academy of Management Review, 16*(2), 340–361.

Sahlman, W. (1990). The structure and governance of venture-capital organizations. *Journal of Financial Economics, 27*, 473–521.

Sapienza, H., & Gupta, A. (1994). Impact of agency risks and task uncertainty on venture capitalist-CEO interaction. *Academy of Management Journal, 37*(6), 1618–1632.

Sapienza, H., Amason, A., & Manigart, S. (1994). The level and nature of venture capitalist involvement in their portfolio companies: A study of three European countries. *Managerial Finance, 20*(1), 3–17.

Sapienza, H., Manigart, S., & Vermeir, W. (1996). Venture capitalist governance and value added in four countries. *Journal of Business Venturing, 11*(6), 439–469.

Scott, W.R. (1995). *Institutions and organizations.* Thousand Oaks, CA: Sage.

Securities and Exchange Board of India (SEBI). (1999).

Short, H., Keasey, K., Wright, M., & Hull, A. (1999). Corporate governance: From accountability to enterprise. *Accounting and Business Research, 29*(4), 337–352.

Sparrow, P., & Budhwar, P. (1997). Competition and change: Mapping the India HRM recipe against world-wide patterns. *Journal of World Business, 32*(3), 224–243.

Sweeting, R. (1991). UK Venture capital funds and the funding of new technology based businesses: Process and relationships. *Journal of Management Studies, 28,* 601–622.

Sweeting, R., & Wong, C. (1997). A UK "hands-off" venture capital firm and the handling of post-investment investor-investee relationships. *Journal of Management Studies, 34*(1), 125–152.

Venkata Ratnam, C. (1998). Multinational companies in India. *International Journal of Human Resource Management, 9*(4), 567–589.

Verma, J.C. (1997). *Venture capital financing in India.* London: Sage.

Virmani, B., & Guptan, S. (1991). *Indian management.* New Delhi: Vision Books.

Wright, M., & Robbie, K. (1998). Venture capital and private equity: A review and synthesis. *Journal of Business Finance and Accounting, 25*(5 & 6), 521–570.

Wright, M., Karsai, J., Dudzinski, Z., & Morovic, J. (1999). Transition and active investors: Venture capital in Hungary, Poland and Slovakia. *Post-Communist Economies, 11*(1), 27–46.

Zutshi, R., Tan, W., Allampalli, D., & Gibbons, P. (1999). Singapore venture capitalists investment evaluation criteria: A re-examination. *Small Business Economics, 13,* 9–26.

Part III

CASE STUDIES IN TECHNOLOGICAL ENTREPRENEURSHIP: MANAGING IN TURBULENT ENVIRONMENTS

CHAPTER 9

CRITICAL INCIDENTS IN HIGH-TECH START-UPS

A Singapore Study

Maw Der Foo and Hwee Hoon Tan

ABSTRACT

This study explores the critical incidents faced by high-tcch start-ups in Singapore in their first two years of operation. The results show that human resource management issues dominate at the start-up phase. This contrasts with past research that finance, sales and marketing issues are the most important in all stages of development (e.g., Kazanjian, 1988; Terpstra & Olson, 1993). The findings suggest that the speed of new business development has escalated the types of critical incidents faced in high-tech start-ups. Implications and suggestions for future research are raised.

INTRODUCTION

This study explores the critical incidents faced by high-tech start-ups in their first two years of operation. The popular press has given considerable attention to the growth-related strategic and managerial issues of technology-based firms. Researchers such as Kazanjian (1988) note that high-tech

185

firms face issues that are exacerbated by the need to grow quickly. How an entrepreneur handles issues at the early stages of the firm can determine long-term performance and firm survival (Stearns, Gilbertson, & Reynolds, 1997). While the study is only on high-tech businesses, these firms are particularly interesting because they account for a disproportionate number of high-growth firms. High-tech firms play a key role in the commercialization of new products, processes, technologies and the creation of new industries such as computers, genetic engineering, machine vision, and robotics (Kazanjian, 1988).

Cowan (1990) argues that much of the executives' time is spent on identifying and attempting to solve problems. Further, the way an executive interprets a problem affects subsequent information processing, decision-making and behavior. Following Tompkins (2001), we focus on critical incidents and define a critical incident as an event that evokes strong emotions among the founders and has a big impact on the start-up. We prefer to use critical incidents instead of problems because critical incidents refer to both positive and negative events, both of which demand the attention of managers and entrepreneurs. Further, since entrepreneurs spend a large part of their time identifying and solving issues within their start-ups, studying how they interpret critical incidents is a crucial step to understanding entrepreneurial behaviors and decision making.

Some researchers have studied the whole organizational life cycle and this study extends the work by detailing early stage critical incidents. While some studies (e.g., Terpstra & Olson, 1993) have asked the CEOs to reflect on the firms' most significant problems, we selected only firms that are in existence for twenty-four months or fewer to reduce survival and recall biases. *Wall Street Journal* (October 16, 1992) reports that 63% of firms fail within the first six years. This means that firms that have been in existence for several years may not have the same characteristics as firms that have been in existence for one or two years. A long time lag between when the issues occurred and the studies could exacerbate recall biases. The results of our study add to extant work, showing that critical incidents faced by high-tech firms at the early stages could be different from that of firms in general. Entrepreneurs in high-tech areas face issues of manpower (both human resource and the lack of general management skills), operations management and finance, in that order. This is different from that of finance and marketing issues found in other studies. The findings are consistent with evidence from Silicon Valley that people is the source of competitive advantage. In addition, using Fayol's POLC (planning, organizing, leading and controlling) framework, we also found that entrepreneurs faced critical incidents of organizing and planning, with few critical incidents of leading and control.

THEORY DEVELOMENT

We first review the life-cycle literature. Although this literature has its limitations in understanding start-up issues, much of what we know of the early stages comes from this work. Organization development has long been of interest to organizational researchers, and in particular, to scholars of the entrepreneurship phenomenon. Work on the life-cycle literature suggests that organizations evolve in a consistent and predictable nature.

Integrating past research, Churchill and Lewis (1983) posited and found support that organizations go through five major stages, the existence, survival, success, take off and resource maturity stages. Stage 1, existence, is characterized by direct supervision, simple organization structure and minimal to nonexistent formal systems. The key issues facing firms at this stage are getting sufficient customers, delivering products and services, expanding from one key customer to a broader sales base and having sufficient money to cover the considerable cash demands. In stage 2, survival, the main issues are generating sufficient cash to break even, and financing growth. In stage 3, success, the entrepreneur must decide whether to grow the firm or to focus on the firm's niche market. The first professional staff members are hired, usually a controller in the office and perhaps a production scheduler in the plant. In Stage 4, take off, the most important issues are that of delegating responsibilities and getting sufficient cash. Moreover, the key managers must be very competent to handle a growing and complex business environment. Finally, in stage 5, resource maturity, the biggest concerns are consolidating and controlling the financial gains brought on by rapid growth and retaining the entrepreneurial spirit. Eggers, Leahy and Churchill retested the model in 1994 and found support for it.

Focusing on technology-based new firms, Kazanjian (1988) found four stages of development, namely, conception and development, commercialization, growth and stability. In stage 1, conception and development, the focus of the entrepreneur is on the invention and development of a product and the technology. The major issues are developing the business idea, constructing the prototype and selling the business idea to financial backers. In stage 2, commercialization, the entrepreneur focuses on developing the product or service for commercialization. The issues are gearing up for manufacturing, first sales and developing the nucleus of the administrative system. Stage 3, growth, is characterized by the issues of manufacturing in volume, manufacturing efficiently, establishing market share, and managing the personnel issues associated with high growth. Stage 4, stability, is characterized by the need to launch a second-generation product while managing efficiency of existing products.

The review shows that the life-cycle of firms, including high-tech firms, are that of start-up, growth and maturity. The early issues are that of finance, particularly getting funds to start operations, and to develop the markets to generate revenue. Terpstra and Olson (1993) studied the first year of firm operations and found similar problems in the early start-up phase. They used a sample of 115 from *Inc.* magazine and asked the CEOs to state the most significant problem faced by their firms in the first year of operation. The dominant issues in the first year of operations, in order of frequency, were sales/marketing, internal financial management, obtaining external financing, general management, product development, human resource development, production/operations management, economic environment and regulatory environment. However, one limitation of the study was that the median age of the firms in the sample was 9 years, with a mean age of 9.4 years and there could be severe recall biases. The study was also limited to the more successful firms, as this was a criterion to be included in the *Inc.* magazine listing. These limitations make it difficult to generalize the findings to start-ups firms, but only to those that had successfully grown over a number of years.

Sexton, Upton, Wacholtz, and McDougall (1997) found that high-growth firms faced issues of getting funds, developing strategies for increasing sales, and acquiring and efficiently using human resources. They conclude that these findings support that of Terpstra and Olson (1993). However, a closer examination shows that human resource issues, which typically appears later in the organizational life-cycle, is now important at the start-up phase. Stearns et al. (1997) also found that fast growing firms that fail to understand the need to recruit talented resources are more likely to fail. Consistent with the findings of Sexton et al. (1997) and Stearns et al. (1997), the popular press has highlighted the dearth of skilled personnel in the high-tech field, resulting in high levels of turnover among employees, poaching among firms and other strategies to attract technically trained personnel (e.g., *Financial Review,* October 31, 2000).

While Terprstra and Olson's model (1993), together with the life-cycle models suggest that finance and marketing are the main issues in the early stages, studies on high-growth firms suggest that human resource development is just as important at the start-up phase. All the studies above have classified entrepreneurial issues in terms of functional departments such as marketing, finance and human resources. However, the literature on managerial activities has primarily used the planning, organizing, leading and controlling (POLC) framework to understand organizational activities. This framework provides clear and discrete methods of classifying the thousands of different activities that managers carry out and the techniques they use to achieve organizational goals (Carroll & Gillen, 1987). Thus in the reminder of this section, we review the POLC framework and use it to understand key activities undertaken by entrepreneurs.

The POLC framework is based on Henri Fayol's work and represents the most useful way of conceptualizing the manager's job and perhaps the most favored description of managerial work in current management textbooks (Carroll & Gillen, 1987). They found that of 21 management books published between 1983 and 1986, 17 used at least four of the classical Fayol functions and three used three of these functions. The co-author of this paper identified ten management books published between 1997 and 2000. All ten included the classical management functions of planning, organizing, leading and controlling (POLC). This suggests that the framework continues to be accepted as the dominant way of describing managerial activities. In addition, many studies have found that managers who spend more time and have more skills in the POLC functions experience higher unit performance in terms of profitability and productivity (e.g., Bray, Campbell, & Grant, 1974; Gillen & Carroll, 1985; Miner, 1982; Stagner, 1969). Gillen and Carroll (1985) found that supervising and planning skills were significantly related to unit productivity-efficiency. Time spent in organizational planning was also found to be related to the firm's profitability. Bray et al.'s (1974) study on 8000 entry level managers in AT&T found that skills in planning/decision making was one of the strongest predictor of managerial success. While there are other ways to conceptualize managerial work such as Mintzberg's (1971) managerial roles, Carroll and Gillen (1987) argue that these are less useful than Fayol's classical approach in understanding how organizations function and what managers do. It is therefore surprising that no research to our knowledge have used the classical approach to understand issues faced by start-ups.

According to Robbins and Coulter (1999) planning includes "defining goals, establishing strategy, and developing plans to coordinate activities," organizing includes "determining what tasks are to be done, who is to do them, how the tasks to be done are grouped, who reports to whom, and where decisions are to be made," leading includes "motivating subordinates, directing others, and resolving conflicts," and controlling is the monitoring of "activities to ensure that they are being accomplished as planned and correcting any significant deviations." An article in the *Economist* (November 11, 2000) asserts that while the skills needed by senior management in this Internet age are changing and that senior managers can no longer run the business as a tight-ship from day to day, when the Internet revolution has stabilized and transformed the business landscape, organizations would still need managers who can manage to run a tight-ship. Hence we contend that the planning, organizing, leading and controlling model would continue to provide the perspective for understanding management functions.

In sum, we expect that in the early start-up phase of high-tech firms, human resource management issues will be as important as the traditional issues of finance and marketing. To study critical incidents, we use the framework developed by Terpstra and Olson (1993). This framework was developed to understand the key issues faced by start-ups and the issues raised were supported by other studies (e.g., Sexton et al., 1997). In addition, consistent with the dominant way of classifying managerial activities, we use the POLC framework to classify the critical incidents.

METHODS

Samples and Procedures

The sample comprised 67 high-tech start-ups in Singapore. Given the limited lists of high-tech start-ups, research assistants were told to gather the contact information of the start-ups from a wide range of sources such as the web, centers in Universities that have contacts with start-ups (e.g., the Centre for the Management of Innovation and Technopreneurship at the National University of Singapore), government agencies that assist start-ups (e.g., the Singapore National Science and Technology Board) and newspaper reports. High-tech start-ups were defined to include but were not limited to start-ups in the computer (e.g., business to business, business to consumer, hardware, software) and life-sciences (e.g., medical technologies, genetic engineering) fields.

Following Terpstra and Olson (1993) and Hood and Young (1993), we adopted an open-ended interview approach to our study. This approach avoids imposing limitations on perceptions on the founders (Hood & Young, 1993) on the types of events that could be considered as critical incidents. The study uses interviews to answer the questions "what are the critical incidents faced by firms in the first two years of operation" and "what are the main activities carried out by the firms in this period" and can be considered as an exploratory case study (Yin, 1994).

The lead founder, defined as the key person driving the firm's strategic direction and who had an equity stake in the start-up, was contacted. The lead founder was asked to provide the most critical incident faced and told that a critical incident was an event that happened at the start-up which strong emotions were evoked (e.g., puzzled, confused, shocked, happy etc.) and had a strong impact on the firm. The lead founder was also asked to outline the history that led to the event and to include as many details as he or she could remember. This technique of obtaining critical incidents was adapted from Tompkins (2001). The selection of one individual (typically the CEO in previous studies) as the single respondent has ample pre cedent in the organization and strategy fields (Kanzanjian & Drazin, 1990). To provide comparative data and to reconfirm that the firms were less than two years old, the founders were asked to state the date in which the firm became a legal entity and the type of legal entity (e.g., partnership, private limited company). If no legal entity had been formed, they were asked when members decided to work on the business (date).

The interviewers were instructed to read the definition of a critical incident to the lead founders and to record their answers. These steps were to establish a common understanding of what constituted a critical incident and to ensure that the answers were the statements of the interviewees and not the impressions of the interviewers. These help to increase the construct validity of cases (Yin, 1994). Every interviewer was provided with the protocol defining a critical incident, a lead founder and the questions that they should ask in the semi-structured interview. This protocol increases the reliability of case study research in providing interviewers with a guide in carrying out the study, and providing documentation to ensure that others can repeat the same study using the same procedures (Yin, 1994). The protocol increased the confidence that the results were not due to idiosyncratic practices of the interviewees. The reliability and construct validities were also increased by transcribing the interviews with each interview coded by at least two persons.

Data Coding

The average length of the interview was 32 minutes, with a median of 30 minutes. Most of the interviews were tape recorded and the transcripts of these interviews were prepared. The average length of the transcript was five pages, and more than 300 pages of transcripts were produced. We coded the data according to Terpstra and Olson's (1993) ten categories of types and classes of entrepreneurial issues. The data were also coded with Fayol's POLC framework.

Two business school students familiar with the Terpstra and Olson (1993) and POLC frameworks, but who were otherwise not familiar with the entrepreneurship literature, coded the data. First, the coders randomly chose ten cases and both of them coded these cases. Differences were resolved after the initial coding to reach a common understanding of the categories. They then proceeded to code the data separately.

For each critical incident, the coders first distilled in a sentence the critical incident faced by the start-up. For both the Terpstra and Olson and the POLC framework, in all but 16 cases (hence 76% simple agreement), the coders agreed on the coding of the critical incident. The level of agreement between the coders ensures that the study is systematic and objective and that valid references are made from the transcripts of the interviews. In all cases, they wrote essentially the same sentence but in some cases, disagreed on the locus of the critical incident. For example, in one instance, they agreed that the critical incident was one of "clinching first deal due to stiff competition from other market players." The first coder classified it as a planning critical incident while the other classified it as an organizing critical incident. To resolve the differences, a third person coded the data. In all cases, this coder was in agreement with at least one of the two coders. Thus, when there were differences, we used the third coder's classification. The level of agreement between the coders ensures that valid references are made from the transcripts of the interviews.

RESULTS

Table 1 reports the profile of the start-ups in this study. The start-ups had an average size of 22 persons, with a range of 2 to 165, a median of 12 and standard deviation of 28.9. On average, the start-ups had incorporated for 13 months, with a range of 2 to 24 months, a median of 12 and a standard deviation of 7.1. 43 start-ups had asked for external funding while 23 did not (one firm did not provide this information).

Table 1.   Summary Information of the Start-up Firms

	Number	Percent
Legal Entity		
Private limited	49	73
Partnership	12	18
Sole proprietorship	2	3
No legal entity	2	3
Public limited	1	1
Not available	1	1
Industry		
E-commerce	22	33
E-Magazine and entertainment	10	15
IT services and solution portal	8	12
Online services	7	10
Application Software Provider (ASP)	5	7
Wireless telecommunciations	5	7
Web-software design	4	6
Others	4	6
Life sciences—Medical insurance	2	3

Size: Mean 22 (range of 2 to 165 with median of 12, s.d. 28.9)
Months legal entity formed: Mean 13 (range of 2 to 24 with median of 12, s.d. 7.1)

Twenty-two were e-commerce firms, ten provided e-entertainment, 8 in IT services and solutions, 7 in online services, 5 application software providers, 5 in wireless telecommunications, 4 in web-software design, 2 in life-sciences and 4 in other high-tech industries. Most of the founders had invested their own money in the firms (70%), hired employees (70%), prepared business plans (61%) and employed a full-time person in the firm (61%). About half (49%) had asked for funding with 46% receiving external financing support.

Table 2 reports the critical incidents faced by start-ups coded into both the Terpstra and Olson (1993) and POLC frameworks. To determine if the critical incidents differed across firm characteristics, we also compared and contrasted the types of critical incidents faced for three different categories of start-ups: (1) those who had asked for external funding versus those who had not (1 if they did and 0 otherwise), (2) smaller versus larger start-ups (median split, with firms of size 12 and smaller coded as 0 and firms with more than 12 persons coded as 1 and (3) start-ups in operation for less than a year versus those who had been in operation for over a year (coded as 1 for the former and 0 for the latter). Only the bivariate correlation between asked for external funding and size of the firm was statistically significant ($r = 0.35$, $p < 0.01$).

The Terpstra and Olson Framework

Using the framework first developed by Terpstra and Olson, the number one critical incident identified was that of Human Resource Management (33%) and included recruitment, selection, turnover, retention, satisfaction, employee development and other general human resource management issues. The second most common critical incident was that of General Management (24%). This included the lack of management experience, managing growth and administrative problems. The third most common critical incident was Production and Operations Management (15%) such as the establishment and maintenance of quality control. Financing, was the fourth most cited critical incident (12%) and this included financing for growth and general financing problems. The rest of the categories had 3 or fewer cases out of the 67 instances identified (internal financial management, sales/marketing, economic environment and organization structure). None of the start-ups named the Regulatory Environment as a key issue.

Of the firms in the sample, 43 firms had asked for external funding while 23 did not (one firm did not provide this information). There was a significant difference between start-ups that asked for external funding and the types of critical incident that they cited ($\chi^2 = 20.29$, df = 8, $p < 0.01$).

Table 2a. Coding Critical Incidents into the Terpstra and Olson and POLC Frameworks

	Planning	Organizing	Leading	Controlling	Total
1. Obtaining external financing e.g. Obtaining financial for growth, Other or general financing problems	6	1	0	1	8
2. Internal financial management e.g. Inadequate working capital, Cash flow problems, Other or general financial management problems	1	0	0	2	3
3. Sales/Marketing e.g. Low sales, Dependence on one or few clients/ customers, Marketing or distribution channels, Promotion/Public relations/Advertising, Other or general marketing problems	2	1	0	0	3
4. Product development e.g. Developing products/services, Other or general product development problems	1	0	1	0	2
5. Production/Operations management e.g. Establish-ing or maintaining quality control, Raw materials/resources/supplies, Other or general production/ operations management problems	1	4	0	5	10
6. General management e.g. Lack of management experience, Only one person/no time, Managing/controlling growth, Administrative problems, Other or general management problems	7	6	3	0	16
7. Human resource management e.g. Recruitment/selection, Turnover/retention, Satisfaction/ morale, Employee development, Other or general human resource management problems	0	20	2	0	22
8. Economic environment e.g. Poor economy/recession, Other or general economic environment problems	0	0	1	0	1
9. Regulatory environment e.g. Insurance	0	0	0	0	0
10. Organization structure/design e.g. New division, Changing from custom programming to product, Other or general organization structure/design	1	1	0	0	2
Total	19	33	7	8	67

Table 2b. Coding Critical Incidents into the Terpstra and Olson Framework by Request for External Funding, Size and Length of Operation

Overall	Funding		Size		Length of Operation
	Request for External Funding (N=43)	Did not Request for External Funding (N=23)	Smaller Firms (N=33)	Larger Firms (N=34)	No difference for firms in operation for 1 year and less and those in operation for over a year
1. Human Resource Management	1. Human Resource Management	1. Production and Operations Management	1. Production and Operations Management	1. Human Resource Management	1. Human Resource Management
2. General Management	2. General Management	2. Human Resource Management	2. General Management	2. General Management	2. General Management
3. Production and Operations Management	3. External Financing	3. General Management	3. Human Resource Management	3. External Financing/ Internal Financial Management/ Sales and Marketing	3. Production and Operations Management

The top three critical incidents for the firms that had asked for external funding were Human Resources Management (35%), General Management (23%) and obtaining External Financing (19%). For firms that had not asked for external funding, the three most frequently cited critical issues were that of Production and Operations Management (30%), followed by Human Resources Management (22%) and General Management (22%).

The data also showed some differences between smaller and larger firms in the critical incidents cited (χ^2 = 14.34, df = 8, p < 0.10). The firms were classified using the median split; 33 firms of size 12 or fewer persons were classified as smaller firms while 34 with more than 12 persons as larger firms. The top three critical incidents cited by the smaller firms were those of Production and Operations Management (27%), General Management (24%) and Human Resources Management (21%). For the larger firms, the top two critical incidents cited were Human Resources Management (41%) and General Management (21%). There was a three-way tie among obtaining External Financing, Internal Financial Management and Sales and Marketing (9% each).

We also split the sample into firms that were in operation for less than a year and those in operation for over a year. Thirty-two firms were in each group, while three firms did not disclose this information. There were no significant differences in the types of critical incidents cited (χ^2 = 4.33, df = 8, n.s.). The three most cited critical incident in each group were Human Resources Management (31% in each group), General Management (16% in each group) and Production and Operations Management (16% in each group).

The POLC Framework

Using the POLC framework, organizing and planning were the main critical incidents faced by the start-ups. Organizing defined as the process of determining what tasks were to be done accounted for 33 out of the 67 incidents (49%). Of the 33 organizing activities, 22 were in the Human Resources area. Planning defined as the process of defining goals and establishing a strategy for achieving these goals accounted for 19 incidents (28%). Only 7 (10%) mentioned Leading and 8 (12%) Controlling incidents. Table 3a and Table 3b report the description of the critical incidents developed by the coders in relation to Human Resources and Planning activities.

Table 3a. Critical Incidents in Human Resources

Recruitment/Turnover Issues (12)

23	Recruiting of staff that are not capable enough due to lack of talent in market
26	Chief designer left company due to better offers
30	Lack of concensus in hiring new staff
44	Difficult to recruit the right people to do the job
47	HR issue—co-founder was offered a teaching position and wanted to quit startup
50	High turnover due to unglamourous location
51	New staff did not turn up for work & equipments had been bought for them
52	Deal called off due to lack of full time programmers to complete client's work
56	Manpower shortage and succession problem as staff are on volunteer basis
59	Difficulty in getting skilled manpower
69	Difficulty in finding employees with the right attributes
71	Lack of local IT talents

Lack of Management System/Backup Procedures (8)

20	Lack of backup person in the absence of founder
22	Employing a GM that did not fit into the company culture and was fired
29	Not distinguishing between friendship & professionalism in recruitment of partners
38	No proper system of work delegation
40	Lack of proper recruitment criteria
55	Conflicts between partners—due to different ways of thinking and commitment
58	Uncompleted work left behind when 1 partner left
64	Conflicts in appointment of financial manager

Table 3b. Critical Incidents Related to Planning

Internal and External Financing (7)

7	Funding problem—rejected by VCs due to their lack of experience and credibility (students)
9	Merger—it supplied much needed operating working capital
11	Acquisition offer—founder decide not to accept in the end
28	Funding problems—Infrastructures were expensive and involved high risk commitments
53	Funding issue—2 of the partners do not have enough money for equal ownership in company

Table 3b.   Critical Incidents Related to Planning (Cont.)

57   Funding issue—lack of investors due to company being a new startup

66   Impressive initial presentation—client willing to invest in them to start a company providing such services

General Management (7)

 3   Management conflict—differences in management policies and business directions

15   Changes in company strategies—e-commerce venture rejected by fellow team members initially

18   Differences in company business direction by top management

36   Poor business alliance—other party did not fulfill promise

41   Changes in business plan—conflict with original business partners

61   Poor management of company—lack clearly defined business strategy, ineffective work management, insufficient planning

62   Administrative problem—lots of regulations to follow to obtain the necessary permits

Others (5)

21   Lack of industry recognition—due to startup being newly established

43   Wrong business plans and revenue model—competitors offering same product for free

45   Wrong business plans and revenue model—high fees turned customers off

67   Marketing strategies—adopting aggressive marketing strategies to increase sales

70   Incompatibility of product—failure of product when hosted on a different server

We also analyzed the differences between the critical incidents using the POLC framework and whether the firms had asked for funding, firm size and length of operation (less than one year versus more than one year). There were no significant differences in the critical incidents cited for firms who had asked for external funding and those that did not ($\chi^2 = 4.87$, df = 3, n.s.). In each case, Organizing was the most important (47% and 43% respectively) followed by Planning (33% and 22% respectively). Again no differences with firm size and critical incidents cited were found ($\chi^2 = 0.47$, df = 3, n.s.). For the larger firms, the two most important critical incidents were those relating to Organizing (50%) and Planning (26%). The corresponding figures for the smaller firms were that of 42% and 30% respectively. Again, no difference between firms in operation for more than a year and those less than a year were found ($\chi^2 = 5.60$, df = 3, n.s.). Organizing was the most often cited issue (38% for firms more than a year and 53% for firms less than a year), followed by Planning (25% for firms less than a year and 34% for firms less than a year).

Matching the Terpstra and Olson and POLC Frameworks

In matching both the POLC and Terpstra and Olson's framework, we found that Human Resource Management accounted for 61% of the organizing critical incidents. These were mostly related to recruitment and turnover (see Table 3a). Recruitment critical incidents included, "recruiting staff that are not capable due to lack of talent in market," "lack of consensus of who to hire," "difficulty of recruiting the right people to do the job," and "difficulty of finding employees with the right attributes." Examples of turnover critical incidents included "employees who left company due to better offers" and "difficulty to retain the right people to do the job" and "manpower shortage and succession problem as staff are on volunteer basis." General Management and Production and Operations Management accounted for 18% and 12% of organizing critical incidents respectively. Together, these three factors accounted for 91% of the organizing critical incidents.

Planning incidents accounted for 28% of the entire sample. Given earlier work by Carroll and Gillen (1987), it appears that the start-ups in this study face a rather high number of critical incidents which could possibly affect their viability in the long run. The main planning critical incident involved General Management. This accounted for 7 out of 19 of the planning critical incidents (or 42%). General Management critical incidents included the lack of management experience, managing and administrative problems. These included "differences in management policies and business directions," "changes in business plan after original revenue model was not viable" and "founder disagrees with consultant over business plan."

Financial critical incidents were ranked second in planning critical incidents. While only 11 out of the 67 critical incidents identified were Financial (both internal and external financing), of these, 7 were in the planning category. Several lead founders mentioned that they had planning critical incidents with regard to obtaining external financials including, "rejected by venture capitalists due to the lack of experience and credibility" and "deciding whether to accept an acquisition offer."

DISCUSSION

The study used critical incidents to reflect the key issues that occupy the attention of entrepreneurs. Critical incidents refer to dominant problems as defined by Kazanjian (1988) but could also include opportunities for the firm. The lead founders could name any incident which they felt to be critical and no framework was provided to them. This approach is an improvement over some research where respondents were asked to identify issues in hypothetical cases (e.g., Dearborn & Simon, 1958; Walsh, 1988). Our sample also differs from previous studies as we interviewed lead founders, not managers enrolled in MBA programs (e.g., Cowan, 1990) or CEOs of firms that have already been in existence for a number of years (e.g., Terpstra & Olson, 1993).

Contrary to findings in the life-cycle literature, critical incidents identified in this study were not in the finance and marketing areas. Instead, issues in human resource management loomed as the greater worry. This is the main finding of both classifications via the POLC model and the Terpstra and Olson framework. However, the results are consistent with research in high-growth firms. Hanks, Watson, Jansen, and Chandler (1994) found that it was not uncommon for high-technology firms to grow from start-up to maturity in a few years. Anderson and Dunkleberg's (1987) study of CEOs of fastest-growing public firms also found that management and employee development were the greatest challenges to maintaining growth. A reason for the findings is that the life cycle of high-tech start-ups may have shortened due to the need for fast growth. Thus, high-tech firms may face a huge ramp up in the types of human and management systems required—crises related to growth stages of firm development.

When we divided the firms into those who had asked for funding and those that had not, critical incidents in human resource management and general management remained as the top two areas of concern. However, in the former, funding issues was the third most often area for critical incidents While this is perhaps not surprising, what is significant is that in the latter, critical incidents in production and operations management became the most important concern. When we divided firms by size (using median split), human resources and general management were the two most important, followed by financial and sales and marketing issues. There was a three-way split among obtaining external financing, sales and marketing and internal financial management. For the smaller firms, production and operations management was the most important followed by general management and human resources management. What surprised us was that production and operations management was more a critical incident for smaller firms than larger firms. We had expected the opposite because larger firms would face greater problems in maintaining quality control. One possibility is that larger firms are further along the organizational life-cycle than the smaller firms and would have established procedures to maintain quality of raw materials and resources. We did not study the life-cycle of the firm but this suggestion is supported by the positive and significant correlation between firms that had asked for funding and firm size. The findings taken together suggest that at the early stage of firm existence, management should give at least equal focus to the three aspects of management, namely, human resources, general, and production and operations.

The low incidence of marketing critical incidents was also not expected. Past studies have shown that gaining market acceptance was one of the key issues for start-ups. Although the reasons for this are beyond the scope of the study, the findings are consistent with Hood and Young (1993) that leadership, communication (both oral and written), human relations and management skills are the four most important skills of an entrepreneur. Production and operations management was found in this study to be one of the critical incidents faced by high-tech start-ups. This is an area that has received little attention in the life cycle and organizational problem literature. One reason is that high-tech firms, particularly those developing products, have to develop the prototype, make it commercially viable and develop efficient ways of manufacturing it.

Although human resource management, in particular the need to attract and retain the best people, is the critical incident found in this study, some may question if this will remain critical given the retrenchment of staff in some Internet and high-tech companies. For instance, in early 2001, Amazon.com retrenched about 15% of its employees. We expect that human resource issues will continue to be a crucial issue. High-tech firms are being formed in emerging areas, such as biotech, where skilled manpower remains scarce. In these firms, human resource should remain important, although the focus might be different. For instance, managing employee expectations and motivating them to work despite the slim chances of getting rich through stock options may be crucial.

One reason why finance was not a major critical incident could be the institutionalized means of getting funding. For instance, the Global Entrepreneurship Monitor (Reynolds et al., 2000) reports that venture capital plays a vital role in providing funding for start-ups. In the first six months of 2000, 80% of venture capital in the United States was invested in firms with Internet-related products or services. In the same year, the Singapore government provided U.S. $1billion of venture capital funds to support high-technology start-ups. The Singapore government also encourages individuals to invest in start-ups, and reduces the risk by allowing these individuals to write-off losses against personal income taxes (Wong et al., 2000).

Since no study to our knowledge used the POLC framework to study start-ups, we could not compare the results to existing studies. However, given the early stage of the firms, it is probably not surprising the critical incidents of deciding what to do (i.e., planning) and how to do it efficiently (i.e., organizing) loomed large in the responses. In addition, as discussed earlier, time devoted to planning and planning skills have implications for the performance of the firms in terms of profitability and productivity (Carroll & Gillen, 1987). The results in the POLC framework were consistent when we divided the sample in different ways, including firm size, year in operation (more than versus less than a year) and whether the firm had asked for external funding. The findings give us greater confidence in concluding that firms face issues of organizing followed by planning at the start-up phase. Hence, this study highlights start-ups' need for more and better planning to enhance their survival. Future research should continue to use the POLC, and collect bottom line measures that could validate studies by Bray et al. (1974), Stagner (1969) and Gillen and Carroll (1985) on the relationship between the POLC functions and firm viability.

Future research can determine if the recent retrenchment by the Internet and high-tech companies might increase the number of control issues faced by start-ups. In some cases, e.g., Amazon.com, both revenues and losses continued to increase. These losses cannot be sustained as the companies could run out of funds. *Barron Magazine* reported in 2000 that 273 of the 339 Internet firms surveyed burned more cash than they took in, spending $1.8 billion in the first three months of 2000. Managing burn rate and expenditures, both control issues, are increasingly important.

In sum, using two validated frameworks, we examined critical incidents faced by high-tech start-ups in Singapore in their first two years of operation and found that contrary to previous research, human resource management are most dominant at the start-up phase. Planning and organizing are also the most crucial activities. These findings suggest that start-ups should develop their human resource systems at the initial planning and organizing phases and should not delay these activities.

ACKNOWLEDGMENTS

We would like to thank the participants of the Conference on Technological Entrepreneurship in the New Millennium and two anonymous reviewers for their helpful comments on earlier drafts of this paper. Funding support by the National University of Singapore is also gratefully acknowledged.

REFERENCES

Anderson, R.L., & Dunkleberg, J.S. (1987). *Managing growing firms.* Englewood Cliffs, NJ: Prentice-Hall.
Barron Magazine. (2000, March). Burning up.
Bray, D.W., Campbell, R.J., & Grant, D.L. (1974). *Formative years in business: A long-term AT&T study of managerial lives.* New York: Wiley.

Carroll, S.J., & Gillen, D.J. (1987). Are the classical management functions useful in describing managerial work? *Academy of Management Review, 12,* 38–51.

Churchill, N., & Lewis, V.L. (1983). The five stages of small business growth. *Harvard Business Review, 61,* 30–50.

Cowan, D.A. (1990). Developing a classification structure of organizational problems: An empirical investigation. *Academy of Management Journal, 33,* 366–390.

Dearborn, D.C., & Simon, H.A. (1958). Selective perception: A note on the departmental identification of executives. *Sociometry, 21,* 140–144.

Economist. (November 11, 2000). Tough at the Top.

Eggers, J.H., Leahy, K.T., & Churchill, N. (1994). Stages of small business growth revisited: Insights into growth path and needed leadership/management skills in low and high growth companies. *Frontiers of Entrepreneurship Research, 14.*

Financial Review. (October 31, 2000). Desperately seeking high-tech talent.

Gillen, D.J., & Carroll, S.J. (1985). Relationship of managerial ability to unit effectiveness in more organic versus more mechanistic departments. *Journal of Management Studies, 22,* 668–676.

Hanks, S.H., Watson, C.J., Jansen, E., & Chandler, G.N. (1993, Winter). Tightening the life-cycle construct: A taxonomic study of growth stage configurations in high-technology organizations. *Entrepreneurship Theory and Practice,* 5–29.

Hood, J.N., & Young, J.E. (1993). Entrepreneurship's requisite areas of development: A survey of top executives in successful entrepreneurial firms. *Journal of Business Venturing, 8,* 115–135.

Kazanjian, R.K. (1988). Relation of dominant problems to stages of growth in technology-based new ventures. *Academy of Management Journal, 31,* 257–279.

Kazanjian, R.K., & Drazin, R. (1990). A stage-contingent model of design and growth for technology based new venture. *Journal of Business Venturing, 5,* 137–150.

Miner, J.B. (1982). *Theories of organizational structure and process.* Chicago: Dryden.

Mintzberg, H. (1971). Managerial work: Analysis from observation. *Management Science, 18,* 97–110.

Reynolds, P.D., Hay, M., Bygrave, W., Camp, S.M., & Autio, E. (2000). *Executive Report, Global Entrepreneurship Monitor 2000.* **City:** Kauffman Center for Entrepreneurial Leadership.

Robbins, S.P., & Coulter, M. (1999). *Management* (6th ed.). Engelwood Cliffs, NJ: Prentice-Hall.

Sexton, D.L., Upton, N.B., Wacholtz, L.E., & McDougall, P.P. (1997). Learning needs of growth-oriented entrepreneurs. *Journal of Business Venturing, 12,* 1–8.

Stagner, R. (1969). Corporate decision making. *Journal of Applied Psychology, 53,* 1–13.

Stearns, T.M., Gilbertson, D.L., & Reynolds, P.D. (1997). The effects of managerial problems on new venture start-ups. *Frontiers of Entrepreneurship Research, 17,* 288–302.

Terpstra, D.E., & Olson, P.D. (1993, Spring). Entrepreneurial start-up and growth: A classification of problems. *Entrepreneurship Theory and Practice,* 5–20.

Tompkins, T.C. (2001). *Cases in management and organizational behavior.* Engelwood Cliffs, NJ: Prentice-Hall.

Wall Street Journal. (1992, October 16).

Walsh, J.P. (1988). Selectivity and selective perception: An investigation of managers' belief structures and information processing. *Academy of Management Journal, 31*, 873–896.

Wong, P., Foo M., & Wong, F. (2000). *Global entrepreneurship monitor, Singapore executive report.* CMIT & NSTB.

Yin, R.K. (1994). *Case study research* (2nd ed.). Thousand Oaks, CA: Sage.

CHAPTER 10

A PROCESS STUDY OF NEW VENTURE CREATION AT AN INTERNET START-UP COMPANY

Rueylin Hsiao and Chee-Leong Chong

ABSTRACT

This qualitative study examines the process of new venture creation in an Internet start-up. It traces in detail the evolution of different business models and the associated changes in products, alliances and outcomes of the new venture. The aim is to report how the company responded to new environmental changes, assessed its progress, and adapted to new competitors. Most important, the findings highlight a contrast between traditional views on new venture creation and the experience of the selected Internet start-up. They indicate an alternative pattern of new venture creation characterized by business model renewal, rapid scale-up and accelerated adaptation. This perspective adds valuable insights to the theoretical understanding of new venture creation by relating to the emerging e-commerce context.

INTRODUCTION

The phenomenon of dot.com (Internet start-up) growth requires entrepreneurs and researchers to reconsider the task of new venture creation. Market analysts have claimed three particularly important aspects of the new dot.com enthusiasm. First, small start-ups can now shorten the painstaking learning curve and enter global markets at affordable costs; second, dot.com firms need not wait for years to build a customer base of thousands but can gain millions of customers within months; third, small ventures can achieve market valuations as high as that of established corporations. Market analysts also suggest that a paradigm shift is taking place so that the traditional rules of competition are no longer applicable. Although these assessments may not fully reflect the reality of incorporating a dot.com, they do indicate that the subject of dot.com new ventures is an area that requires systematic examination.

At present, there remains a conspicuous lack of empirical studies apart from a few anecdotal accounts (e.g., Hagel & Armstrong, 1997; Werbach, 2000). Increasingly, there is a need to explore the entrepreneurial process and examine the functions, activities and actions associated with the creation of dot.com ventures. Harvey and Evans (1995) further suggest that researchers should treat entrepreneurship as a dynamic system and adopt a more holistic analysis of the process elements of start-ups.

This motivates us to explore the dynamic process of new venture creation in a selected Internet startup. We gathered data from Media-Ring.com (the first IPO-listed dot.com start-up in Singapore specializing in Internet Telephony) since its incorporation in 1999. The primary advantage of such a qualitative case study is that it provides rich data for an indepth understanding of a specific case, thereby enabling further theoretical development of the phenomenon under study (Yin, 1989). This method is also suitable for exploring underdeveloped subject areas when researchers need to identify theoretical constructs and build (rather than test) formal theories.

The paper is structured as follows. First, we review the current literature on the venture creation process, which offer a conceptual background. Secondly, we explain the use of case study method and process analysis, which guide our data collection and analysis. Thirdly, we describe an analytical framework developed inductively from the field data. This framework guides the tracing of the case in real time with reference to four tracks: context, business model, alliances and outcome. Finally, we discuss how our results relate to those of previous studies by comparing traditional views of venture creation with the experience of the selected dot.com. We also summarize practical lessons based on our field observation for prospective dot.com entrepreneurs.

NEW VENTURE CREATION PROCESS

There is a growing interest in process studies in the current literature on entrepreneurship (Burgelman, 1983; Kamm et al., 1990). Researchers have come to acknowledge the benefit of process studies as a complement to the hypothesis-testing, factor-based approach in the venture creation literature (e.g., Herron & Sapienza, 1992; Shane, 1994). A review of process-related studies reveals that there are in fact four broad categories of venture creation model: static frameworks, stage models, quantification sequences, and process dynamics. These four approaches offer diverse perspectives that enhance our understanding of venturing. We will review each of them in turn in order to provide a conceptual orientation for the present study, which emphasizes the fourth category.

First, *static frameworks* characterize the overall process of venture creation without examining the sequence of activities involved. Typically, this type of process model consists of a limited set of variables connected by speculative causal links (Greenberger & Sexton, 1988). For example, Gartner (1985) suggests a new venture creation model that includes four variables: the characteristics of entrepreneurs, the organization of the new venture, the environment around the new venture, and the new venture launch. Busenitz and Lau (1996) develop a venture creation model based on a cognitive perspective, explaining why some individuals across different cultures tend to be more prolific than others in starting new ventures. While these studies are process-oriented, the resulting frameworks are static and do not capture the specific sequences of activities that occur during venture creation.

Secondly, some researchers divide the venture creation process into a priori stages or phases. For example, Webster (1976) proposes a life-cycle model which covers the pre-venture set-up, the period of struggling, and the venture termination. VanderWerf (1993) develops a stage model to understand product innovation activities during a new venture creation. Bhave (1994) suggests a process model of venture creation divided into three stages: the opportunity stage, the technology set-up stage, and the exchange stage. Although stage models describe the process of new venture creation, one major weakness is that they tend to narrow the scope of investigation, and researchers often find that the temporal order of events does not fit the proposed stages.

The third approach uses *quantification* techniques to examine the sequences of events that occur over a venture's history. For example, MacMillan et al. (1987) examined 150 proposals submitted by entrepreneurs in order to understand the venture screening process. Carter et al. (1996) studied 71 entrepreneurs to reveal the activities initiated during the start-up process, and they identified three broad activity profiles: up-and-running, still-trying, and given-up. The analysis of event sequences allows researchers to describe the processes that actually lead to the outcome of interests. But this quantification approach does not allow researchers to understand the dynamics of how antecedent conditions shape the present and the emergent future within the process.

The fourth approach is *process dynamics*, which often employs qualitative methods to examine how and why variations in context and process shape outcomes such as the pace of change and the firm's performance (Pettigrew, 1992, p. 7). For example, Gersick (1994) maps out the strategic change process of one new venture and discovers two forms of pacing: one time-based, with reorientations initiated at temporal milestones; the other event-based, with actions initiated when the right event occurred. Badguerahanian and Abetti (1995) offer an interpretative account of Merlin-Gerin, a leading French manufacturer of electrical apparatus, over a 15-year period. From the process story, they develop theories that explain the success and demise of this business. Similarly, Greening et al. (1996) investigate the process of geographical expansions in small start-ups and develop theories that elaborate venture growth.

These process-oriented studies decompose data into successive adjacent periods in order to enable an explicit analysis of how the actions of one period lead to changes in the context that affect actions in the subsequent period (Langley, 1999, p. 703). One key purpose of process analysis is to build theories from the ground up through the process data that have been gathered. Such theories adopt the process as the phenomenon of interest. Therefore, a theory emerging from process methods can often contribute to theory building and also offer practical insights. For example, Mezias and Kuperman (2000) examine in great detail the collective process of entrepreneurship in the context of the formation of new industries. By examining the community dynamics of the American film industry, they are able to formulate two propositions that help us to rethink the role of community in entrepreneurship. By examining the social process, their study suggests that individual entrepreneurs may be more successful in the venturing process if they can leverage on their social networks.

The present study therefore has two primary purposes. First, it seeks to examine new venture creation process in the e-commerce emergent context. Secondly, most current studies on venture creation of Internet start-up seem to emphasize recipe models, anecdotal stories, and practical advice (e.g., Earle & Keen, 2000; Fisher, 2000; Kambil et al., 2000). Thus far, the actual process of dot.com venture creation remains insufficiently understood. For this reason, this study attempts to advance the theory of entrepreneurship by examining the process of new venture creation in a selected dot.com. The purpose is to describe this emerging context's process dynamics and to develop relevant theoretical propositions.

RESEARCH METHODS

The Research Setting

Mediacom Technologies, a start-up incubated by KRDL (Kent Ridge Digital Lab, Singapore), was founded in 1993. The company holds several cutting-edge patents of Internet-related applications such as electronic transparency, real-time application sharing and file transfer. In February 1999, the entrepreneurs identified the business opportunity presented by Internet Telephony and decided to transform the high-tech company into a dot.com. Within nine months, MediaRing.com (hereafter MediaRing) became the first dot.com company to be listed on the Stock Exchange main board in Singapore.

Since its incorporation, MediaRing's Voice-over-Net products and services have received the highest ratings by TUCOWS, ZDNet and Download Planet. In terms of "user stickiness" (i.e., how often online users visit a web site), MediaRing.com has outperformed some well-known names such as America Online and Net2Phone. MediaRing quickly became a recognizable name in voice communications over the Internet. Since IPO launch, MediaRing has adjusted its business models to respond to the dynamic market challenges.

We select this case because it provides a relevant context in which distinct periods of new venture creation can be identified. It must be stressed that the case is not intended to represent a successful example of dot.com entrepreneurship. Rather, the purpose is to examine the new venture process resulted from ongoing strategic responses and environmental challenges. By so doing, we attempt to understand how this selected dot.com achieved survival in the face of turbulent Internet competition.

Process Analysis Process Methods

The case is examined by means of two qualitative methods: the case study method (Yin, 1989) and process analysis (Langley, 1999; Pettigrew, 1990, 1997). We use an in-depth case study approach because it has the potential to develop contextual details and thereby provide a rich understanding of our research question. It also provides a way to add incrementally to more robust theory development (Dyer & Wilkins, 1991). We adopt process analysis because it helps us to understand the temporal dynamics within the process of new venture creation.

Data collection. Our main informants consisted of three groups: top operating teams (excluding the vice-president level as these executives were not involved directly in the operation), operational staff (including

senior managers and marketing/technical personnel), and business partners. Although we also interviewed customers who used MediaRing's services, this only helped us to appreciate the product characteristics. We
conducted semi-structured interviews, each lasting for two to three hours
(the scheme is shown in Table 1). One important note is that our research
emphasized the venture creation process of the company and not customers' perceptions of MediaRing's products.

The first author also stayed in the company and participated in three
internal meetings lasting for three to four hours each. We also examined
internal archives, with a focus on the company's IPO proposal, news
releases, and quarterly reports to investors. The multiple sources of data
collection helped to enhance the data integrity. We conducted fieldwork in
a real-time tracing from October 1999 to November 2000 (we visit the company in average every three weeks). We also traced events retrospectively
(from February to October 1999) in order to understand the activities that
took place during the pre-launch period.

Table 1.   Persons Interviewed, by Job Titles

	Number	Frequency
CEO	1	3 times
Chief Technology Officer	1	2 times
Chief MIS Officer	1	3 times
Chief Officer of Web Operation	1	2 times
Chief Marketing Officer	1	2 times
Chief Officer of Internet Lifestyle	1	2 times
Senior Managers	6	Once each
Marketing and PR staff	4	at different
Technical (R&D) staff	8	time periods
Business Partners	4	
	28	

Data analysis.   We adopted an inductive approach to the examination
of the field data. At first, we tried not to rely too much on the current literature on new venture creation in order to develop concepts and theories
grounded in the field data (Glaser & Strauss, 1967, p. 37). Data were collected until distinct patterns had clearly emerged and additional data no
longer added to the refinement of the concepts.

Business model is an emergent theoretical element which is used exten-
sively in our study. Since the concept of a dot.com "business model" is relatively new, we begin this study by adopting the definition offered by Afuha
and Tucci (2001, p. 4):

A business model is about the value that a firm offers its customers, the scope of products/services it offers to which segment of customers, its sources of revenue, the prices it puts on the value offered its customers, the activities it must perform in offering that value, the capabilities these activities rest on.

According to this definition, the renewal of business models will thus impact on pricing and revenue, and will define options for how a firm can adopt a given product/service in the online market (Applegate & Collura, 2000).

In order to understand the dynamics of this dot.com venture, we analyze the new venture activities with the aim of describing the major transitions in business models. The data analysis investigates the natural occurrence of activities within the dot.com entrepreneurial process. Inductively, four theoretical constructs emerged and were used to document the venture activities: context, business models, business growth and outcome (a method suggested in Van de Ven et al., 1999). The first construct (context) refers to the internal and external conditions that trigger strategic actions; the second construct aims to capture the variations in business models and the associated adjustment of products and services; the third construct traces how the dot.com achieved rapid growth by setting up business and technological alliances; and the fourth construct describes the outcome of the overall performance in each time period.

RESEARCH FINDINGS AND ANALYSIS

The research findings are presented in four time periods to show how MediaRing had to respond constantly to market challenges by renewing its business models. A more detailed mapping of MediaRing's business growth is shown in Figure 3.

Period 1: e-Telephony Model (February to December 1999)

Context.   Internet telephony, also known as Voice-Over-IP (Internet Protocol), provides a low-cost alternative to the traditional phone. Using Internet telephony, long-distance calls can cost as little as 3 cents a minute. Increasingly, voice communication is becoming an integral part of the Internet experience. New venture financing for Internet start-ups was active in early 1999 in Singapore. In part, this was due to the enviable record of early dot.com successes in the U.S. market. In both the public and private sectors, and for both large and small firms, Internet venture incubation attracted the attention of every aspiring entrepreneur.

It was in this context that MediaRing decided to convert its communication-related products, such as video conferencing, into a dot.com venture, with financial support from both the public and private sectors. However, although the enthusiasm for dot.com ventures was high, most entrepreneurs had few ideas what should be the focus of performance. Most market analysts considered a critical mass of users as a useful indicator to evaluate the fitness of a dot.com. It was common knowledge that the stock market often rewarded dot.com start-ups with high market valuation even if they did not show profits (e.g., the case of Amazon.com). Therefore, many venture capitalists and entrepreneurs believed that the key need for dot.com was to gain the critical mass of users (not paying customers) in order to launch IPO (Initial Price Offering) and survive in the face of intensive competitions.

In October 1999, one month before the IPO launch, MediaRing was under stress to show a rapid scale-up of users in order to win confidence from market analysts and venture funding parties. Therefore, MediaRing's primary target was to attract as many online visitors as possible to demonstrate the potential for IPO.

Business model.   MediaRing's initial success stemmed from a business model which generated online advertising revenue through MediaRing Talk™, an Internet Telephony technology. MediaRing Talk™ created two major products: VoizMail and ValueFone. VoizMail is a voicemail messaging system. It enables MediaRing users to send voicemail messages to any party with an email address by simply clicking on an icon on the MediaRing client software interface. The recipient is prompted by an email message to click on an Internet link to retrieve the voicemail message at the MediaRing website. ValueFone is a PC-to-Phone system which allows users to make calls from their personal computers to telephones anywhere in the world via the Internet, at a cost of a local phone call.

To prepare a viable IPO launch, MediaRing needed to show a strong stream of site visits. The company decided to offer the downloaded software and the Internet telephony infrastructure free of charge in order to attract online visits. In October 1999, the top team of MediaRing further applied the Internet telephony to provide different versions of e-services. Five more services were added: TalkZone, Voice Persona, Co-Webbing, MyOrganizer, and E-Conferencing (see Table 2 for details of these services). The top team intended to expand the product line to attract more traffic to MediaRing's website.

Business growth.   The challenge was to scale up site traffic. To achieve this, MediaRing swiftly set up alliances with three computer manufacturers—Simens AG (in February 1999), Legend (March 1999) and Compaq (in June 1999)—and bundled VoizMail and ValueFone with the computers sold by these three companies. Global expansion was another strategy to

Table 2.   Extending e-Services

TalkZone. Participants can anonymously post their nicknames, personal profiles and interests at the TalkZone web page. When a TalkZone participant wishes to engage in voice chat, the web page allows the initiating participant to select and invite another participant to join based on that participant's profile and listed interests. The invited TalkZone participant can then choose to decline or accept the invitation.

Voice Persona. The features allow users to disguise their voice by modulating it to five disguised pitches when making a voice call or creating a voicemail message. This option seeks to enhance the entertainment value of MediaRing's voice communication experience.

Co-Webbing. This service seeks to enable two MediaRing users simultaneously to visit the same websites while engaged in a PC-to-PC conversation. This is to enhance the voice communication experience of the users as they can discuss and share the information they view on the web sites.

MyOrganizer. This is a web-based personal organizer which enables a MediaRing user to organize call contacts into user-defined categories. The software also transfer the call contact into the user's personal organizer.

E-Conferencing. This conferencing service allows up to 96 MediaRing users to engage in real-time voice communication with up to four persons speaking simultaneously during the conference session. To participate in the conferencing service, a MediaRing user is required to access a participating website and click on the web site provided by the conference organizer.

---

scale up the site traffic. By exchanging membership, MediaRing collaborated with Mail.ru (targeted at the Russian market), SINA.com (aimed at the Chinese market), Community Connect Inc. (an Asian-American community portal) and Daum Communications (for the Korean market).

MediaRing also faced heightening competition from other Internet telephony service providers, such as Net2Phone, iBasis (formerly VIP Calling), G3 (owned by Global Gateway Group Consortium), GlobalVoice, ICG Netcom, I-Link Worldwide, and Globalnet. The company also had to complete three areas of technological enhancement. First, it transferred the "Modem Bridge" technology from GVC (a Taiwanese Modem manufacturer) with the aim of improving the quality of transmission for those who use the modem as a medium to access the Internet. Secondly, MediaRing improved the voice quality of its products by working with Delta Three (for PC-to-Phone systems) and Ericsson (for the API platform, an infrastructure to enable voice transmission over the Internet). Thirdly, another alliance with Conexant System allowed the latest version of its modem chipsets to work with MediaRing's software. This enabled users to connect modems to a telephone handset and initiate conversations-over-net (instead of using a microphone). Moreover, modem manufacturers who bought Conexant's chipsets were able to offer VoizMail and ValueFone to their customers.

In October 1999, MediaRing initiated a potential collaboration with IBM on a new product idea: RingCash (an online coupon). Online users from IBM's online shopping mall could use RingCash to purchase items without submitting credit cards. Although RingCash was not yet a fully-fledged idea, this incentive program was designed to build trust with online shoppers. Ultimately, this IBM alliance brought reputation and drove site traffic to MediaRing.

To ensure that all these e-service products functioned effectively, Media-Ring collaborated with Creative Technologies (a sound card maker) to enhance the technology of MediaRing Talk™. This alliance also allowed MediaRing's software to be installed together with Creative Technologies' software driver (which boosted its sound interface card). In November 1999, MediaRing set up another alliance, with China Netcom and CE-INFOCOM Network, which gave the company a huge exposure to the Chinese market. Subsequently, MediaRing aligned with ITXC.net, a company that hosted PC-to-Phone services to more than 73 cities around the world in order to provide an infrastructure that could alleviate MediaRing's traffic load. The additional benefit was that this alliance also offered MediaRing an opportunity to gain access to ITXC.net's worldwide customer base.

Outcome. Within the first seven months (by early September 1999), MediaRing had created its dot.com venture and had quickly boosted its growth in membership to about two million registered users around the world. Although there were no clear revenue incomes, this impressive critical mass of users was a key thrust to help MediaRing launch IPO. On 19 November 1999, MediaRing was listed on the Singapore Stock Exchange and thus completed the IPO journey. By the end of 1999, MediaRing had managed to obtain a user base of 2.8 million.

Period 2: E-Advertising (January to March 2000)

Context. More and more dot.com entrepreneur began to consider online advertising as a major source of revenue. Advertisers also came to recognize the value of Internet telephony in interacting with potential customers, evaluating the advertising result, and renewing advertising messages with greater frequency. MediaRing faced a growing number of voice-over-IP service providers who rivaled its own PC-to-PC voice communication capability. The range of products included Microsoft's NetMeeting, Vocaltec Communications' Internet Phone, Netscape's Cool Talk, Tribal Voice's Pow Wow, and NetSpeak's Webphone. Other telecommunication equipment providers were also sources of competition. Companies like Ericsson, Alcatel, Cisco, and Lucent planned to build telephony networks and gateway devices to provide voice communication over the Internet.

These developments would influence the technology used for voice transmission over the Internet (e.g., in terms of voice transmission quality).

On the market side, most dot.com investors became less tolerant of profit loss and demanded to see stable revenue streams. To satisfy the stock market's expectation, dot.com entrepreneurs constantly had to announce novel business models. The expectation of revenue stream and innovation on business model gradually became two major indicators in the dot.com industry. They significantly influenced the strategic agenda of MediaRing's top team.

Business model. As traditional telephone charges came down and new competitors emerged, MediaRing decided to adjust to a new business model known as e-Advertising. The top team hoped to leverage on MediaRing's online community (i.e., user base) and attract online advertising. In early 2000, MediaRing's main source of revenue began to shift to sales of advertising slots. Its advertising revenue was categorized into streamed advertisements and sponsorship arrangements. The former offered a series of advertisements that are delivered through the RingCast window (a software product, see Figure 1) to users while they are using Internet telephony. Sponsorship arrangements enabled sponsors to post advertisements through the RingCast for a certain agreed period. The key advertisers included Pacific Century CyberWorks, Creative, and Lycos Bertelsmann.

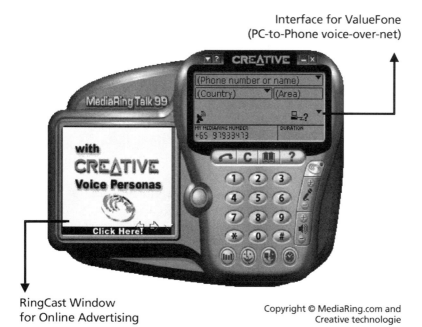

Interface for ValueFone
(PC-to-Phone voice-over-net)

RingCast Window
for Online Advertising

Copyright © MediaRing.com and
Creative technologie

Figure 1.   RingCast—Online advertising (as appeared on the computer screen).

The e-Advertising business model had a different focus than the e-Telephony model. While the latter emphasized the advance features of technology to attract investors, the former focused on securing a stable revenue stream from online advertisers. Under this business model, MediaRing still offered all the voice-related services free to online users, while it leveraged on the online community to attract advertisers. With a 30-plus team in the MIS (Management Information Systems) department, MediaRing helped advertisers to build up segmented databases and deliver unique advertising contents to their target customers (this was known as one-to-one marketing). In this way, MediaRing acted less like a technology firm but more like an advertising agency by leveraging on its voice-over-IP technology.

Business growth.   The business model based on e-Advertising required MediaRing to sustain a steady growth in its customer base in order to gain advertisers' confidence. In January 2000, MediaRing had a chance to help SeedNet (Taiwan) provide online advertisements for presidential candidates in Taiwan, where they packaged voicemail services as a tool to communicate with prospective voters. This voice campaign via the Internet was unprecedented in Taiwan, and the use of this unique technology resulted in a rapid growth of registered users.

Later, MediaRing again employed a product-bundling strategy with companies such as Gigabyte Technology (Taiwan) and HP (Pavilion personal computers) to enlarge its customer base. In order to expand further to the Australian and Chinese markets, the company also aligned with LookSmart.com (Australia) and CNT (China). This achieved a synergy with these two firms and provided a smooth entry into the two markets.

The size of site traffic was a necessary condition to attract online advertisers, but it also gave rise to the need of a robust infrastructure. In early January, MediaRing collaborated with Bell Systems to upgrade the technology platform. Later, two more new ideas were proposed: first, to enable users to turn text e-mail into voice data via VoizMail (working with IBM); and secondly, to link up VoizMail with ICQ, an online chatting software, so as to attract the huge base of existing ICQ users (collaborating with Shenzen Tencent Computer Systems, China).

Outcome.   The result of this growth was astronomical. By the end of 1999, the number of China-based users had more than doubled from 5% to 11% (5.9 million) of the total user base. MediaRing's revenue income reached $2.5 million and its market capitalization reached $670 million in spite of an expected loss in 2000 of $34 million.

Period 3: E-Commerce (April to June 2000)

Context.   One major problem for all Internet start-ups is the issue of intellectual property rights. This problem was particularly alarming in the U.S. market in 2000, when the level of competition was growing rapidly. In February 2000, Multi-Tech Systems, a U.S. company, sued MediaRing for alleged infringement of its patents. This involved a copyright dispute over a hardware design for Internet telephony products.

These crises made MediaRing's top team consider a business transformation: to position MediaRing as an Internet telephony service provider rather than a high-tech firm. Increasingly, while the investors demanded to see a steady growth of revenue, the heightened competition in online advertising also slowed down the revenue incomes. MediaRing now had to consider other sources of revenue. The solution was to exploit the e-commerce (electronic commerce) opportunities as more and more companies began to realize the benefit of Internet telephony.

Business model.   The copyright disputes and pressures from investors urged MediaRing to shift to a less technology-oriented business model and concentrate more on the e-commerce model. With the large membership base (buyer side) and advertisers (seller side), the top team aimed to run a virtual mega-shopping mall. The idea was to recruit business partners (mainly from the current advertisers) and to sell their products or services over the Internet through MediaRing. For this business model to work, the major income would have to come from commissions from the global transactions between buyers and sellers.

The top team perceived that this was the right timing for MediaRing to extend the RingCash project to enable e-commerce (see period 2). Online surfers could use RingCash coupons to shop around. Early participants included IBM, Creative Technology, Epson, Canon, and Kodak. MediaRing also integrated its existing products (RingCast and other e-Services) to promote the shopping mall. It expected to generate a revenue stream from the commissions derived from every online transaction made. However, it would generally direct customers' complaints about defective goods to the principal vendors.

Business growth.   To make the e-commerce model viable, MediaRing decided to create a global brand and focus on research and development in technology. Global expansion could quickly obtain economies of scale for its e-commerce business model. For MediaRing, this meant capturing the China and U.S. market share by leveraging on its large user base in these two countries.

In April 2000, a major joint partnership with ITXC, CNC, GTE, and CNT offered free Internet call services to the Chinese market. This alliance leveraged on the partners' integrated network infrastructure, and offered exclusive access to CNC's marketing channels. Similarly, MediaRing set up another joint venture with TransCosmos (Japan) in order to gain access to Japanese online users.

In June 2000, MediaRing formed another alliance, with USAGreetings.com, in order to transfer a technology that supported voice-enabled greeting cards. The purpose was to provide customer relationship management for the e-commerce model. Customers could receive seasonal voice-enabled greeting cards as well as product information and special sales notices from MediaRing's online shopping mall.

Outcome. By the end of June 2000, MediaRing had recruited 7.6 million registered users (including 32% in the United States and 50% in Asia). Although the company managed to grow to $7.1 million revenue (with a major share coming from e-commerce transactions), the loss was close to $21.7 million.

Period 4: E-Builder (July to October 2000)

Context. The middle of 2000 heralded a new era of competition for MediaRing. As voice-based e-mail became more an integrated experience of daily communication, most of the telecommunications carriers (such as AT&T, MCI, British Telecom, and Deutsche Telecom) began to participate in the voice-over-net market. These telecommunication companies competed by lowering the charge for local and international telephone calls. Companies like AT&T Jens (a Japanese affiliate of AT&T) and British Telecom also built network infrastructure to provide Internet telephony within limited geographical areas. Thus, the dot.com players no longer had a cost advantage.

The competition in online advertising and e-commerce also increased. When all kinds of dot.coms poured into the online market, online advertising charges also dropped drastically. To gain profit from online advertising was difficult even for major players like Yahoo. Even worse than this competition was the consolidation of the Nasdaq market in March-April 2000, leading to the demise of many dot.coms. Investors generally began to lose confidence in information intermediary players (i.e., dot.coms that sold information-based products/services and had no physical presence). MediaRing was severely affected by this dot.com crash.

Business model. In early July 2000, the top team undertook another reorientation of MediaRing business model to e-Builder. One important reason for doing this was to reposition MediaRing not as a pure dot.com but as a technology company capable of offering an Internet-based voice solution. MediaRing also realized that it had to avoid direct competition with telecom giants (like Singtel) and many pure dot.coms. The emphasis was shifted from general customers (online users) to corporate customers by providing Internet Voice Services. The key aim was to generate quickly a steady revenue stream to boost business growth. The business idea behind this was to leverage on the previous products and services for revenue generation and reorient marketing efforts to corporate accounts.

Figure 2 illustrates MediaRing's e-Builder model, which divides the marketing efforts into three segments: Free Consumers, Paying Consumers and Corporate Accounts. This e-Builder model invovled three operational logics. First, MediaRing distributed the existing e-Services free to online users in order to gain exposure and enlarge its installation base. The large customer base in turn would help to attract online advertising. The free service would also help MediaRing to identify problems through users' feedbacks and thus improve the technology so as to generate "proven solutions." Secondly, MediaRing promoted ValueFone (with local charges for long-distance telephone calls) through technology providers by product bundling. ValueFone then created revenues from users who made cross-continental telephone calls via MediaRing. Thirdly, all the e-Services (voice-over-net) were offered to corporate clients according to their special needs. The underlying purpose was to sell the proven solutions of "Internet Voice Services" to corporate clients.

This new business model generated revenue from three sources (see Figure 2): first, advertising revenue from RingCast services; secondly, telephony revenue from general users and corporate accounts through prepaid calling cards (including PC-to-Phone, Phone-to-Phone); thirdly, from messaging services, which included installation, hosting and licensing fees

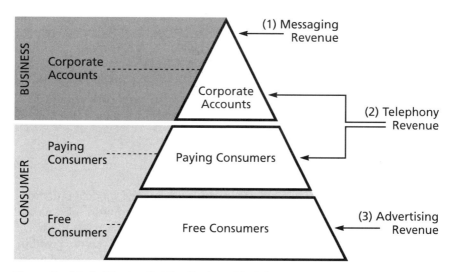

Figure 2.   MediaRing's e-Builder Business Model.

(MediaRing charged set-up and usage fees for telephony solutions). The underlying rationale of this e-Builder model was a "free-to-profit" strategy. As the CEO explained:

> Our concept [of the e-Builder model] is to leverage our installed base: 7.6 million customers worldwide. We offer free product download and use it to attract more exposure. In the meantime, we also use the general users to experiment with our voice-related products. We will find out their needs and the potential flaws in our products. We can then package the "proven" solutions and sell it for $10–30K... And this is our Internet strategy—you have to be free to be profitable.

Business growth. The e-Builder model required MediaRing to enhance its technology and provide more product options for corporate clients. Therefore, in this period, most activities were centered on technology alliances. For example, MediaRing collaborated with Askey to develop voice-enabled modems, with IBM to design VoizLetter (a voice-enabled e-Newsletter for corporate communications), and with TransCosmos to set up telephony-enabled Call Centers. Moreover, in the hope of expanding into the Chinese market, MediaRing extended its collaboration with China Netcom and offered sales of prepaid ValuePhone cards.

Outcome. Under the new business model, MediaRing gradually created a new market in providing Internet-based voice solutions to corporate accounts. The shift to the e-Builder model also boosted investors' confidence. By the end of September 2000, MediaRing had achieved a revenue of S$22m, with a net loss of S$37m. However, its market capitalization had reached $209m.

DISCUSSION

Based on the process model presented above, we first suggest three theoretical implications of new venture creation with reference to strategic focus, business growth and pace of change.

Implications for Theory

This research provides an exploratory study of a process model of new venture creation of an Internet start-up. We investigate the nature of dot.com entrepreneurship and observe the strategic agenda that is necessary to survive in high-velocity environments. To better understand the new venture creation process in the Internet context, we propose to analyze three theoretical propositions: strategy focus, business growth and pace of change (see Table 3).

Table 3.   Three Propositions on New Venture Creation

Three propositions	New venture creation: current understanding	What we observe in the dot.com context
Strategic Focus	New ventures aim to develop a sustainable strategy based on a durable business model (e.g. Porter, 1985).	New ventures achieve strategic changes oriented by renewable business models.
Business Growth	New ventures grow organically by prudent planning (e.g. acquire physical assets such as McDonald outlets; see, Greening, Barringer, and Macy, 1996).	Rapid growth by scale-up (e.g. by exploiting existing technology and aligning with partners).
Pace of Change	New ventures devise planned/emergent strategy by years (e.g. Bhide, 1996; Mintzberg and Waters, 1985).	Accelerated adaptation of business models by days; cf. the adaptation in the computer industry by weeks (Eisenhardt, 1989).

Strategic focus.   Researchers of new venture creation suggest that entrepreneurs need to formulate a sustainable strategy in order to achieve a competitive position (Eisenhardt & Schoonhoven, 1990; Romanelli, 1989; Stuart & Abetti, 1987). These positioning strategies have been classified in different ways. For example, Miles et al. (1978) suggest four strategic types named as defender, prospector, analyzer and reactor. Porter (1985) proposes three positioning strategies in terms of low cost, market focus and product differentiation. Maidique and Patch (1982) distinguish between first mover advantage, cost-minimization (via economies of scale in production), fast-follower, and niche strategy (identifying specific segments with products). On the basis of this thinking, entrepreneurs have to find a sustainable strategy anchored on a durable business model (Bhide, 1996, p. 125). The traditional view on new venture creation is that entrepreneurs should develop sustainable strategies according to the market competition but maintain a durable business model.

In this case, a first glance at periods 1–4 suggests that the main strategy was simply to diversify from narrow revenue sources (e.g., advertising) to include other sources (such as messaging and Internet-based long distance telephony). However, on a closer examination, we observe an alternative proposition in which entrepreneurs begin to think more about business models to guide their complex response to environmental challenges. For instance, in period 1 MediaRing was in a context where the launch of IPO required a critical mass of users. The e-Telephony model thus had a technology focus and the products/services were offered to attract site traffic. Shifting to period 2, MediaRing had to react to the stock market's changing expectation (with a focus on revenue stream). The e-Advertising model required a new product platform (RingCast) in order to integrate the e-services provided in period 1.

In addition, the emphasis on setting up alliances also changed accordingly (e.g., MediaRing worked with Creative Technologies to develop software that enhanced web advertising features). Another contextual change then emerged in period 3, and required MediaRing to show more revenue generation strength and depend less on advertising incomes. The top team then had to leverage on the two online communities (users and advertisers) and devise an e-Commerce model that created revenue from transactions.

Finally, the stock market expectation changed again in period 4. The market analysts expected dot.com firms to show profitability. Pure dot.com players began to be seen as lack of sustainability. MediaRing had to embark on a new business model (e-Builder). It had to act more like an application service provider specializing in Internet-based voice solutions to demonstrate a physical presence, and less as a pure dot.com. The shift to the e-Builder model required MediaRing to minimize incomes from previous e-services and focus more on Internet infrastructure and server hosting capabilities. MediaRing then had to redefine its target customers (from general users to corporate customers) in order to make the e-Builder model viable in driving profits.

Thus, competing in the dot.com context requires entrepreneurs to rethink the "business model" in order to reshape their organizations, to change the way they interact with customers and partners, and to pioneer new ways of collecting revenues and earning profits. This points to a new pattern of new venture creation that requires systematic investigation by researchers. MediaRing's experience encourages us to think about *business model renewal*, rather than simply developing a sustainable strategic position.

Dot.com entrepreneurs need to focus on their business model rather than strategy for two reasons. First, in contrast to traditional strategy formation, entrepreneurs employ a business model as a guide to navigate the uncertainties and rapid changes in the dot.com environment. Business models help entrepreneurs to develop strategies to cope with competition and contextual variations (as shown in Periods 2, 3, and 4 in this case). It will be difficult for entrepreneurs to respond to environmental change if they depend on static strategy positions.

We also observe that entrepreneurs used business models as a strategic framework to create value for customers and investors by enhancing the company's Internet-based services (for free) and leveraging on the network effect (by rapid scale-up a critical mass of users through strategic alliances). Additionally, entrepreneurs used business models to innovate different versions of e-services that could transmit voice information (this versioning strategy is discussed in Shapiro, 1998). We also observe Media-Ring's strategic response in pioneering new business models in order to generate new sources of revenue and renew its distinctiveness as new forms of competition emerged. For example, MediaRing had to shift from the e-Advertising model to the e-Commerce model in order to respond to the increased competition from portal players and Internet telephony providers.

As a result, it can be seen that managing a dot.com venture requires entrepreneurs to adapt constantly by renewing their business models in order to identify a strategy that builds upon previous competence and strength. Moreover, new business models provide a useful mental framework that entrepreneurs can employ to guide innovation on products/services, to respond to market challenges, and to define directions for business growth (see Table 4).

Table 4.   New Venture Creation through the Renewal of Business Models

Business models	Purpose of change	Key performance measures
Period 1: e-Telephony	Launch IPO and achieve high market valuation	Site traffic (enlarge user base by offering free services)
Period 2: e-Advertising	Maintain rapid growth and generate revenues	Advertising revenues (attract advertisers through a critical mass of users and product and service extension)
Period 3: e-Commerce	Build business networks and generate revenues	Commissions based on transaction fees (leverage on the communities of users and advertisers)
Period 4: e-Builder	Provide voice solution to business sectors and generate revenues	Profit and sustainability (show physical presence and position as a high-tech dot.com)

Business growth.   Previous studies of venture growth suggest that most ventures have to grow organically, using operating profits from early customers to fund expansion through, for example, product innovation, acquisition, franchising, and geographic expansion (e.g., Greening, Barringer, & Macy, 1996; Orsino, 1994; Roberts, 1980). Underlying this assumption is a rational growth model in which new ventures have sufficient control over the required resources to escape the tight control of external constraints. Thus they can engage in strategic choices to grow new ventures (see a review of this argument in Burgelman, 1983). For new start-ups, entrepreneurs are encouraged to undertake "prudent growth," i.e., pace business growth with the ability to control the level of expertise, training activity, and careful planning (Greening et al., 1996; Schuman et al., 1985).

This study identifies a different pattern of business growth characterized by rapid scale-up through strategic alliances. The dot.com has to achieve rapid growth in terms of site traffic in order to maintain market expectation and derive future revenues. The real difficulty lies in achieving this rapid growth within a relatively short time frame, aiming at a change cycle of approximately 100 days. The objective of business growth is to enlarge the virtual marketplace through many alliances in a matter of days, rather than expanding physical outlets over years.

Dot.com entrepreneurs thus need to target two strategic goals: first, they need to exploit existing competence in exchange for complementary know-how; secondly, they have to grow by assimilating memberships with other dot.coms. In this case study, MediaRing emphasized maintaining growth by transferring new technical know-how from partners (technology alliances) and exchanging new services with partners (business alliances). Figure 3 categorizes the two streams of alliances and outcomes over the four periods.

MediaRing employed a network synergy method (a concept which is relevant to network externalities as discussed in Kaufman et al., 2000; Katz & Shapiro, 1992; Riggins, Kriebel, & Mukhopadhyay, 1994). The idea is that the value of a network (an online community) depends on the scope of network adoption. More adoption by users will increase the total value of the network (user base). The value may result in a virtuous circle of getting more user adoption, more alliances and then higher market valuation. To achieve rapid network adoption, MediaRing employed network synergy to acquire new users worldwide with minimal costs in a short time period.

The idea of MediaRing network synergy was to expand networks by leveraging on other networks. The logic of rapid growth is as follows: first, MediaRing acquires the first 1.5 million registered users; secondly, it has the bargaining power to talk to another dot.com in a different market segment, with an established membership of 2.2 millions (for example); thirdly, the exchange of membership (databases) will give both parties a membership of 3.7 million. The fourth stage then requires some time for both parties to convert their merged membership. Fifthly, with some losses, both parties may have 3 million members each. In this way, MediaRing is able to double its membership in a short time period.

Pace of change. The current literature suggests a planned mode of change which requires setting a deliberate, long-term strategy, as elucidated by Bhide (1996, p. 124):

> The strategy should integrate entrepreneur's aspirations with specific long-term policies about the needs the company will serve, its geographic reach, and its technological capabilities.

Alternatively, entrepreneurs can improvise and experiment with strategies as they move the venture ahead (Mintzberg & Waters, 1985). The

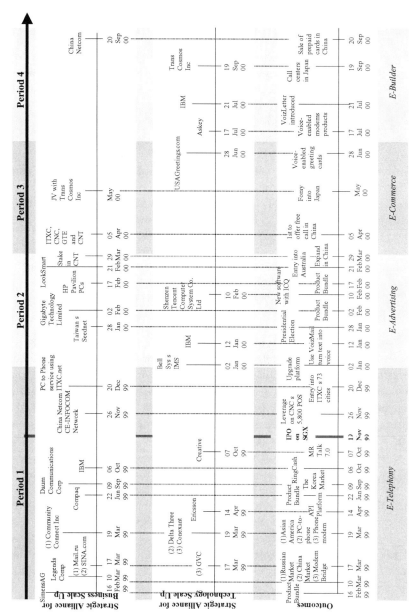

Figure 3. Mapping the events of key strategic alliance.

225

pace of this change is usually measured in *years* in more stable contexts (e.g., 3–5 years is suggested by Mintzberg and Waters, 1982; and 5–7 years by Roberts, 1980).

By contrast, we describe a process that requires adaptive change in business models, not just strategies. Dot.com entrepreneurs need to change their business model at a pace that matches the dynamism in their market. They have to tolerate ambiguities and compete on a *daily* basis by continuously evaluating business models to adapt to variations in the market, the competitive environment, and technological changes

Our results also relate to the theory of adaptation in the broader strategic literature. The current discussion of this subject has shifted from whether adaptation happens to how and when it occurs (Eisenhardt & Tabrizi, 1995; Gersick, 1994). Researchers consider punctuated equilibrium to be a useful model to understand adaptation in new venture creation, as elaborated in Gersick's (1994, p. 11) study:

> ...organizations evolve by alternating between relatively long periods of convergence, during which interdependent underlying structures permit only incremental change, and relatively compact periods of metamorphosis, or reorientation, during which fundamental change occurs.

Yet this study suggests that adaptation can also occur through small, frequent shifts in business models in order to compete effectively. This echoes Eisenhardt and Tabrizi's (1995) findings, which focus on accelerating the adaptation processes of new product development in the computer industry (see also Brown & Eisenhardt, 1997; Eisenhardt, 1989 on the computer industry; Schoonhoven et al., 1990 on the product innovation; Nicholls-Nixon et al., 2000 on a start-up context).

In this case study, we report new venture processes that may provide the same type of rapid adaptation as that of high-tech industry (e.g., computers). We also observe a type of accelerated adaptation (Eisenhardt & Tabrizi, 1995) in which dot.com firms need to respond to the constant flux of the evolving market and changing technologies by melding with one another in ever-changing networks. Companies thus need a continuous, rapid flow of innovative business models that reposition themselves and leverage on their existing resources.

Can this case be generalized to other dot.com venture creations? This question is important in view of the current cynicism regarding the prospects of dot.com firms. The "business models" of such companies have recently been called into question, especially with the demise of promising start-ups such as eToys and Priceline. Therefore, a key concern shared by researchers is: should the case of MediaRing be viewed as a "success" dot.com venture, since, even though its rapid membership expansion is an impressive achievement, the company still lost a lot of money. Increasingly, a rapidly expanding user base alone no longer commands high market valuation. This raises the issue of the generalizeability of the findings in this study: to what extent is this case specific to dot.com firms or to the period of the Internet bubble?

The question denies simple answers. Researchers are not advised to consider MediaRing as a successful model for managing a dot.com venture. Rather, this study aims to illustrate the strategic change process of a dot.com in the early developmental stage of Internet-based industries. To this end, the case study places more emphasis more on describing the interaction of changing contexts and a dot.com's adaptive actions for survival. Although researchers may anticipate a different pattern of dot.com competition in the future, the underlying operational logic—use business models as strategic frameworks for adaptation in dynamic contexts—will be the same.

Moreover, researchers are not encouraged to consider that a dot.com will adopt one "right" business model and then achieve success. Operating businesses in the Internet context involves confronting uncertainties and risks at a much higher speed than traditional industries. Although many dot.com entrepreneurs often use the rhetoric of "business model" simply to attract market attention, researchers should not ignore its value in orienting the change agenda. In this case study, we report how MediaRing relied on renewing business models to coordinate entrepreneurial activities with reference to pricing voice-based services, versioning products, attracting memberships, and building alliances (see the discussion of these issues in Shapiro & Varian, 1999).

It must be stressed that MediaRing should not be viewed as a "success" even though the company achieved a rapid expansion of membership. On the other hand, we cannot describe MediaRing as a failed dot.com just because it was not achieving any profit at period 4. The outcome reported in this case study is intended to show how MediaRing achieved different measures according to the expectation of the market and investors. We need to note that MediaRing had different focuses at different periods. For example, at period 1, getting IPO was the main goal and MediaRing had to live up to market expectation by achieving high user adoption. Under this condition, profit loss was a desirable measure. Shifting to period 4, the investors' expectation then changed to profitability. This also explains why MediaRing had to adjust its business model to react to this change. Under this new condition, the e-Builder model began to direct MediaRing's resources in order to provide system integration services to corporate members. The purpose was to achieve profits while maintaining steady growth in the user base. However, a rapidly expanding user base does not guarantee a high market valuation (as in period 1) and revenue streams (as in period 2 and 3). In period 4, it became a necessary condition to show a healthy dot.com as *perceived* by investors.

Therefore, it is not desirable to generalize the findings of this study to more universal statements about how one can best manage a successful dot.com entrepreneurship. Instead, this case study should be generalized *analytically* (Mitchell, 1983; Yin, 1989) by examining the strategic change process which captures the critical entrepreneurial activities needed to maintain survival in a high-velocity context. The process itself describes the period of the Internet bubble but the three propositions that are analyzed offer generic lessons for how dot.com firms derive strategic actions, grow businesses, and adapt to changes in a matter of days.

Implications for Practice

We learn from this case study that managing a dot.com venture takes more than web sites and passion. Furthermore, this study demystifies the proclaimed "paradigm shift" induced by the Internet gold rush. For prospective dot.com entrepreneurs, three practical lessons can be extracted from this case study. For the sake of convenience, we discuss these insights under the headings of shift, scale and speed.

1. *What* to change (*shift*):   Entrepreneurs need to recognize that they are managing a new type of venture creation. They should no longer focus simply on strategies that are sustainable and business models that are durable. Managing a dot.com requires the constant renewal of business models in order to derive strategies that can leverage on core competence and build upon previous actions. Entrepreneurs can then begin to develop products and services that can respond to market challenges. To compete effectively, entrepreneurs need to change their lens from *strategy* to *business model*—a shift that is less about technological advancement than about a new way of managing a venture.

2. *How* to change (*scale*):   Entrepreneurs also need to rethink the scale of growth of new ventures. The traditional wisdom is to have prudent growth through geographical expansions, acquisition and franchising. In dot.com competition, entrepreneurs need to think about network effects and rapid scale-up. They can achieve this by setting up alliances with two strategic goals: to enlarge the user base (through business alliances), and to trade their core competence in exchange for technological know-how (through a technology alliance) that can provide a better infrastructure or launch new products. Eventually, once a critical mass is achieved, the real challenge for dot.com

entrepreneurs is to convert the network effect into profits. This denies any particular prescription for success and requires entrepreneurs to adapt (our next advice).

3. *When* to change (*speed*):   The long planning cycle advised by traditional wisdom allows new ventures to predict changes or alternatively improvise actions to counter market challenges. For traditional ventures, a typical planning cycle can last from three to seven years. In high-velocity industries (such as computers), entrepreneurs may still keep two or three contingency-plans to hand and respond to competition through weekly planning (Eisenhardt, 1989; Eisenhardt & Tabrizi, 1985). In the dot.com context, where rapid growth is a precondition, the change is best characterized as accelerated adaptation. Managing a dot.com (with specific reference to information intermediary business) calls for a rapid scale-up. Within a period of approximately 100 days, entrepreneurs need to concentrate solely on one business model and keep the venture moving. Subsequently, they have to anticipate change that is discontinuous by renewing business models and products/services.

Limitations and Future Directions

The observation in this study is limited to the period of the early developmental stage in the dot.com industry. There are two areas that need to be improved in the future. First, we need to maintain closer contact with the entrepreneurs and conduct more participatory observations in order to capture the dynamics of adaptive change occurring in the dot.com. Due to limitations of access and the constant renewal of personnel, a more detailed observation of the organization was impossible. Furthermore, it is also useful to enhance this study by exploring the issues of leadership, team formation and organizational change (as suggested by Bruyat & Julien, 2000).

Secondly, our results offer a description of the selected dot.com's strategic change process. However, we cannot assert whether the process observed relates directly to the firm's success. Future studies may consider linking the change process research to the literature on performance (e.g., Gartner, Starr, & Bhat, 1998; Hofer & Sadberg, 1986) so that we can better understand how the adaptive process of change relates to effective new venture creation. In addition, we need to trace the dot.com's entrepreneurial activities beyond period 4. Such additional data would allow us to examine the issues relating to business models and new venture survival before and after the Internet bubble period.

CONCLUSION

Internet start-ups changed our perception of how to manage new venture creation. In this study, we offer a process account of a dot.com's strategic change journey. We construct a descriptive story from process data. The chronicle analysis of the case study reach toward theory building by clarifying sequences of events across four levels of analysis (context, business model, business growth and outcome). These also help us to establish early analytical themes about venture creation and strategic change.

Because of its focus on contextual details, this study concentrates on one case of a dot.com venture. We describe a process that deals with the entrepreneurial work of the selected dot.com, with strategic renewal and rapid growth, and with emerging business models guiding the venture's formation. The aim of this process analysis is not just to produce a case history but also to search for patterns (e.g., adaptation of change over a 100-day cycle), to link process to outcome, and to generate theories (in three areas: strategic focus, business growth and pace of change).

Evidence is also drawn together to examine how the context affects these processes. As suggested by Pettigrew (1990), one benefit of such an analysis is to enable researchers to examine how discontinuity (at the present time) emerges from previous continuity (the evolving, disruptive business models). We conclude that the management of a dot.com new venture requires entrepreneurs to build on traditional wisdom and exploit the three emerging principles suggested by our empirical observation.

ACKNOWLEDGMENT

Portions of the research reported here were supported by the National University of Singapore research grant (RP 314-000-031-112). We thank Ede-Phang Ng, Eng-Choon Loh, Alvin Chew, Richard Chua and Yew-Cheng Yak (MediaRing top management team) for their collaboration on the project.

REFERENCES

Afuah, A., & Tucci, C.L. (2001). *Internet business models and strategies: Text and cases.* Singapore: McGraw-Hill.
Applegate, L.M., & Collura, M. (2000). *Overview of e-business models.* Harvard Business School Case (9-801-172).

Badguerahanian, L., & Abetti, P.A. (1995). The rise and fall of the Merlin-Gerin Foundry business: A case study in French corporate entrepreneurship. *Journal of Business Venturing, 10*(6), 477–494.

Bhave, M.P. (1994). A process model of entrepreneurial venture creation. *Journal of Business Venturing, 9*(3), 223–243.

Bhide, A. (1974). The questions every entrepreneur must answer. *Harvard Business Review, 6*, 120–131.

Bird, B.J. (1992). The operation of intentions in time: The emergence of the new venture. *Entrepreneurship Theory and Practice, 17*(1), 11.

Brown, S.L., & Eisenhardt, K.M. (1997). The art of continuous change: Linking complexity theory and time-based evolution in relentlessly shifting organisation. *Administrative Science Quarterly, 42*, 1–34.

Bruyat, C., & Julien, P. (2000). Defining the field of research in entrepreneurship. *Journal of Business Venturing, 16*, 165–180.

Burgelman, R.A. (1983). A process model of internal corporate venturing in the diversified major firm. *Administrative Science Quarterly 28*(23), 223–224.

Burgelman, R.A. (1994). Fading memories: A process theory of strategic business exit in dynamic environments. *Administrative Science Quarterly, 39*(1), 24–57.

Busenitz, L.W., & Lau, C-M. (1996). A cross-cultural cognitive model of new venture creation. *Entrepreneurship Theory and Practice, 20*(4), 25–39.

Bygrave, W.D. (1993). Theory building in the entrepreneurship paradigm. *Journal of Business Venturing, 8*(3), 255–281.

Carter, N.M., Gartner, W.B., & Reynolds, P.D. (1996). Exploring start-up event sequences. *Journal of Business Venturing, 11*(3), 151–167.

Charkravarthy, B.S., & Doz, Y. (1992). Strategy process research: Focusing on corporate self-renewal. *Strategic Management Journal, 13*, 5–14.

Dyer, W.G., & Wilkins, A.L. (1991). Better stories, not better constructs, to generate better theory: A rejoinder to Eisenhardt. *Academy of Management Review, 16*(3), 613–619.

Earle, N., & Keen, P. (2000). *From .com to .profit: Inventing business models that deliver value and profit.* New York: Jossey-Bass.

Eisenhardt, K.M. (1989). Making fast strategic decisions in high-velocity environments. *Academy of Management Journal, 32*(3), 543–576.

Eisenhardt, K.M., & Tabrizi, B.N. (1995). Accelerating adaptive processes: Product innovation in the global computer industry. *Administrative Science Quarterly, 40*(1), 84–110.

Eisenhardt, K., & Schoonhoven, C. (1990). Organizational growth: Linking founding team, strategy, environment, and growth among ussemiconductor ventures, 1978–1988. *Administrative Science Quarterly, 35*(1), 504–529.

Fisher, L.M. (2000). Product or service? Choosing the right e-business model. *Strategy & Business*, 4th Quarter(21), 77–87.

Gartner, W.B. (1985). A conceptual framework for describing the phenomenon of new venture creation. *Academy of Management Review, 10*(4), 696–706.

Gartner, W.B., Starr, J.A., & Bhat, S. (1998). Predicting new venture survival: An analysis of "anatomy of a start-up" cases from Inc. magazine. *Journal of Business Venturing, 14*, 215–232.

Gersick, C.J.G. (1994). Pacing strategic change: The case of a new venture. *Academy of Management Journal, 37*(1), 9–45.

Glaser, B.G., & Strauss, A.L. (1967). *The discovery of grounded theory: Strategies for qualitative research.* Chicago: Alding Publishing.

Greenberger, D.B., & Sexton, D.L. (1988). An interactive model of new venture initiation. *Journal of Small Business Management, 26*(3), 1–7.

Greening, D.W., Barringer, B.R., & Macy, G. (1996). A qualitative study of managerial challenges facing small business geographic expansion. *Journal of Business Venturing, 11,* 233–256.

Hagel, J., & Armstrong, A.G. (1997). *Net gain : Expanding markets through virtual communities.* Boston: Harvard Business School Press.

Harvey, M., & Evans, R. (1995). Strategic windows in the entrepreneurial process. *Journal of Business Venturing, 10*(5), 331–348.

Herron, L., & Sapienza, H.J. (1992). The entrepreneur and the initiation of new venture launch activities. *Entrepreneurship Theory and Practice, 17*(1), 49.

Hofer, C.W., & Sadberg, W.R. (1986, Summer). Improving new venture performance: Some guidlines for success. *American Journal of Small Business,* 11–25.

Kambil, A., Eselius, E.D., & Monterio, K.A. (2000, Summer). Fast venturing: The quick way to start web business. *Sloan Management Review,* 55–67.

Kamm, J.B., Shuman, J.C., Seeger, J.A., & Nurick, A.J. (1990, Summer). Entrepreneurial teams in new venture creation: A research agenda. *Entrepreneurship Theory and Practice,* 7–17.

Katz, J.A. (1993). The dynamics of organizational emergence: A contemporary group formation perspective. *Entrepreneurship Theory and Practice, 17*(2), 97.

Katz, M.L., & Shapiro, C. (1992). Product introduction with network externalities. *The Journal of Industrial Economics, 40*(1), 55–84.

Kaufman, R., McAndrew, J., & Wang, Y.M. (2000). Opening the black box of network externalities in network adoption. *Information Systems Research, 11*(1), 61–82.

Langley, A. (1999). Strategies for theorizing from process data. *Academy of Management Review, 24*(4), 691–701.

MacMillan, I.C., Zemann, L., & SubbaNarasimha, P.N. (1987). Criteria distinguishing successful from unsuccessful ventures in the venture screening process. *Journal of Business Venturing, 2*(2), 123–138.

Maidique, M., & Patch, P. (1982). Corporate strategy and technological policy. In Tushman & Moore (Eds.), *Readings in the management of innovation* (pp. 273–285). Marshfield, MA: Pitman.

Mezias, S.J., & Kuperman, J.C. (2000). The community dynamics of entrepreneurship: The birth of the American film industry, 1985–1929. *Journal of Business Venturing, 16,* 209–233.

Miles, R.E., Snow, C.C., & Meyer, A.D. (1978). Organizational strategy, structure, and process. *Academy of Management Review, 3*(3), 546.

Mintzberg, H., & Waters, J. (1985). Of strategy, deliberate and emergent. *Strategic Management Journal, 6,* 257–272.

Mintzberg, H., & Waters, J.A. (1982). Tracking strategy in an entrepreneurial firm. *Academy of Management Journal, 25*(3), 465–500.

Mitchell, J.C. (1983). Case and situation analysis. *The Sociological Review, 31*, 187–211.

Nicholls-Nixon, C.L., Cooper, A.C., & Woo, C.Y. (2000). Strategic experimentation: Understanding change and performance in new ventures. *Journal of Business Venturing, 15*, 493–521.

Orsion, P. (1994). *Successful business expansion.* New York: John Wiley and Sons.

Pettigrew, A.M. (1985). *The awakening giant: Continuity and change in ICI.* Oxford: Blackwell.

Pettigrew, A.M. (1990). Longitudinal field research on change: Theory and practice. *Organization Science, 1*(3), 267–292.

Pettigrew, A.M. (1992). The character and significance of strategy process research. *Strategic Management Journal, 13*, 5–16.

Pettigrew, A.M. (1997, Autumn). What is processual analysis? *The Scandinavian Journal of Management* (Special Issue on Conducting Process Research), 337–348.

Porter, M.E. (1985). *Competitive advantage: Creating and sustaining superior performance.* New York: Free Press.

Riggins, F.J., Kriebel, C.H., & Mukhopadhyay, T. (1994). The growth of interorganizational systems in the presence of network externalities. *Management Science, 40*(8), 984–995.

Roberts, E.B. (1980, July-August). New ventures for corporate growth. *Harvard Business Review, 134–41.*

Romanelli, E. (1989). Environments and strategies of organization start-up. *Administrative Science Quarterly, 34*(3), 369–388.

Sch , D.A., & Rein, M. (1994). *Frame reflection: Toward the resolution of intractable policy controversies.* New York: Basic Books.

Schoonhoven, C.B., Eisenhardt, K.M., & Lyman, K. (1990). Speeding products to market: Waiting time to first product introduction in new firms. *Administrative Science Quarterly, 35*(1), 177–208.

Shane, S. (1994). Cultural values and the championing process. *Entrepreneurship Theory and Practice, 18*(4), 25.

Shapiro, C., & Varian, H.R. (1999). *Information rules: A strategic guide to the network economy.* Boston: Harvard Business School Press.

Stuart, R., & Abetti, P.A. (1987). Start-up ventures: Towards the prediction of initial success. *Journal of Business Venturing, 2*, 215–230.

Suchman, J., Shaw, J.J., & Suissman, G. (1985). Strategic planning in smaller rapid growth companies. *Long Range Planning, 18*, 48–53.

Van de Ven, A.H., Polley, D.E., Garud, R., & Venkatraman, S. (1999). *The innovation journey.* Oxford: Oxford University.

VanderWerf, P.A. (1993, Winter). A model of venture creation in new industries. *Entrepreneurship Theory and Practice, 39–47.*

Webb, D., & Pettigrew, A. (1999). The temporal development of strategy: Patterns in the U.K. insurance industry. *Organization Science, 10*(5), 601–621.

Webster, A. (1976). Models for new venture initiation—A discourse on rapacity and the independent entrepreneur. *Academy of Management Review, 1*(1), 26.

Werbach, K. (2000, May-June). Syndication: The emerging model for business in the internet era. *Harvard Business Review, 85–93.*

Yin, R.K. (1989). *Case study research: Design and methods.* Newbury Park, CA: Sage.

CHAPTER 11

FROM FLYPAPER TO GLOBALIZATION

Zobele Chemical Industries (1919–2001)

Pier A. Abetti[1]

ABSTRACT

This case history of Zobele Chemical Industries, which encompasses more than eight decades, has rich implications for technological entrepreneurs, particularly those who intend to compete in a fairly stable consumer market dominated by major multinational distributors. The evolution of the company can be studied according to Greiner's (1972) theory of growth punctuated by critical events. Some of the challenges and key success factors for technological entrepreneurs in stable industries are simple product technology driven by industrial design and uniform high quality; manufacturing technology based on automation, rapid cost reduction and quality control; marketing through the creation of long-standing relationships as world preferred suppliers and cooperation with clients in product design; organizational structure that combines strategic, marketing and technical skills with fast informal decision making and high sensitivity to changes in the international marketplace.

INTRODUCTION

On a beautiful day in May 2001, Enrico Zobele, principal stockholder and CEO of Zobele Chemical Industries, was sitting in his office of the main factory in Trento, Northern Italy. He looked at the Italian Alps where he had wandered often with his father, an experienced climber, and remembered the Psalm "I lifted my eyes into the mountains, whence cometh my strength" (*Holy Bible*, 1992) and felt elated. He had good reasons for rejoicing. The 15-year long transition of powers from his father had finally been completed, and he had been appointed Chairman of the Board after being CEO for five years. Under his leadership, the family company had grown rapidly to sales of $75 million, profits of $5.1million, 700 employees, factories in Italy, Spain, Brazil, Paraguay, India, Hong Kong, Mexico, Malaysia, and expansions underway in Italy, China, and possibly in the United States. The Zobele company was considered the leading world supplier of mosquito and insect repellants and similar household hygienic products. It was also the preferred world supplier to a $6 billion marketing and distribution American company, Stevenson Home Products.

From a personal perspective, Enrico was regarded as the leading industrial executive in Trento. He was President of the Confederation of Industries of the province. In recognition of his contributions to the local economy and public service, the President of the Italian Republic had named Enrico "*Cavaliere del Lavoro*" ("Knight of Industry"), the youngest one in Italy. As owner of 50% of the shares of Zobele Chemical Industries, the value of his estate was substantial, and he had just acquired a large villa in the wooded hills above Trento, where he was planning to move from his penthouse apartment in the city. Enrico looked at the picture of his grandfather and namesake, who had founded the company 82 years earlier, in 1919, and then to the picture of his father, who had transformed the company from a local business to international, and finally to the picture of his 16-year-old son Thomaz, whom he hoped to train as his successor.

All the shares of the Zobele company had belonged to the founder, Enrico's grandfather. He had distributed them equally to his two sons, Luigi and Fulvio (see the Zobele family tree, Figure 1). In time, Luigi had passed on all his shares to Enrico,[2] and Fulvio had distributed his shares to his two sons, Franco and Giovanni. Therefore, the Zobele company was now owned by Enrico (50%) and his two cousins: Franco (25%) and Giovanni (25%). However, the Board still had only four members: Enrico, his father Luigi, his uncle Fulvio, and his cousin Franco. To maintain the balance of votes between the two branches of the family, Giovanni, the younger son of Fulvio, had been excluded.

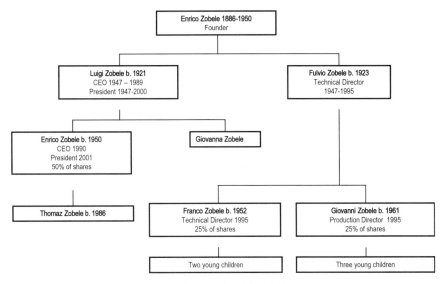

Figure 1.   Zobele family tree and shares held in 2001.

HISTORY OF ZOBELE CHEMICAL INDUSTRIES (1919–2001)

The history of Zobele Chemical Industries may be divided into three phases separated by critical events (Greiner, 1972) as shown in Table 1.

Table 1.   Stages of Growth and Critical Events of Zobele Chemical Industries

Date	Critical Event	Stage of Growth	Actions Taken
1919	Birth	Artisan Growth	
1942–1946	World War II and DDT		Closing of factory Flypaper obsolete
1947–1994		Re-birth and growth with new products	
1995	Failure to establish own brand		No direct sales, production for major distribution
1996–2001		Expansion of production and globalization	

First Phase: Birth and Artisan Growth (1919–1941)

The Zobele family has always been a family of entrepreneurs (Figure 1.) The father of the founder, Fortunato Zobele, earned his living by delivering goods by mule from Calliano station on the first railway in the region of Trento to the villages in the adjacent valleys. His son Enrico (1886–1950) studied at a business school in Trieste. Until the end of the World War I, Trento and Trieste, although geographically Italian, were part of the Austro-Hungarian Empire. Thus, Enrico Zobele's first job was at the Länderbank in Vienna. Soon thereafter, World War I broke out and he served in the Austrian army on the Russian front. After the collapse of the Austro-Hungarian empire, Trento was reunited with Italy.

When he returned from the front, the situation in Trento was chaotic. The ties with Vienna had been cut, and new ties with the rest of Italy were not yet operational. There was a shortage of all kinds of household goods, from soap to floor wax, shoe polish, shoe grease, steel wool, metal polish, etc. Therefore, in 1919 the Zobele company was founded to import household goods built by the Austrian SOLO company that was owned by the Länderbank. As the business grew, the founder decided to manufacture some of the imported products in the cellar of his home. His son Luigi remembered a large cauldron of melted wax heated by an open gas flame. In those days, there were no rules for fire prevention … or they were not enforced!

In 1930 the founder started manufacturing a new line that made his fortune: flypaper. There was only one product, called "spiralette = little spirals" and only one packaging: boxes of 100 pieces which, in turn, were packaged in cartons of 12 boxes. Traveling salesmen on commission solicited orders in autumn. Manufacturing was from April to July. The workers were furloughed in August until the following spring.

The key to success was mechanization of production. A broken-down machine prototype was bought in Czechoslovakia, fixed up by the factory mechanic, who then built eight more. The Zobele company became the undisputed leader in Italy and exported to Albania and other Mediterranean countries, all infected by flies.[3]

First Critical Event (1942–1946): World War II and DDT

World War II ended all this. In 1942 there was a shortage of raw materials, and the founder feared that the factory would be destroyed by air raids. Thus, he cleared the factory and hid the machinery in farmhouses. In fact, in 1946, when his son Luigi came back home after completing his chemical engineering studies at the Polytechnic of Milan, he found that the factory had been partially destroyed and was slowly being rebuilt. His father was despondent and sick, passed on what was left of the business to him, and retired.

Luigi had inherited a very difficult situation. Ninety per cent of his revenue was due to flypaper, which now had become almost useless since DDT had killed most of the flies. There were only five employees: two clerks, the mechanic, and two workers. Luigi had the brilliant idea of replacing flypaper with steel wool, which could be sold and distributed through the same channels. Luckily he found a machine to start the new line. In the meantime his younger brother Fulvio, a mechanical engineer, had joined him. The two brothers were complementary in skills and character. Luigi did the planning, marketing and sales; Fulvio designed the production lines, acquired old and new machines, adapted them, and was responsible for production. But sales were difficult to restart. Luigi and Fulvio carried cases of samples and visited wholesalers and retail shops all over Italy who were not too interested in their products. They were happy when they could sell five dozen boxes of shoe polish or 50 kilograms of floor wax.

Second Phase: Rebirth and Growth with New Products (1947–1994)

During the 1950s, the Zobele Company was born again and started growing thanks to new products. New production lines were set up to make all kinds of steel wool. Hard to believe, there was also a rebirth of flypaper, a product that will never die! The last advice from the founder, who did not want to manufacture insecticides, to his sons was "keep offering flypaper, as long as some people still ask for it!" In fact, in 2001 Zobele Chemical Industries is marketing increasing quantities of flypaper in Italy and other countries, imported from Japan, Czechoslovakia and Thailand.

In 1960, a new product was introduced which is now the workhorse of the company—mosquito repellent spirals. The Zobele brothers found out from their salesmen that the Zampironi company of Venice, the oldest producer in Italy of these spirals, was going to shut down. For a small sum they acquired the machinery, which was technically obsolete and hardly operational. Fulvio Zobele completely redesigned the machinery and built two automated production lines.

In the 1970s, some strange new products had appeared in the stores, mosquito-repellent heated mats with the Japanese trademark, Fumakilla. Luigi bought a few samples, guessed the chemical formula, which was then confirmed by laboratory analysis, and registered the formula with the Italian Ministry of Health. With his son Enrico, still a business school student, he traveled to the Far East to collect ideas and offers from potential suppliers. In Taiwan, they found a small heater, which is now displayed in Luigi's office. From this prototype, Fulvio developed the concept of the electrical heater "Spira" which is inserted directly into an electrical outlet. According to the well-known "razor and blades" approach, one mat was used every night, to obtain a mosquito free room. The mats were initially produced by a Japanese company, but the Zobele brothers bought their machinery and know-how and conceived the present production line that manufactures more than half a million mats per 8-hour shift with only three operators. (There are now five lines in Trento and three in Verona.)

Their new product boosted sales and the present modern factory was built in 1979 and expanded in 1985. An adjacent building, the warehouse, was purchased in 1995. Since 1975, the third generation started working in the company; first Enrico, the son of Luigi who had completed his studies at the leading Italian business school, Bocconi; then, Franco, the son of Fulvio, who has studied mechanical engineering and later his brother, Giovanni, who had studied political economics at the University of Trento.

The Zobele brand names were already established on the Italian market but the company sought multinational partners for attacking the global markets, Ciba-Geigy in Switzerland and Stevenson Home Products in the United States. The Zobele company was the first to obtain approval for its mosquito repellent heaters and mats by the health authorities in the United States and Canada.

Several other products were added in the 1980s such as liquid insecticides that are evaporated using an electric plug-in heater. Since the insecticide market is highly seasonal, like flypaper, from May to September, the company was searching for products that could be sold throughout the year. Enrico Zobele found out, by chance, during a business trip, that a Danish company was producing a detergent for dishwashers in tablet form, while only powder was available on the Italian market. These tablets were considered nonionic and "baby-proof" since they were individually packaged.

In 1989, the company spent 12% of its revenue to launch the new product and the initial results were favorable. Demand exceeded the production capacity, but the sales campaign fizzled. The main reason was that Zobele's brand name "Qubì" was no match to the brand name of the main competitor, Finish, the powder detergent produced and marketed by a German multinational firm with 90% market share.

Second Critical Event: Failure of Brand Identity and Withdrawal from Direct Sales (1995)

In the late 1980s and 1990s, the market expanded and became gradually globalized due to the increasing demand from industrializing and developing countries. The demand for better protection from the insects was increasing in parallel with the requirements for improved health standards. Previously closed markets, like China, Brazil, and India were opening up. Local production became strategically important in order to take advantage of the low labor and production costs and of government incentives. However, in parallel, distribution became globalized and was dominated by five major worldwide companies from the United States, UK, and Germany. These "big five" had their own preferred suppliers selected after rigorous testing and preliminary contracts, often insisted that their smaller suppliers work exclusively for them, and were wary of suppliers that also served their competitors. Therefore, there was the danger that Zobele Chemical Industries would become too dependent on one client, and would not be able to sell to other major potential clients.

Responding to this threat, in 1994, Enrico came to the conclusion that Zobele could not fight the "big-five" in Italy or abroad. His strategy was now to be the world leader in innovative new products and the leading supplier to the "big-five" for the global market. The first step in the implementation of the new strategy was to dismiss all his sales representatives in 1995. The second step was to enter into a long term contract with one of the "big-five," an American company, LS, which would market all of Zobele's branded products in Italy. Naturally, this reduced the marketing and selling costs, but also the gross margins, because of the discounts to LS. However, the sales volume increased so that net sales billed were the same as in the preceding year.

Third Phase: Expansion of Production and Globalization (1996–2001)

In order to implement his strategy of becoming the world-leading supplier in selected market niches, Enrico decided to first become the uncontested leader in Italy, and then to seek partners for globalization of production.

Zobele Chemical Industries had purchased in 1970 the Siapi company, their main competitor in mosquito-repellent spirals. The next step was to acquire the Palma company of Verona, the main competitor in mosquito-repellent mats. The two acquisitions almost doubled production capacity, and enabled the Zobele company to become in 1996 the preferred world supplier to the Stevenson company for three branded products to be sold world wide: heaters and mats, spirals and liquid insecticides for evaporation.

In parallel, Enrico wanted to expand in Southern Europe, the Mediterranean countries and Latin America, where the demand for home hygiene products was growing rapidly. The first-step was to set up in 1988 a partnership with a Japanese company, Zobele's main supplier of chemicals for insecticide manufacturing. In turn, this partnership owns 50% of the IRIS company in Paraguay. The second step was the creation of the Zobele do Brazil company, 100% owned by Zobele.

The third and major step in globalization was the creation in 1999 of a partnership with the Spanish group DBK, with sales of $30 million and 470 employees, led by an engineer and entrepreneur, Jordi Basaganas (Franco, 1999). While both Zobele and DBK produced insecticides and deodorants, Zobele is more specialized in insecticides and DBK in deodorants. The two companies are also geographically complementary. Zobele's factories are in Italy, Brazil, and Paraguay, and DBK's in Spain, Brazil, Mexico and India. There seems also to be complementary skills in the two CEOs: Enrico Zobele is oriented toward marketing and sales, while Jordi Basaganas is more oriented toward technology and new product development and engineering. The new partnership was established in the Netherlands as the BiZeta (from the initials of the two principals) alliance BV, owned 51% by Basaganas and 49% by Zobele through its international company, Zobele International BV. In turn, BiZeta alliance owns 80% of DBK, with a German multinational chemical company owning the remaining 20%.

With this partnership, Enrico Zobele was able to create a group with $75 million in sales, 700 employees and 8 factories in 7 countries, with expansion underway in 2 more countries (a geographic overview of the Zobele group is shown in Figure 2). It should be noted, however, that in the Netherlands and Great Britain there are only holding companies without engineering and production facilities.

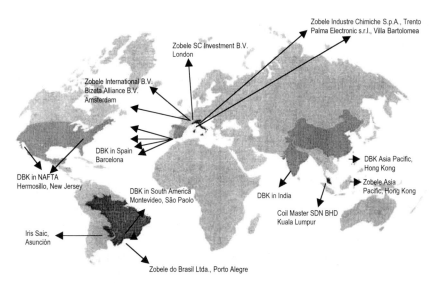

Figure 2.   Overview of Zobele Group.

ZOBELE CHEMICAL INDUSTRIES: SITUATION ANALYSIS

The status and prospects of Zobele Chemical Industries in 2001 may be summarized as follows.[4]

Mission

Zobele Chemical Industries is the leading international designer and manufacturer of selected innovative home hygiene products, marketed worldwide by major distributors.

Products

The products produced and marketed by Zobele are grouped into five major product lines (Zobele Chemical Industries, 2000).

1. Electric devices to be used in conjunction with mosquito mats, liquid insecticides refills, air freshener refills, air freshener pads, etc. The devices may be electrical or battery operated, may have different add-on features like pilot lamp, night light, switch timer, etc.
2. Mosquito coils (spirals) and sticks—insect repellent for outdoor use.
3. Mosquito mats insect repellent for indoor use, to be used with electrical devices as above as well as in conjunction with candles or other heating systems.
4. Insecticides and/or air freshener liquid refills to be used in conjunction with electrical devices for continuous evaporation.
5. The Home line consisting of steel wool rolls, gold and wax sponge packets, steel wool, soap pads, no-scratch sponges, firelighter cubes, spray starch for ironing, spray oven and furniture cleaners, spot removers, Qibì dishwasher detergent in tablets and rinse agents.

In total, the five product lines include only 56 items. However, due to different electrical connector requirements and packages in many different languages, the overall number of different products, as seen by the end customer, amounts to more than five hundred. In addition, there are similar products, which are produced for the major distributors under their brand names. In total, there are more than 2,000 different packagings.

Markets Served

As described above, Zobele markets only to distributors, the "big five" multinationals, and major national distributors worldwide. Consequently, Zobele does not advertise. The Italian market represents 20% of sales, and the foreign market 80% of sales in more than 50 countries.

Production

With the exception of a few purchased items, Zobele manufactures all its products in its two main factories in Italy and subsidiaries in Brazil, Paraguay, and Malaysia with China and the United States to follow. The main factory in Trento, Italy is highly automated with advanced product lines designed in-house with ISO 9001 quality control.

Research and Development, Design and Engineering

The Zobele products are researched, developed and engineered in house, often with the help of leading Italian industrial designers. Similarly, production lines are designed and built in house with machinery built to order by Italian and foreign firms.

Organization and Personnel

The Board of Directors includes four family members: Luigi, Fulvio, Enrico, and Franco Zobele. Since May 2001, Enrico Zobele is chairman of the board and CEO. As shown in the simplified organization chart (Figure 3), Enrico is also Director of Marketing, with three departments: Foreign, Italian and Special Clients (Stevenson Company). Enrico's cousin Franco Zobele is Technical Director, with three departments: R&D, Maintenance and Technical Office, and Outside Contracting. Enrico's cousin Giovanni Zobele is director of Operations, with four departments: Production, Production Programming, Quality Control, and Purchasing. Giovanni Zobele is also Director of Human Resources (Zobele Chemical Industries, 2000).

Dr. Andrea Caserta is the only Director who is not a member of the Zobele family. He is in charge of Administration with four departments: Accounting and Administration, Control of Operations, Information Systems, and Administration of Companies within the Zobele Group. Two additional positions report to the CEO: quality control and security, and innovative technologies.

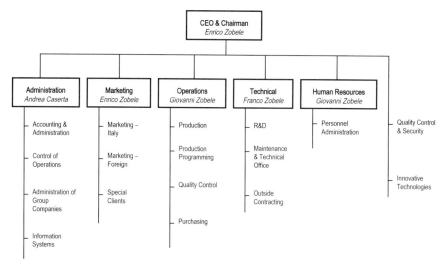

Figure 3.   Simplified organization of Zobele Chemical Industries.

The Zobele Group

As shown in Figure 4 the Zobele Group consists of the Zobele Chemical Industries of Trento, the 100% owned Palma Electronics near Verona, and Zobele International BV incorporated in the Netherlands. In turn, Zobele International BV includes Zobele do Brazil (100% owned), Coil Master in Malaysia (29% owned), Zobele Asia Pacific Hong Kong (80% owned), and Zobele SC Investments in London, which owns 50% of the Paragyan subsidiary IRIS. Zobele International BV owns 49% of the BiZeta Alliance BV, also incorporated in the Netherlands, which in turn owns 80% of DBK holdings BV with subsidiaries in Spain, Brazil, Hong Kong, India, and Mexico. In total, the Zobele Group included, in the year 2001, almost 1000 employees in ten locations.

Financial Summary

For the year 2000, the Zobele Group had revenues of $75 million and net profit of $5.1 millions,[5] corresponding to a return on sales (ROS) of 6.8% (Gruppo Zobele, 2001). Compared to 1999, the financial results of 2000 are impressive. Revenue increased by 47%, net income by 70%, and ROS by 0.9%. Sales were distributed geographically as follows: Europe 46%, South America 8%, NAFTA 19%, and other 27%. The Group investment in 2000 amounted to $15 million, 11% higher than in 1999, and stockholders equity of $117 million, 13% increase from 1999. Net financial

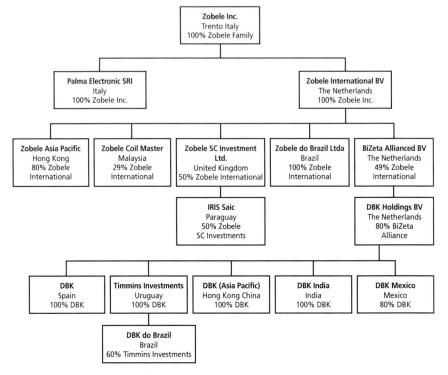

Figure 4.   Zobele Group.

investment was $8 million, 16% higher than 1999. Finally, productivity (sales/employee) was $114,000 with no significant change from 1999.

These results show that the impressive increase and especially profits were achieved with only a modest increase in investment and personnel; in fact, return on investment (ROI) increased from 22% in 1999 to 34% in 2000, and return on equity (ROE) from 22% to 30%. In conclusion, the financial situation of the Zobele Group at the beginning of 2001 was very favorable.

Personnel and Labor Relations

Zobele Chemical Industries is considered one of the leading companies in Trento, a fairly small city of 100,000. Because of its 82-year presence and the reputation of family members and their leadership in community projects it is considered a very desirable place to work. Relationships with the union, often strained in Italy, are excellent. In Italy, it is almost impossible to dismiss or even furlough workers for lack of work. Because many of its products are seasonal, Zobele negotiated an innovative contract, vertical part-time, whereby some workers are employed for six months per year and furloughed for the other six months without losing benefits and continuity of service.

Zobele pays average salaries higher than other local employers. Factory workers receive a monthly production premium (amounting to 10–15% of salary) based on production results, which are posted every morning. Managers and office employees receive a year-end bonus of 25–30% of salary as set by the board, that is, by the Zobele family, but this bonus is by now expected and not directly related to individual achievements. Needless to say, there are no stock options. Because of the international strategic orientation, free English language courses are given individually and to small groups.

In summary, the Zobele company is considered a solid business of international reputation with excellent working conditions, the most modern technology and machinery, the best opportunity for traveling abroad and prospects of career and professional growth thanks to recent expansion. As a result, turnover of office and factory workers is only 2% per year, compared to an average of 5% for similar Italian firms.

Decision Making Process

In the first phase of artisan growth, all decisions were made by the founder and sole owner. After the critical event of the war and appearance of DDT, decisions were made jointly by his two sons, Luigi and Fulvio, who each owned half the shares. In turn, Luigi turned over his shares to his son Enrico, and Fulvio to his sons Franco and Giovanni. Luigi and Fulvio kept their seats on the Board, while Giovanni was excluded in order to maintain the parity of votes between the two branches of the family. Since all four board members and Giovanni have adjacent offices, it is very easy for them to discuss problems and challenges and come to a decision. During these meetings, the first objective is always to maintain family harmony, and then to come to a decision. In practice, consensus is first reached among the three younger members of the family (Giovanni, Franco, and Enrico) who then consult with the two senior members, Luigi and Fulvio who act as advisors, and then obtain their agreements as members of the Board. Since the CEO, Enrico, is not always available, in some cases the four family members get together informally, prepare a proposal, and then discuss it with Enrico who makes the final decision after consultation with Dr. Caserta, the financial director.

At the present, there has never been a case where the Board has been asked to vote formally. However, there is a provision in the bylaws to give authority to the Chairman to decide in case of a tie. When they sit on the Board, Enrico and Franco have to play the roles of shareholders and managers, which may not always be fully compatible. The position of Giovanni, the only family member who does not have a board seat, is interesting. He participates in all board meetings and acts as a business advisor to his brother Franco, who is more oriented toward technology. Therefore, Giovanni is able to separate and emphasize his role of manager. The employees understand his position. While they respect the owners or former owners (Luigi and Fulvio), they take order from the directors.

Although family harmony is the dominant theme, this does not impose conformity or group think, and there are often heated discussions to stimulate creativity, for as we have seen, the five family members have complimentary skills and interests: Luigi and Enrico, strategic planning and marketing; Fulvio and Franco, technology and machinery; Giovanni, production and human resources. There is however, some tension between the second generation, more conservative and risk-adverse, still conscious of the post war difficulties, and the third generation, more innovative, aggressive and oriented toward global expansion.

Working for a Family Company

There is always the possibility that non-family members working in a family company are considered second-class citizens, and that some high-level decisions are made to benefit the family rather than all the employees (Kuratko & Welsch, 2001; Neubauer & Lank, 1998). This does not appear the case with Zobele Chemical Industries. First, the three persons interviewed who are not family members, stated that all positions and responsibilities are based on merit and competencies and not on family membership. Second, daily direct contact with the shareholders is a positive factor, since the situation is more dynamic, there is less bureaucracy and decisions are reached in a short time by the five family members, whose culture emphasizes fast and efficient decisions. Third, compensation of managerial personnel is fair, based on merit, and is higher than in comparable local industries. Since stock options are not customary in Italy, they are not needed to attract and retain outstanding employees.

CRITICAL SUCCESS FACTORS

The continuing success of Zobele Chemical Industries may be attributed to several critical factors, external and internal, as with other entrepreneurial ventures previously studied such as the Toshiba Laptop and Notebook (Abetti, 1997b), the Toshiba Japanese Word Processor (Abetti, 1999), and the Steria Company (Abetti, 2002). However, the internal factors are more important in the present case, because Zobele is a family company.

The most important external factors that impacted, positively or negatively, on the growth of Zobele Chemical Industries are: (1) the evolution of the market, (2) changes in the technology, (3) location of the company in Italy, more specifically in Trento, and (4) the globalization of distribution and the specialization and automation of manufacturing.

Evolution of the Market

Flies, mosquitoes, cockroaches, moths and other insects have always plagued the world's population. Not much could be done to combat them in the rural environment. Urbanization has increased dramatically since World War II, first in developed countries, and now in developing countries, contributing to a concentration of these pests in areas where they can do the most damage. In parallel, people have become more health conscious, and more proactive in fighting these pests. At the same time, the average buying power of the consumer has increased, and some of the discretionary income could be devoted to protect the family and the home. Thus, the market is growing very fast, particularly in Latin America, Southern Asia, and the Pacific Rim.

Changes in Technology

During the first artisan period, the technology was quite simple. The main products (shoe polish, floor wax, shoe grease, metal polish, and aluminum varnish) were manufactured in batches first in the family cellar, then in the factory under license from an Austrian chemical company.

The next step was to automate the production of fly paper, by acquiring obsolete machinery and redesigning it completely, thereby achieving cost leadership in a rapidly expanding market.

The technology for fighting flies and mosquitoes changed rapidly and drastically from flypaper to DDT, which, as we have seen, almost destroyed the Zobele company. After DDT was found to be harmful to the environment and DDT-resistant insects had developed through genetic mutation, the emphasis was on repelling rather than exterminating mosquitoes, using natural products (pyrethrum) and less harmful chemicals. This was the origin of the spirals, heated mats and vaporizers, the present flagship products of Zobele.

The two technological entrepreneurs with degrees in chemical and mechanical engineering, improved the production technology from individually operated machines to fully automated production lines with minimum operator intervention, and rigorous quality control, according to ISO 9001 standards.

Location in Italy and Trento

The location of Zobele Chemical Industries in Italy has contributed to the international growth of the company. Given the rather small size of the Italian market and its seasonality, Zobele was forced to target much larger markets where Italy had close geographical commercial and cultural relationships (the Mediterranean countries and Latin America) or where the major distributors were located (United States). Italy is considered one of the world leaders in small and medium enterprises specializing in specific fields (fashion, furniture, machine tools, etc.), which serve global markets (Porter, 1990). Also, Italian design, simple and practical but aesthetically pleasant, is appreciated throughout the world, and Zobele products are no exception. Finally, location in Trento, a provincial city in the Alps, is a major advantage for Zobele. Costs are lower than in large metropolitan areas, such as Turin, Milan and Genoa, unions are less politically motivated and less hostile to multinationals. There is less mobility of personnel, because there are few industrial companies in the area. Also, persons born in Trento are very attached to their city and prefer local employment, seeking opportunities to return home from other parts of Italy or foreign countries, after they have gained industrial experience.

Globalization of Distribution

Since pests are similar all over the world, the same products can be used in principle in many different countries. The main differences as shown by the Zobele product brochures are in the electrical connections and packaging with various languages. As the world became a global village and trade barriers were reduced or removed, it became feasible, indeed necessary for achieving economies of scale and scope, to create worldwide distribution networks. Five multinational companies emerged as leaders, thanks to their worldwide brands and efficient distribution systems. As we have seen, the Zobele company could not compete with these powerful brands and instead became a preferred supplier to these distributors.

Specialization and Automation of Manufacturing

The globalization and concentration of distribution, in turn, caused major changes in manufacturing. The distributors have high purchasing power and demand large quantities of uniform products at low prices. At the same time, these distributors are concerned about maintaining reliability of supply and high quality standards; therefore, they seek longer term contracts based on partnerships in product, process, and technology development. Thanks to Italian ingenuity and their postwar experiences, Fulvio Zobele and his son Franco were able to first adapt old machinery and then to design and install modern automated production lines in their main factory. The knowledge gained in Italy was later transferred to factories overseas in order to be closer to customers and reduce transportation costs. Thus, production has become more specialized (a few product lines with minor variations in electrical connectors and packaging) and automated. The next step would be the rationalization and further specialization of production through agreements with other multinational producers, such as DBK. Naturally, this specialization of production would increase the bargaining power of the suppliers in dealing with the major distributors.

The most important internal factors are: (1) family harmony, (2) personality of the entrepreneurs and (3) changing strategy in congruence with changes in the market and in industry structure.

Family Harmony

Zobele Chemical Industries has always been a family company, with a very limited number of stockholders, who are all actively engaged in managing the company. Up to now, family members who do not work in the company have not been granted shares. The Board of Directors has no outside members. One reason for the exclusion may be that, since the shares and the Board seats are equally divided among the two branches of the family, the outside members would control the deciding votes in case of conflict, and thus acquire excessive power. This may also be the reason for the reluctance to enter the stock market and bring in outside shareholders, even with limited voting rights.

Given this balance of power between the two family branches, preservation of family harmony has been the controlling imperative and the foundation of the successful growth of the company. In addition to the strong family ties and family loyalty that are typically Italian, the family harmony is strengthened by several factors:

1. The complementary roles of the family members, with one branch concentrating on planning and marketing, and the other on technology and production with minimum overlap of competencies and duties.
2. The fact that all family members who are (or were) shareholders are also full-time directors and they must always give priority to the needs of the business above family interests.
3. The proximity of the offices of the five family members, that facilitates formal and informal communication.
4. The residence of all members and their families in Trento, with frequent opportunities for social interaction and participation in community initiatives.

There are also well known business advantages in dealing with a family company, compared to a public company (Brokaw, 1992; Kets de Vries, 1993) such as long-term orientation, greater independence of action due to no pressure from the stock market and no risk of takeovers, stability and continuity of leadership. In turn, this stability is a source of confidence for employees and consumers. For instance, since 1977, Luigi and Enrico have been developing relationships with their major customer Stevenson Home Products and are now world-preferred suppliers. In contrast, the interfaces of a public company with customers change every few years, as general managers, marketing and sales managers come and go.

Lead Entrepreneurs

The role of lead entrepreneur (Timmons, 1994) passed naturally from the founder to his first son Luigi, and from Luigi to his only son Enrico. However, the personalities of the three entrepreneurs were quite different.

The founder had studied at a business school and worked in a bank. He became an entrepreneur by necessity and he became an artisan manufacturer in order to increase his low margins through import substitution. He then conceived and developed his "killer product" flypaper and thanks to his mechanical ingenuity, built up a production line of nine machines. He was satisfied with the seasonality of the product, and did not start other product lines in order to operate all year. During the war, he closed down the factory, to save the machinery. At the end of the war, he slowly rebuilt the factory, but DDT had replaced flypaper. He did not want to manufacture and market insecticides. He became ill and passed on the business to his first son Luigi, three months after he had graduated in engineering and started working as a salesman in the family company. Luigi was 26 years when he was suddenly named CEO.

Luigi's personality was truly entrepreneurial. Faced with the demise of flypaper and his father's hostility to insecticides, he decided to move to an entirely different product, which could be marketed and sold through the available channels—steel wool. Here again, thanks to the mechanical expertise of his brother Fulvio, he built an automated production line. In contrast to his father, Luigi was always on the lookout for new products that would expand his limited business scope, regardless of the technologies to be adopted. First, he acquired the broken-down machinery for making mosquito repellent spirals and then Fulvio built two automated production lines. Second, Luigi bought a few Japanese mosquito-repellent heated mats, guessed the chemical formula, registered it in Italy and went to Taiwan and Japan to collect information and find manufacturers. Based on this competitive intelligence, Luigi and Fulvio built up an efficient production line and achieved world leadership.

In his personal life as in his business strategy, Luigi was always looking for new opportunities and challenges that would test his leadership. An experienced mountain climber, hiker and explorer he toured the world during his vacations and became familiar with many different cultures. Therefore, he had few difficulties in negotiating with the Japanese, Latin Americans and North Americans. In fact, he built up long-lasting relationships with two major American distributors and many local distributors in developing countries. Luigi was considered a civic leader in Trento, as Board member of the Confederation of Industries of the province and as President of SAT (Società Alpinisti Tridentini) a world famous organization of hikers and mountain climbers. He completely rebuilt a renaissance palace in Trento, which is now the society's headquarters and museum.

The transition of power from Luigi to Enrico was gradual and slow. While his father and uncle were engineers, Enrico attended the leading business school in Italy and started working for the company in 1977, at the age of 27. One year later he was named Director of Marketing, with emphasis on the development of foreign business. He was promoted to General Manager in 1989 and to CEO in 1995. Finally, in 2001, he became Chairman of the Board, completing a transition of powers from his father that had lasted 24 years.

In contrast to his father, an entrepreneur, Enrico appears to be more of a statesman, a marketing and business manger, rather than an innovator in technology. However, he is still an entrepreneur in implementing his vision of globalization. He inherited a growing company, leader in a chosen market niche, which had to become international in order to grow, indeed to survive. An ambitious person by nature, Enrico aspired to become a world leader in a broader market as preferred supplier to at least two major multinational distributors. Thanks to his strategic vision and thorough personal knowledge of the market, he is now embarking on a major thrust of globalization through alliances and expansion through local production. In parallel, Enrico followed his father's footsteps as civic leader, as President of the Industrial Association of the Trento Province. When he was named "Cavaliere del Lavoro" he obtained national recognition, and created important relationships with Italian industrial and political leaders. He is now in the process of achieving increased international recognition, particularly in Europe (the Netherlands and Spain), the United States, South America, and China.

Evolution of the Strategy of Zobele Chemical Industries

During it's 82 years of existence, the strategy of the Zobele Chemical Industries has evolved in congruence with changes in technology and especially in the international markets, which in turn, have induced changes in industry structure. Entrepreneurs and CEOs have shown an uncanny ability to sense these changes and take advantage of them by developing and implementing new strategies to achieve leadership in the targeted market niches.

The original strategy of the startup was imports and import substitution. Then came the first innovation: flypaper. After the war, the technology changed and the company sought new technologies to satisfy its traditional markets: steel wool, anti-mosquito coils, mats, and vaporizers for insecticides. The strategy was to be the technological and production leader in the selected narrow market niche. This strategy corresponds to that of the prospectors in the Miles and Snow (1978) typology. "Prospectors are organizations that almost continually search for market—opportunities, and they regularly experiment with potential responses to emerging environmental trends." Smith, Guthrie, and Chen (1986) analyzed further the prospectors among a sample of 47 electronic manufacturing firms. These firms had "an unstable customer base, a changing product mix, a competitive edge in innovation, a 'creating change' approach to their customer base and an aggressive attitude toward growth."

These two quotes appear to describe clearly the tactics and strategies of the Zobele company during the 1947–94 phase in Table 1.

As we have seen, by 1995 the industry structure had changed and the market, by now globalized, was dominated by the brand names of the "big five." Enrico changed his strategy from prospector to analyzer, as described by Miles and Snow (1978). "Analyzers are organizations that operate into two types of product market domains, one relatively stable, the other changing. In their stable areas, their organizations operate routinely and efficiently, through use of formalized structure and processes. In their more turbulent areas, top managers watch their competitors closely for new ideas, and they rapidly adopt those that appear to be the most promising." In fact, for Zobele Chemical Industries, the stable area is the 25-year relationship with Stevenson company, as preferred world supplier of few high-volume stable items produced both in Italy and abroad with very efficient production lines. In contrast, the turbulent areas correspond to new products (such as the night light—heated mat combination), and new product lines (such as deodorants in cooperation with the DBK group) and new opening markets, such as China.

Recently, Gimenez (2000) studied the strategies of the 150 Brazilian family firms. The prospectors corresponded to 23% of the total, the analyzers to 41%. However, the prospectors had a higher ratio of growing firms during the last 5 years (75%) and a lower ratio of stable firms (21%) and a very low ratio of decreasing firms (4%). In contrast, the analyzers had a somewhat lower ratio of growing firms (69%) and higher ratios of stable firms (25%) and decreasing firms (6%). Among the 150 companies involved, 15 operated in the chemical sector. Of these, 40% were analyzers, 20% prospectors, 20% defenders, and 20% reactors. From this, and other studies (Hambrick, 1983) it appears that the more successful chemical ventures start as prospectors and then move on gradually to analyzers.

The technological strategy adopted by Zobele was always a divergent strategy (Abetti, 1997a) since different technologies were needed for pest-control. However, the market strategy evolved from divergent distribution channels (selling direct and through distributors) to convergent channels (selling only through distributors). As shown by Abetti (1997a), this convergence increases the probability of success for the form. At the same time, this combination of divergent technological and convergent market strategies enhances the core competencies of the firm and contributes to the achievement of sustained market leadership in the industry (Abetti, 1996).

IMPLICATIONS FOR TECHNOLOGICAL ENTREPRENEURS: KEY SUCCESS FACTORS

This case history, encompassing more than eight decades, is rich with implications for technological entrepreneurs, particularly those intending to attack a fairly stable consumer market dominated by major multinational distributors. Following are some of the most important challenges faced by the Zobele entrepreneurs and the corresponding key success factors:

1. *The product technology* is rather simple given the transparent function-ality and low cost per item. The key success factors are therefore industrial design, ease of use, safety and uniform high quality.
2. In contrast, the *manufacturing technology* evolved rapidly from batch to continuous manual processing and then to automated produc-tion. The key success factors are the know-how in designing auto-mated lines, enabling progressive cost reductions with rigorous quality control while meeting the demands of the rapidly expanding international market.
3. *Marketing and sales* evolved from seasonal direct sales in Italy and Mediterranean countries to year-round sales of complementary products under Zobele's brand names. Zobele was unable to com-pete with multinational distributors and became by necessity a sup-plier to them. The key success factors were the creation of long-standing relationships as world preferred supplier and cooperation in designing and launching new product lines.
4. The second and third generation of *technological entrepreneurs* led the Zobele company from its rebirth after second World War to global-ization. The key success factors were the preservation of family har-mony, the complementarity of strategic, marketing and technical skills between the two branches of the family, fast informal decision making and high sensitivity to the changes in the international mar-ketplace.
5. Recruiting and qualification of *human resources* was no problem in spite of the changes in strategy. The key success factors were the loca-tion in Trento, the equal status of all managers, whether family mem-bers or not, the excellent relationships with the unions, wages tied to productivity and the opportunity for career growth in Italy and abroad.
6. The *financial aspects* have always been favorable and expansion has until now been self financed. The key success factors were family ownership, without the need to satisfy outside stockholders and mar-ket analysts, conservative spending patterns, reinvestment of earn-ings in the company, and outstanding credit ratings in Italy and abroad.
7. Perhaps the most important key success factor was the *strategic and human evolution* of the company from artisan to a leader in Italy in its market niches and then to global leader for production in selected market niches. In parallel, the family entrepreneurs expanded their skills from technical to marketing, from national to international suppliers, and from functional to general managers.

8. Finally, the relatively smooth *transition between generations* has been a determining success factor since Zobele is a long-lived family company.

CONCLUSION

In spite of the venerable age of 82 years, the Zobele company is still very dynamic and in full expansion. Thus, it would appear that the company will continue with its successful analyzer strategy, perhaps attacking more aggressively the new turbulent markets through the DBK connection. There is no evidence that it will reach maturity as long as Enrico is CEO and move to a "defender" strategy, or worse, to a "reactor" strategy (Miles & Snow, 1978). In parallel, the Zobele company will continue to enhance its technological and marketing core competencies by fine tuning the present divergent technological and convergent market strategies.

The evolution of Zobele Chemical Industries can also be studied according to Greiner's (1972) theory of growth punctuated by crises or, in our case, by critical events, as shown in Table 1. The first critical event (1942–46) almost destroyed the company, and was overcome by the ingenuity of the second CEO and his brother and their prospector strategy. The second critical event (1995) was less traumatic, because the third CEO realized fairly early that the industry structure had changed and redirected his strategy from prospector to analyzer. The next critical event may coincide with the transition from Enrico Zobele, 51 years old, to his successor (in 2015–2020?).

Enrico Zobele looked again at the picture of his son. He knew that only 30% of family companies reach the third generation, and less than 15% the fourth generation (Phan, 2001). On the other hand, in nearby Gardone Val Trompia, the Beretta company, founded in 1450 to supply guns to the republic of Venice, was still prospering under the same family, and had become a leading international supplier of light arms (Beretta, 1989). The two key issues in Enrico's mind was how to build and structure Zobele Chemical Industries into a leading global company, and how to gradually transfer the ownership and management to his son, who had expressed a desire to succeed his father.[6]

APPENDIX

Persons Interviewed

Enrico Zobele	CEO and Chairman of the Board, Director of Marketing, Principal Shareholder (50%)
Gino Zobele	Former CEO and Chairman of the Board
Fulvio Zobele	Former Technical Director, Vice-President of the Board
Franco Zobele	Technical Director, Major Shareholder (25%)
Giovanni Zobele	Director of Production and Human Resources, Major Shareholder (25%)
Andrea Maria Caserta	Financial Director
Stefano de Florian	R&D Project Manager
Maria Cristina Pedrazza	Account Manager
Thomaz Zobele	Son of Enrico Zobele, high school student

ACKNOWLEDGMENTS

This research was sponsored by the John Broadbent Endowment for Research in Entrepreneurship. The author wishes to thank Dr. Ing. Luigi Zobele, former CEO of Zobele Chemical Industries, for sharing his experiences since 1960 in numerous meetings in Italy and the United States, and his son, CEO Dr. Enrico Zobele, for his support in organizing interviews with key persons on May 20–24, 2001 and for providing ample documentation.

NOTES

1. The persons interviewed for this research are listed in the appendix. For confidentiality, a few company names have been changed.
2. At Enrico's request, his sister Giovanna had not received any shares, but had been compensated with other family assets.
3. The author, nine years old in 1930, remembers country general stores and taverns with door curtains of bamboo sticks to keep out the flies and spirals of fly paper hanging from the ceiling that had to be changed frequently.
4. The DBK Group, where Zobele is a minority stockholder will not be discussed further.
5. Calculated at the exchange rate of 1$ = 2048 Italian Lire.
6. Interview with Thomaz Zobele, Trento, Italy, May 24, 2001.

REFERENCES

Abetti, P.A. (1996). The impact of convergent and divergent technological and market strategies on core competencies and core rigidities. *International Journal of Technology Management, 11*(3/4), 412–424.

Abetti, P.A. (1997a). Convergent and divergent technological and market strategies for global leadership. *International Journal of Technology Management, 14*(6/7/8), 635–657.

Abetti, P.A. (1997b). The birth and growth of Toshiba's laptop and notebook computers. *Journal of Business Venturing, 12*(6), 507–529.

Abetti, P.A. (1999). The birth and growth of the Japanese language word processor. *International Journal of Technology Management, 18*(1/2), 114–132.

Abetti, P.A. (2002, in press). The entrepreneurial control imperative: A case history of Steria (1969–2000). *Journal of Business Venturing.*

Brokaw, L. (1992, March 20–22). Why family businesses are best. *Inc.*

Franco, E. (1999, November 9). Zobele creates a group with 700 employees. *L'Adige,* 27.

Gimenez, F.A. (2000). The benefits of a coherent strategy for innovation and corporate change. *Creativity and Innovation Management, 9*(4), 235–244.

Greiner, L.E. (1972, July-August). Evolution and revolution as organizations grow. *Harvard Business Review,* 37–46.

Gruppo Zobele. (2001, May 15). *Bilancio Consolidato 3/12/2000* (Annual Report 2000). Trento, Italy.

Hambrick, D.C. (1983). Some tests of the effectiveness and the functional attributes of Miles and Snow's strategic types. *Academy of Management Journal, 26*(1), 5–26.

The Holy Bible. (1982). Psalm 121. Nashville, TN: Thomas Nelson.

Kets de Vries, M.F.R. (1993, Winter). Dynamics of family controlled firms: The good and bad news. *Organizational Dynamics,* 61.

Kuratko, D.F., & Welsch, H.P. (2001). *Strategic entrepreneurial growth.* Fort Worth, TX: Harvard College Publishers.

Miles, R.E., & Snow, C.C. (1978). *Organizational strategy, structure and process.* New York: McGraw-Hill.

Neubauer, F., & Lank, A.G. (1998). *The family business.* New York: Routlegde.

Phan, P.H. (2001, March 23). *CEO succession at GE.* Lecture at Gordon Institute of Tufts University, Boston, MA.

Porter, M.E. (1990). *The competitive advantage of nations.* New York: Free Press.

Smith, K.G., Guthrie, J.C., & Chen, M-J. (1986). Miles and Snow's typology and strategy, organizational size and organized performance. *Academy of Management Proceedings,* 45–49.

Timmons, J.A. (1994). *New venture creation* (4th ed.). Burr Ridge, IL: Irwin.

Zobele Chemical Industries. (2000). *Manuale della Qualit', Unien ISO 9002 (Quality Manual).* Trento, Italy.

Zobele Chemical Industries. (2000). *Product specifications brochures.* Trento, Italy.

ABOUT THE CONTRIBUTORS

Pier A. Abetti holds a Ph.D. in Electrical Engineering from Illinois Institute of Technology. Prior to joining Rensselaer Polytechnic Institute in 1982, he worked 32 years for the General Electric Company (USA). He was manager of the Electrical and Information Advance Technology Laboratories and manager of General Electric's Europe Strategic Planning Operation. Author of more than 150 technical and management papers in five languages, he is a Fellow of the Institute of Electrical and Electronic Engineers and a former member of the Research and Development Council of the American Management Association, and the recipient of the 1993 Kaufman Foundation Award as University Entrepreneurship Professor of the Year.

Michael Armstrong is an Assistant Professor at the Sprott School of Business of Carleton University, where he teaches courses in operations management. He obtained his Ph.D. in Management Science from the University of British Columbia. In his research he uses mathematical models to learn more about a variety of management topics, including maintenance planning, arbitration procedures, and entrepreneurship.

Chee Leong Chong is Associate Professor and Director of the NUS-PSB Centre for Best Practices in the Faculty of Business Administration at the National University of Singapore. He holds a Ph.D. (Management) from the Sloan School of Management at MIT. Dr. Chong's research interests are in managerial and measurement issues in quality and productivity, managing technological innovations, and human resources planning and skills inventory.

Maw-Der Foo is an assistant professor in the Faculty of Business Administration, National University of Singapore. He holds a Ph.D. in Management from the Massachusetts Institute of Technology. His research focuses on start-up issues in high-technology and high-growth firms. He has published in major journals including *Management Science* and was co-author of the best paper for the 1998 Babson-Kauffman Entrepreneurship Research Conference. Maw-Der is a founding member of Startup@Singapore, a national technoventure business plan competition.

David H. Gobeli is a Professor of Management in the College of Business at Oregon State University. He has 15 years of industry experience as a design engineer and R&D executive. He does research and teaches in the areas of management of technology, venture planning, and strategic management. Related publications include articles in *Sloan Management Review, Journal of Product Innovation Management, Journal of Private Equity,* and *Journal of Managerial Issues.* He has been active in developing partnership programs between the College of Business and the College of Engineering to foster entrepreneurship.

Lisa Gundry, Ph.D., is Professor of Management in the Charles H. Kellstadt Graduate School of Business and the Director of the Ryan Center for Creativity and Innovation at DePaul University, where she teaches courses in Creativity in Business and Entrepreneurship Strategy. Her research centers on creative and innovative processes in entrepreneurial firms, and on entrepreneurial growth strategies. She has published three books and numerous articles in journals including the *Journal of Business Venturing, Journal of Small Business Management, Journal of Management, Human Relations,* and *Organizational Dynamics.*

Rueylin Hsiao is an assistant professor in the NUS Business School at the National University of Singapore. He receives his Ph.D. from Warwick Business School, University of Warwick (England). Rueylin's research interests are in information technology enabled organizational change. His current research involves Business-to-Business electronic commerce (in Asia) and information technology failure.

Jill Kickul, Ph.D., is Assistant Professor of Management in the Charles H. Kellstadt Graduate School of Business at DePaul University where she teaches courses on Entrepreneurship and New Venture Management and Entrepreneurship Strategy. Her research interests include entrepreneurial intentions and behavior, strategic and innovation processes in start-up ventures, and organizational and procedural issues within entrepreneurial firms. Her research has been published in the *Journal of Management, Jour-*

nal of Small Business Management, Journal of Managerial Issues, Journal of Business and Psychology, and *Organizational Dynamics.*

Bruce A. Kirchhoff is Distinguished Professor of Entrepreneurship and Director of the Technological Entrepreneurship Program at New Jersey Institute of Technology in Newark, NJ. His prior credentials include service as Chief Economist for the U.S. Small Business Administration and as Assistant Director of the Minority Business Development Agency in the U.S. Department of Commerce. He was Director of the Center for Entrepreneurship and Public Policy at Fairleigh Dickinson University; and Director of Research in Babson College's Entrepreneurship Center. He has also served on the faculties of Chalmers University of Technology and Jonkoping International Business School of Sweden, the University of Nebraska at Omaha, Purdue University, California Polytechnic State University and the University of Utah.

Harold F. Koenig, Ph.D. is an associate professor of marketing in the College of Business at Oregon State University. At Oregon State University Professor Koenig teaches Marketing Research, Retail Management, and Customer Relationship Management to undergraduates and MBA students. His academic research focuses on content issues dealing with consumer satisfaction, brand equity, and network connections between firms. He has published in *Journal of Marketing, Journal of Product Innovation Management, International Journal of Research in Marketing,* and *Public Opinion Quarterly.* He is often consulted on statistical issues, survey design, and scale development.

Moren Lévesque holds a Ph.D. in Management Science from the University of British Columbia and is an Assistant Professor at the Weatherhead School of Management, Case Western Reserve University an. She has published in the *European Journal of Operational Research, IEEE Transactions on Engineering Management, Journal of Business Venturing, Entrepreneurship Theory and Practice,* and *Business Ethics Quarterly.* She has taught at Universit' Laval, Carnegie Mellon University, Rensselaer Polytechnic Institute and Humboldt Universität zu Berlin. Her research applies the methodologies of analytical and quantitative disciplines to the study of entrepreneurial decision-making. She won the 1999 Best Dissertation Award from the Technology Management Section of INFORMS.

Andy Lockett is a lecturer in Strategy at Nottingham University Business School. He received his BA (Econ) from the University of Manchester, MSc from UMIST and Phd from the University of Nottingham. His research interests incorporate the areas of business venturing, venture capital, entrepreneurship, governance, the resource-based view and the strategic implications of technological change. He has published a number of articles in different journals including: *Journal of Management, Research Policy, OMEGA, Small Business Economics, Journal of Technology Transfer, Journal of Marketing Management, Venture Capital,* and the *Journal of Strategic Marketing.*

Qing Lu is currently a doctoral candidate in Business Policy at National University of Singapore. He received his Master's degrees from Fudan University and National University of Singapore. His research interests include venture capital strategy and performance in emerging markets, and entrepreneurship.

Chandra Mishra is Associate Professor of Finance at Oregon State University. His primary teaching assignments are in the areas of corporate finance, new venture finance, and international corporate finance. He has also taught in several joint graduate programs, including the Oregon Executive MBA program, the full time and part-time Master of International Management programs of the Oregon Joint Professional Schools of Business. He has published several research papers in the areas of corporate finance, corporate governance, corporate venture capital, management compensation, and valuation of intangible assets. He is on the board of the *Journal of Private Equity* and a professional reviewer for several refereed journals. He also serves on the boards of local technology companies.

Phillip H. Phan received his Ph.D. from the University of Washington. He holds the Warren H. Bruggeman '46 and Pauline Urban Bruggeman Distinguished Chair in Management and is Research Director of the Paul Severino Center for Technology and Entrepreneurship in the Lally School of Management and Technology at RPI in Troy, New York. He is also Adjunct Professor of Business Policy at the National University of Singapore. Phil's main areas of research are in corporate governance, entrepreneurship, and international business. He has published in such journals as the *Journal of Business Venturing, Academy of Management Journal, Asia Pacific Journal of Management,* and *Corporate Governance: An International Review.* He currently serves on the editorial board of the *Journal of Business Venturing.*

Sarika Pruthi is a doctoral student at the Centre for Management Buyout Research, Nottingham University Business School. She is researching venture capital in an international setting and has published in Small Business Economics.

Dean Shepherd holds a Ph.D. in Strategy and Entrepreneurship and MBA from Bond University, Australia. He is an Assistant Professor at the Leeds

School of Business, University of Colorado. He has published his research in *Management Science, Journal of Management, European Journal of Operational Research, Journal of Business Venturing, Entrepreneurship Theory and Practice, Journal of High Technology Management Research* and *Business Ethics Quarterly.* His research interests include entry strategy, venture capitalists and entrepreneurial decision making, opportunity recognition.

Hwee Hoon Tan is an assistant professor with the Department of Management and Organization, Faculty of Business Administration, NUS. She holds a BBA (Hons) from NUS and a Ph.D. (Management) from Purdue University, USA. Her research interests are in the areas of interpersonal trust, contingent work and emotions. Hwee Hoon has published in major international journals including *Strategic Management Journal* and the *Journal of Business Venturing.* She also teaches executive programs conducted in Mandarin.

Gregory Theyel is an Adjunct Assistant Professor at Worcester Polytechnic Institute. He received his Ph.D. from Clark University, and his research interests are in firm strategy and supply chain management for product and process innovation. His research assesses how management practices, collaboration, and regional resources affect firms' success at innovating new products and processes and improving environmental performance. His publications have appeared in journals such as *Strategic Management Journal* and *International Journal of Operations and Project Management.* He has also been a management consultant for 12 years assisting corporations and governments with their environmental strategy, management, and policy.

Clement Wang received his Ph.D. in Management Sciences (Faculty of Engineering) from University of Waterloo. He is currently an Assistant Professor in the Department of Business Policy, National University of Singapore. His research interests include management of technological change and the interplay between entrepreneurship and venture capital. His publications have appeared in various journals such as *Applied Financial Economics, Competitive Intelligence Review, IEEE Transactions on Engineering Management, Journal of Financial Research,* and *Venture Capital.* Prior to his present position, he worked in R&D engineering and has operated a small manufacturing company. He is also a registered professional engineer in Ontario, Canada.

Steven T. Walsh, Ph.D., is Director of the Technological Entrepreneurship Program and assistant professor in the Anderson School of Management at the University of New Mexico. He is president of the Micro and Nano Technology Education Foundation, and Chair of the international conference on the commercialization of Micro and Nano systems. His current research investigates questions are focused on disruptive technology management, micro and nano systems, competency theory, economic development, entrepreneurship, and R&D management. He has published in such journals as *IEEE Transactions on Engineering Management, SMS, EMJ, Technology Analysis and Strategic Management, MRS, Journal of Business, Frontiers of Entrepreneurial Research, MST, SPIE, MRS,* and *Microsystems Technologies.*

Poh-Kam Wong is Associate Professor, Business School, National University of Singapore, where he directs the Centre for Entrepreneurship since 1990. He was also director of the MSc. Program in Management of Technology at NUS from 1992–2000. He obtained his S.B., S.M., E.E. and Ph.D. from MIT. His current research interests include Management of Technological Innovation, Competitive Strategies in High Tech Industries, S&T and IT Policy, and Technology Entrepreneurship.

Mike Wright is Professor of Financial Studies, Director of the Center for Management Buy-out Research and Research Director at Nottingham University Business School. He is currently a visiting professor at INSEAD, Erasmus University and the University of Siena. His research interests focus on management buy-outs, habitual entrepreneurs, venture capital, privatization, divestment and technology transfer. He has published over 25 books and more than 160 academic papers in such peer reviewed journals as *Academy of Management Journal, Academy of Management Review, Strategic Management Journal, Journal of Business Venturing, Entrepreneurship Theory and Practice,* and the *Journal of International Business Studies.* He served two terms as an editor of Entrepreneurship Theory and Practice during 1994–99 and is a Fellow of the British Academy of Management.